THE UNITED STATES AND THE PALESTINIANS

The United States and the Palestinians

MOHAMMED K. SHADID

ST. MARTIN'S PRESS NEW YORK

Library of Congress Cataloging in Publication Data

Shadid, Mohammed K
  The United States and the Palestinians.

  Bibliography: p. 225.
  Includes index.
  1. United States – Foreign relations – Palestine.
2. Palestinian Arabs – Politics and government.
3. Palestine – Foreign relations – United States.
I. Title.
E183.8.I7S52   1981   327.73017'49275694   80-52166
ISBN 0-312-83315-6

085017

This book is dedicated to the children of Palestine. Their future — and indeed the future of all the children of the region —rests upon the return of the exiles to their homes, to live in peace, justice and liberty.

CONTENTS

Acknowledgements

Introduction   11

1. The Palestinian People   14

2. United States Policy Towards the Palestinians Prior to 1948   24

3. United States Policy Towards Palestinian Refugees   43

4. United States Policy Towards a Palestinian Entity 1967-1976   82

5. The United States and Palestinian Revolutionary Violence
   1968-1980   111

6. United States Policy Towards the Palestinians as a People   133

7. Who Influences American-Palestinian Policy?   160

8. Conclusion   188

Appendices   197

Bibliography   225

Index   247

ACKNOWLEDGEMENTS

There are several people for whose encouragement and assistance throughout my studies and during the preparation of this research I would like to thank.

Mrs Tonsa Jorde and Mrs Mjerial Larson were kind enough to provide the support for my early studies in the United States. Mrs William Siekman helped me through my graduate studies with generosity.

To Professor Bernard Reich of George Washington University I owe a great debt, not only for the energy and expertise with which he provided instruction during my course work, and for the generous assistance with the preparation of my dissertation, but also for his guidance throughout my student days at George Washington. This study, which has grown out of my dissertation, directed by Professor Reich, owes much to his advice and interest in the investigation of this critical area of American foreign policy.

Mrs Violet Tulloch has provided me with endless encouragement and moral support, as well as faithfully typing so many of my early drafts.

Carolyn Gates and Sally Ann Baynard not only edited various drafts of this study but also gave freely of their advice and friendship. Regina Sharif and Anita Vitullo also provided valuable assistance.

Dr Jim Morrell, although more interested in Asia than the Middle East, provided invaluable last-draft editing.

Once again, and indeed always, I owe the greatest debt to Sue and Ahmad Shadid.

INTRODUCTION

It is often said that the United States has no policy towards the Palestinians, only a general policy towards the Middle East. In fact, the United States always has accorded the Palestinians a central role in its considerations of the Middle East. It has variously courted, misunderstood, patronized and accommodated the Palestinians according to perceived US interests.

Prior to World War II, the United States had primarily cultural, philanthropic and economic interests in the Middle East. It relegated strategic interests to the British and French empires and largely stayed out of Middle Eastern affairs.

Since the war, American interests in the Middle East have proliferated into today's enormous economic and strategic stake. The Palestinian issue also has become a central component of US Middle East policy, although invariably policy-makers have sought to portray it as secondary.

US policy towards the Palestinian people went through three stages: it dealt with the Palestinians first as refugees, second, as participants in international terrorism and, third, as an entity.

Chapter 1 identifies the Palestinian people, notes their geographic and demographic distribution, and traces the development of their consciousness as a people. Chapter 2 focuses upon the historical background of US policy and its involvement in the Middle East prior to the creation of the state of Israel. International and domestic factors compelled the Wilson, Roosevelt and Truman administrations to accept the Balfour Declaration, and thus they supported Jewish settlement in Palestine, despite the indigenous Palestinian Arab population's opposition to mass Jewish immigration. The Arabs were taken into consideration only after 1948 when the so-called 'Palestinian problem' emerged as they were forced from their homeland.

The Palestinian problem then presented a humanitarian as well as a political aspect to various American administrations, as discussed in Chapter 3. The US government addressed the humanitarian issue of homeless and economically dependent Palestinians driven from their land. Yet this humanitarian interest had its political side. American policy-makers increasingly feared the repercussions of a sudden influx of Palestinians into neighbouring Arab states. Very much concerned

11

about the political stability of the existing Arab regimes, the US government provided economic aid to the refugees in order to ease the burden on the Arab governments; it also tried to dampen the discontent and hostility among the homeless Palestinians themselves in the refugee camps in Lebanon, Syria, and Jordan.

In 1953, 1956 and 1961, the United States developed specific proposals for water projects to solve the refugee problem by resettlement and integration into the region. The Arabs rejected all the proposals because they failed to treat the political aspects of the problem.

Chapter 4 deals with American recognition of the Palestinians as an entity, a factor that must be part of any viable peace settlement. Chapter 5 analyzes US policy towards Palestinian terrorism. The rise in terrorism has become a major concern and irritant to the United States. The chapter considers trends and objectives of the Palestinians' resort to violence as well as American efforts to counter this activity.

Chapter 6 discusses American recognition of the Palestinians as a people with 'legitimate rights' and the need for a homeland. The American government made tentative approaches to the Palestine Liberation Organization (PLO) in 1976. By 1978, the United States had progressed from total unconcern to halfway recognition.

Chapter 7 discusses the various internal and external pressures on US policy towards the Palestinians. United States' considerations of the Palestinians are subordinated to its policy towards Israel. Policy-makers rationalize this as heeding American public opinion or the influential 'Jewish lobby'. This analysis ignores the significant imperial interests of the United States in the Middle East region.

Huge American economic and strategic interests in the Middle East have stimulated extensive US political involvement. A driving force behind America's desperate efforts to resolve the Palestinian issue in favour of Israeli hegemony is the marriage between US imperial — corporate, military and political — and Israeli Zionist interests. American capital has long penetrated Israel, but, more to the point, if the United States and Israel could pull off some ultimate settlement along the lines of the Camp David process, they would have the economies of the whole region to exploit. Israeli economic, military and political domination of the area would provide market outlets and sources of raw materials for Israel's senior partner, the United States. In addition, the United States could rely on Israel's military advantage in the Middle East to protect its own and American interests in the region. Until the Iranian and Afghan crises, the United States relied heavily on Israel's (and Iran's) military might to secure the region. Even with

President Carter's announcement of the 'Carter doctrine', which backs away from a full reliance on surrogate regional powers to protect American interests, the new American military arrangements in the Middle East – including the Rapid Deployment Force – still force upon Israel the role of regional policeman, albeit in a less obtrusive manner.

This book analyzes America's long string of failures to resolve the Palestine issue. It was a failure not only of policy, but also of understanding. John Foster Dulles once predicted that those Palestinians born outside would soon forget about Palestine if the issue were not resolved. In fact, by 1980, the generation born in exile formed the nucleus of the Palestinian movement. It was they who were willing to risk all to fight for a return to the Palestinian homeland. And, as Mayor Muhammed Milehlm of Halhoul in the Israeli-occupied West Bank noted, after he and two other West Bank leaders were expelled from their homes by Israeli military authorities in May 1980, 'My children are better revolutionaries and will struggle harder than I can.' There was little evidence that the Palestinian people or their struggle would vanish unless Israel embarked on large-scale killings of Palestinians and their supporters, as it began to do in southern Lebanon. And such a policy would only set off the powder keg on the West Bank and indeed within Israel itself. Continued Israeli intransigence, ineffectively opposed by its American protector, could only perpetuate the *status quo*, which at all times threatened regional and international peace.

The revolutionary tide in the Arab world without a doubt slowed during the 1970s. This trend more often than not stemmed from the internal contradictions and necessities of Arab regimes rather than from American and Israeli policies. It was unlikely that the United States and Israel could succeed in the long term in continuing policies that almost by definition countered popular movements in the Arab world.

The United States and its allies stood to be the big losers in the Middle East if the area did explode. American domination of the Middle East, which had brought about devastating tragedy, was accountable for the powder keg that threatened to destroy the whole region. In 1981 there is still time to act. The American people successfully opposed the war in Vietnam through greater active interest. The American people can again help to bring to an end another internationally threatening conflict in their call for a just and equitable resolution of the Palestinian situation.

1 THE PALESTINIAN PEOPLE

Most writers on the Middle East have concerned themselves with issues other than the Palestinian people.[1] Few included within their analytical framework the Palestinians as a people and their role in any future Middle East peace settlement; as if following in the footsteps of the policy-makers themselves, these writers often left out of consideration the very existence of the Palestinian people and failed to grasp their unique history, culture and political ambitions.

Yet events themselves have moved the Palestinians to the fore. The 1967 and 1973 Arab-Israeli wars, the Palestinian-Israeli armed confrontation in South Lebanon in March 1978, and the Palestinians' use of violence to advance their political goals are all gradually gaining the attention and official recognition of the international community for the Palestinians.[2] Many countries have had to adjust their Middle East policies to take into account this missing link. This book traces precisely this adjustment of US policy from the beginning of the century to the present.

While recognition of the Palestinians has been late and grudging, the Palestinians themselves have existed as a people for over two thousand years. An indigenous population of Palestine extends back to the beginning of history in the Middle East. With the Arab conquest of thirteen centuries ago, the people of Palestine, along with other peoples of the region, became Arabized and thereafter came to identify themselves as Arabs. Politically speaking, the region of Palestine 'virtually dropped out of history' following the Arab conquest.[3] During the Ottoman era (1517-1918) Palestine remained Arab in character, as well as an integral part socially, economically and politically of the Fertile Crescent which included what is now known as Syria, Lebanon and Iraq. At that time the Fertile Crescent as a whole comprised several provinces of the Ottoman Empire. West of the Jordan river, the northern half of Palestine was part of the Wilayet of Beirut; the southern half was known as the Sanjak of Jerusalem and was governed directly from Istanbul. The area east of Jordan was part of the Wilayet of Damascus. In fact, Palestine was frequently referred to as Southern Syria.[4]

The Palestinians joined the Arab nationalist resistance to Ottoman Turkish colonialism. They participated in the first Arab Congress held in Paris in June 1913. The congress raised demands for an end to Turkish

14

censorship of the Arabic press, the use of Arabic as the official language in all the Turkish-ruled Arab provinces, and greater Arab self-government. The Palestinians supported these demands; but already they criticized the Arab Congress for failing to note the particular threat which Zionism posed to the Palestinian Arabs. They felt particularly threatened by the Zionists' purchase of land from several wealthy Arab families. Only a few months before the convening of the Arab Congress in Paris, a relatively large land sale to the Zionists prompted the Jaffa newspaper *Filastin* (Palestine) to write, 'If this state of affairs continues – then the Zionists will gain mastery over our country, village by village, town by town; tomorrow the whole of Jerusalem will be sold and then Palestine in its entirety.'[5]

The Palestinians responded to the arrival of European Zionists in Palestine (see Figure 1.1.) with plans to transform it into a Jewish state by forming anti-Zionist societies in Palestinian cities such as Jerusalem and Nablus. They tried to raise money to purchase lands that might otherwise be sold to Zionist colonists. Palestinians rioted in Tiberias in 1914 when Zionists tried to buy the Hulah marshes and their rich mineral concessions from the Turks.[6]

The Palestinian Arabs' aspirations focused on Amir Faisal when he established a government in Damascus in October 1918, and many Palestinian men joined his government and army. The local political clubs that sprang up in the wake of British occupation came together for an all-Palestine conference in February 1919. This conference supported the inclusion of Palestine in an independent Syria, and it elected delegates to the first Arab Congress held in Damascus in the spring of 1919. However, Faisal's fall in July 1920 resulted in a swift reorientation of Palestinian political attention and aspirations. A Palestinian nationalism emerged which was concerned primarily with problems caused by Zionist aspirations, problems that were not faced by the other Arab countries.[7] This sharpening of Palestinian political consciousness became clear as early as the winter of 1920-1 in the demands of the third Arab Congress in Haifa. The demands were presented in the summer of 1921 by the first Muslim-Christian delegation to London in the form of a letter to Colonial Secretary Winston Churchill. These demands may be summarized as: renunciation of the Balfour Declaration, formation of a national government responsible to a parliament elected by the native Jewish, Christian, and Muslim population, implementation of Ottoman rather than British law in the area, and non-separation of Palestine from its neighbours.[8]

Despite its overriding concern with Zionism, Palestinian nationalism initially developed as part of the Arab nationalist movement. Historians generally divide Arab nationalism into three time periods: the first extends up to 1948 – the year of the great Arab 'disaster' that came with the creation of a Jewish state on Arab soil;[9] the second lasted from 1948 to 1967, the year of the second Arab defeat; the third period is 1967 to the present[10] (See Figure 1.2).

Palestinian nationalism existed during all these phases, although the prevailing attitude of Palestinians differed greatly in each. During the first, pre-1948, phase, Palestinian nationalism was an integral part of Syrian-Arab nationalism. Palestinians, such as Ali Nashashibi from Jerusalem, Salim Abd al-Hadi from Janin and Hafiz al-Sa'id from Jaffa, struggled side by side with Syrian nationalists against Ottoman oppression.[11] The British mandate brought about the political separation of Palestine from Syria, forcing the Palestinian Arabs to form their own national organizations. Nevertheless, Palestinian nationalism remained closely allied to Arab nationalism in its struggle against both colonialist rule and Zionist settlement. The second phase of Palestinian national consciousness was characterized by the determination of the indigenous population to liberate that part of Palestine which the great disaster of 1948 converted into the state of Israel. The disaster also brought about the dispersal of the majority of the Palestinian Arab people, marking the beginning of the era of diaspora. More than half of the Palestinian population, which numbered at that time over 1.3 million, became refugees. The other half suddenly found themselves living under Israeli, Egyptian or Jordanian rule.[12] With morale completely shattered, self-respect undermined, and their individual as well as national livelihood severely disrupted, the Palestinians became dependent on others for survival.[13] This dependence was also carried over to the realm of politics, where the few surviving nationalist leaders came to see no other alternative but to join forces with other Arab nationalists. Their awareness and strong belief that Arab unity alone would be able to face the challenge of the technologically superior Israel brought about the Arabization of their Palestinian struggle and displaced the few Palestinian leaders from their role as primary antagonists to Zionism.[14] Palestinian nationalism in alliance with Pan-Arabism thus remained the major characteristic of the second phase of Palestinian nationalism. Yet by the mid-1960s a new generation of Palestinians had emerged, and a new Palestinian leadership came slowly into being. The second great disaster of June 1967 only served to accelerate this trend, causing this new generation of Palestinians to move away from pan-Arabism towards a more distinctly Palestinian national ideology. Meeting in May 1964, the first Palestine National Council committed the Palestinian people to the liberation of their homeland and established the Palestine Liberation Organization as the representative of the Palestinian people. The PLO was expressly charged with the duty to assert Palestinian rights nationally, regionally and internationally and to mobilize the Palestinian people for the task of national liberation.[15] The third phase of Palestinian nationalism thus became the era characterized by independent Palestinian political and military action, designed to achieve the ultimate goal of the liberation of Palestine.[16]

Israel's victory over the forces of Egypt, Syria and Jordan in June 1967 also brought about new realities for the Arabs of Palestine. More than four hundred thousand were again displaced from their homes, about half of them for the second time in twenty years. Most of the new and second-time refugees fled to the East Bank of Jordan where tens of thousands began life in hastily constructed tent camps.[17] In addition to the new generation of Palestinian refugees living outside the boundaries of Palestine, there were now about 1.2 million Arab Palestinians living under Israeli military occupation on the West Bank and in Gaza (see Figure 1.3). Palestinians now lived in a diaspora that is often compared with the Jewish diaspora prior to the creation of the state of Israel.[18] Yet, although dispersed, the Palestinians not only maintained their national consciousness but also built it up further by creating institutions designed to serve the Palestinian community inside and outside of Palestine and to work for the achievement of Palestinian national goals. Thus today's Palestinians not only possess a high level of national consciousness but also the necessary national and political institutions to embody it (see Figure 1.4).[19]

The year 1968, following the second Israeli victory over the joint Arab forces, marked a major breakthrough for the history of independent Palestinian nationalism; this time it completely freed itself from its former Arab tutelage.[20] The Palestinian National Charter of 1968 was formulated by a newly aware people in their struggle for the liberation of Palestine.[21] Paragraph 5 of the charter defines the Palestinian people as 'those Arab nationals who, until 1947, normally resided in Palestine regardless of whether they were evicted from it or have stayed there. Anyone born after that date of a Palestinian father – whether inside Palestine or outside – is also a Palestinian.'[22]

Furthermore, the charter stipulated that 'armed struggle is the only way to liberate Palestine' and that 'commando action constitutes the nucleus of the Palestinian popular liberation war'. Yet the PLO does not merely represent an umbrella organization for various commando groups as it is often portrayed in the West. More importantly, it also incorporates an administrative machinery comparable to that of any government.[23] Economic, educational and cultural institutions function in order to stimulate and foster the national consciousness of Palestinians living outside Palestine (see Figure 1.4).

Although it is now quite clear who and where the Palestinians are, in the period prior to 1948 the United States made no attempt to identify the Palestinians as a distinct group and, consequently, developed no policy toward them. Instead US concerns centred around Palestine as a territory, Zionist aspirations in the area and the Arab governments.

Notes

1. One of the earliest studies focusing on United States policy towards the Palestinian question is that of Frank E. Manuel, *The Realities of American-Palestine Relations* (Washington, DC: Public Affairs Press, 1949). This book is a most helpful source for US policy vis-à-vis Zionism and Jewish settlement in Palestine. Since then many similar studies have been made, i.e. Joseph B. Schechtman, *The United States and the Jewish State Movement* (New York: Herzl Press, 1966); William B. Quandt, *United States Policy in the Middle East: Constraints and Choices* (Santa Monica: The Rand Corporation, 1970); William R. Polk, *The United States and the Arab World* (Cambridge, Mass.: Harvard University Press, 1975); W.A. Beling (ed.), *The Middle East: Quest for an American Policy* (Albany: State University of New York Press, 1973); John A. De Novo, *American Interests and Policies in the Middle East, 1900-1939*, (Minneapolis, Minn.: University of Minnesota Press, 1963); Bernard Reich, *New Directions in US Middle East Policy* (McLean: Strategic Studies Dept., 1971); and *Quest for Peace: United States-Israel Relations and the Arab-Israeli Conflict* (New Brunswick, N.J.: Transaction Books, 1977).

2. At a number of important conferences, such as the Islamic Summit Conference of 1974 in Pakistan and the Nonaligned Conference of 1973 in Algiers, resolutions were passed reaffirming the right of the Palestinian people to self-determination. The majority of the Third World countries also expressed their support for the Palestine Liberation Organization at the Nonaligned Countries Conferences in Lima in 1975 and Belgrade in 1978. Most importantly, however, a number of resolutions passed by the United Nations during 1974 and 1975 called for the right of self-determination and the right of the Palestinians to return to their homeland from which they had been uprooted. The UN General Assembly also recognized in its Resolution No. 3237 (XXIX) the PLO as the legitimate representative of the Palestinian people and invited it to participate in the debates of the General Assembly and Security Council (see UN Documents nos. A/RES/3236 (XXIX) of 25 Nov. 1974, A/RES/3237 (XXIX) of 25 Nov. 1974, A/RES/3376 of 10 Nov. 1975 and A/RES/3375 of 10 Nov. 1975).

3. Cmd. 5479, Palestine Royal Commission Report – 1937, p. 6.

4. Don Peretz, 'The Historical Background of Arab Nationalism in Palestine' in Richard Y. Ward, Don Peretz and Evan M. Wilson (eds.), *The Palestine State: A Rational Approach* (London: National University Publications, 1977), p. 4.

5. *Filastin*, III (25 Jan. 1913), p. 4., quoted in Neville J. Mandel, *The Arabs and Zionism before World War I* (Berkeley, Los Angeles, London: University of California Press, 1976), pp. 138-40.

6. William Quandt, Fouad Jabber and Ann Lesch, *The Politics of Palestinian Nationalism* (Berkeley, Los Angeles: University of California Press, 1973), pp. 15-16.

7. For instance, a large number of Palestinian political organizations emerged such as the National Party, the Youth Congress, the Palestine Arab Party and the National Defence Party.

8. Quandt *et al., The Politics of Palestinian Nationalism*, pp. 15-18.

9. Constantine K. Zurayk, *The Meaning of the Disaster* (Beirut: Khayats, 1956), pp. 2, 34-5.

10. Peretz in Ward, Peretz and Wilson, pp. 3-4.

11. For detailed discussions of Palestinian-Syrian opposition to British rule see George Antonius, *The Arab Awakening* (New York: Capricorn Books, 1976); also Yehoshua Porath, *The Emergence of the Palestinian-Arab National Movement 1918-1929* (London: Frank Cass, 1974).

12. Demographic statistics for the Arab population in Palestine in 1948, before the creation of Israel, are to be found in Janet Abu-Lughod, 'The Demographic Transformation of Palestine' in I. Abu-Lughod (ed.), *The Transformation of Palestine* (Evanston: Northwestern University Press, 1971).

13. Peretz in Ward, Peretz and Wilson, p. 23.

14. Ibid., p. 24.

15. See Palestine National Covenant. Also Rashid Hamid, 'What is the PLO?' *Journal of Palestine Studies*, vol. IV, no. 4, Summer 1975.

16. Ibid.

17. Peretz in Ward, Peretz and Wilson, pp. 43, 44.

18. See map and statistics on page 22. The demographic statistics regarding the numerical distribution of the Palestinians are taken from the *New York Times*, 19 Feb. 1978, p. 16 and Report of the Commissioner General of UNRWA to the UN General Assembly, 30 June 1977, p. 66.

19. The Palestinians have developed educational and social institutions in their homeland as well as in the diaspora, which include women's and student unions, professional organizations, schools and universities such as Bir Zeit University, and Al-Najah University, and cultural institutions such as Dar Al-Tefl in Ramallah and the Shuhada' Families Foundation.

20. In January 1964 an Arab summit meeting in Cairo recommended that a Palestinian entity be formed. In pursuance of this recommendation, Ahmad Shukairy had called for a Palestinian conference to be held in Jerusalem on 28 May 1964, at which the Palestine Liberation Organization was formed under Shukairy's leadership. Blessed by official Arab consent, this new organization was highly influenced by Arab governments and its strategy for liberating Palestine was to follow the conventional warfare strategy of the Arab governments. As a result of the June 1967 war, Shukairy was succeeded by Yasser Arafat, who came to represent the voice of independent Palestinian nationalism as expressed in commando organizations. For the early years of the PLO, see William B. Quandt *et al., The Politics of Palestinian Nationalism*, and Hisham Sharabi, *Palestinian Guerrillas: Their Credibility and Effectiveness* (Washington DC: Centre for Strategic and International Studies, 1970).

21. For the complete text of the Palestinian National Charter, see Zuhair Diab, (ed.), *International Documents on Palestine, 1968* (Beirut: Institute for Palestine Studies, 1971), pp. 393-395.

22. Ibid.

23. Frank H. Epp, *The Palestinians* (Scottdale, Pa: Herald Press, 1976), p. 129; also Judy Bertelson (ed.), *Nonstate Nation in International Politics: Comparative Systems Analysis* (New York: Praeger Publications, 1977), Chapter II.

Figure 1.1: The Arab and the Jewish Populations in Palestine

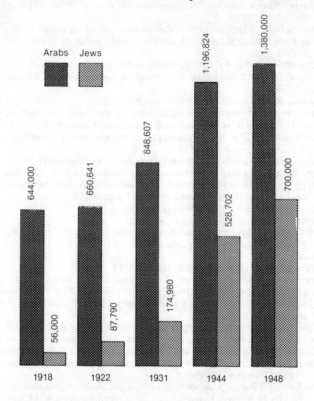

Arabs   Jews

	1918	1922	1931	1944	1948
Arabs	644,000	660,641	848,607	1,196,824	1,380,000
Jews	56,000	87,790	174,980	528,702	700,000

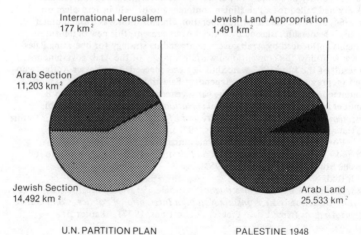

International Jerusalem
177 km²

Jewish Land Appropriation
1,491 km²

Arab Section
11,203 km²

Jewish Section
14,492 km²

Arab Land
25,533 km²

U.N. PARTITION PLAN

PALESTINE 1948

Figure 1.2: Palestinian Nationalism

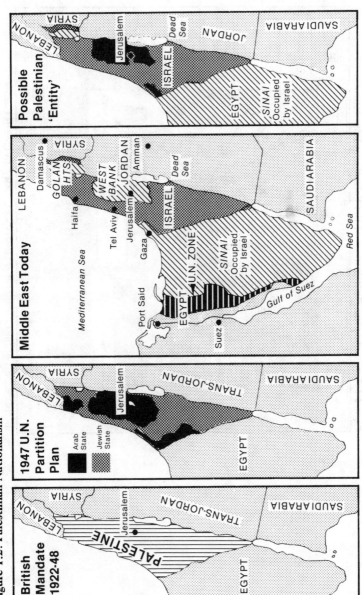

Figure 1.3: Geographic Distribution of the Palestinian Population

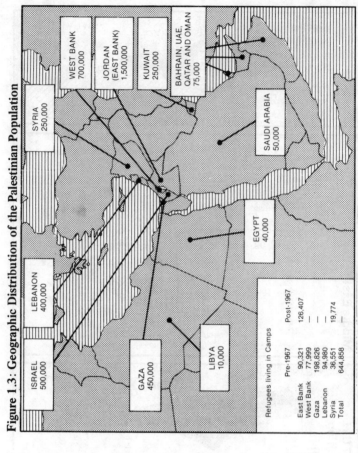

ISRAEL
500,000

LEBANON
400,000

SYRIA
250,000

WEST BANK
700,000

JORDAN
(EAST BANK)
1,500,000

KUWAIT
250,000

BAHRAIN, UAE,
QATAR AND OMAN
75,000

SAUDI ARABIA
50,000

EGYPT
40,000

GAZA
450,000

LIBYA
10,000

Refugees living in Camps

	Pre-1967	Post-1967
East Bank	90,321	126,407
West Bank	77,999	—
Gaza	198,826	—
Lebanon	94,980	—
Syria	36,551	19,774
Total	644,858	—

Source: Report of the Commissioner General of UNRWA to the UN General Assembly, 30 June 1977 p. 66 and *The New York Times*, 19 Feb. 1978.

Figure 1.4: Organizational Chart of the PLO

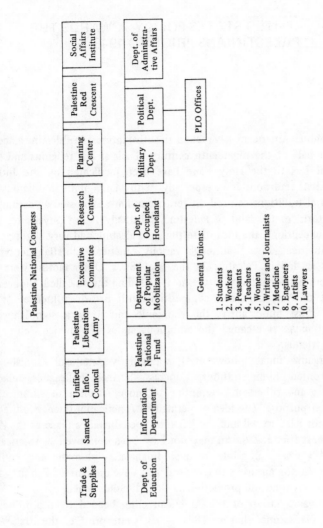

Source: Rashid Hamid, 'What is the PLO?' *Journal of Palestine Studies*, vol. IV, no. 4, Summer 1975.

2 UNITED STATES POLICY TOWARDS THE PALESTINIANS PRIOR TO 1948

Individual Americans have taken an active interest in Palestine since the latter half of the nineteenth century. Their strong religious and emotional ties to the Holy Land have been inculcated by the Judaeo-Christian tradition. Jews especially, with many of their religious and cultural traditions centred on Jerusalem, have expressed a yearning for a 'return' to the land of Palestine, spiritually if not physically. With rare exceptions, the idea of settling in Palestine had very slight appeal to American Jews,[1] although various American Christian denominations settled in Palestine in the late 1800s. Other factors were also responsible for interest in the area, including the so-called 'pioneering' spirit of Americans and competition with British influence for the area; most importantly, the economic and strategic significance of Palestine never escaped the ambitious stares of America's elites and their friends.

Organizationally, however, it was chiefly American Zionists who confronted administrations, Congress, business colleagues, religious leaders and others in attempting to move America to embrace the Zionist purpose. The idea of permanent American influence in the area was not hard to sell and the US soon took Britain's place as the Zionists' best friend. Zionism may not have been conceived in America but the US was responsible, through financial, diplomatic and political channels, for ensuring the survival and development of Zionist ideals and for creating and protecting its Goliath-child, Israel.

It was a group of the American elite, headed by the influential W.E. Blackstone, that in 1891 — six years prior to the first World Zionist Congress — first tried to gain executive support for a proposal for a Jewish homeland in Palestine. The proposal was submitted to President William Henry Harrison in the form of a petition signed by some of the most imposing names of the time: Chief Justice Melville Fuller, House Speaker Thomas Reed, Cardinal Gibbons, banker J. Pierpoint Morgan, John D. Rockefeller, William Rockefeller and financier Russell Sage.[2] Thus began a never-ending campaign to create a homeland — from what was already a homeland — to amalgamate powerful and influential forces in America behind such a scheme, and to support the new state wholeheartedly at every crisis point.

24

In the pre-1948 period, it was the decisions of three American presidents — Wilson, Roosevelt and Truman — that formed the basic foundation of American Palestine policy. There was no policy towards the 'Palestinians' as such; the policy was directed toward the area of Palestine and did not involve its native inhabitants. Concentration of efforts was on methods, techniques and procedures required to create a Jewish homeland in the area. The Palestinians were a 'non-people' in the eyes of the policy-makers.

President Wilson's interest in Zionism was fostered by the men who surrounded him. It was particularly his long and deep friendship with Louis Brandeis, an ardent Zionist, that most influenced him towards this stand. It was said that Brandeis was regarded by Wilson as the man to whom he owed his career. When Wilson succeeded in securing him a seat in the Supreme Court in 1916, Brandeis was President of the Federation of American Zionists. Not only did Wilson sympathize with the purposes of Zionism, but he actually referred to himself as a Zionist in discussions with Brandeis, Felix Frankfurter, Judge Julian Mack, Rabbi Stephen Wise (Chairman of the Provisional Executive Committee for General Zionist Affairs) and other leaders of American Zionism.[3]

Historians give Wilson credit for encouraging Balfour to issue his famous Declaration. Wilson's feelings on the subject, and the opinions of other high American officials, were sought out by the British and given careful consideration at the formation of the declaration. On 4 September 1917 Lord Robert Cecil, the British Under-Secretary of State for Foreign Affairs, had cabled Colonel House as follows: 'We are being pressed here for a Declaration of sympathy with the Zionist movement, and I should be very grateful if you felt able to ascertain unofficially if the President favours such a Declaration.'[4]

President Wilson was quite ready to support the Declaration despite the hesitancy of Colonel House. After delaying his response to Colonel House for almost a month, Wilson replied positively: 'I find in my pocket the memorandum you gave me about the Zionist movement. I am afraid I did not say to you that I concur in the formula suggested by the other side. I do, and would be obliged if you would let them know it.'[5] When the Declaration was issued there were mass celebrations before American consulates in Russia, Australia and China. Scores of telegrams of thanks poured in to Wilson from all parts of the world, almost as if he had issued the Declaration himself.

During the early period of Zionist intrusion into Palestine, American Zionists succeeded in starting America on its long road of involvement in the Palestine question by enlisting Congressional aid. They won the support of some of the most powerful figures in Congress including Henry Cabot Lodge, the Chairman of the Senate Foreign Relations Committee. On 12 April 1922, at the urging of the Zionists, Lodge introduced a resolution into the Senate basically reaffirming the Balfour Declaration:

> Resolved . . . that the United States of America favors the establish-ment in Palestine of a national home for the Jewish people, in accordance with the provisions contained in the declaration of the British government of November 2, 1917, known as the Balfour Declaration, it being clearly understood that nothing shall be done which may prejudice the civil and religious rights of the existing non-Jewish communities in Palestine, or the rights and political status enjoyed by Jews in any other country, and that the holy places and religious buildings and sites in Palestine shall be ade-quately protected.[6]

Later Lodge expounded on his predilection towards a Jewish homeland at a Boston gathering of his constituency:

> I never could accept in patience the thought that Jerusalem and Palestine should be under the control of the Mohammedans . . . that Jerusalem and Palestine, sacred to the Jews . . . a land profoundly holy to all the great Christian nations of the West, should remain permanently in the hands of the Turks, has seemed to me for many years one of the great blots on the face of civilization, which ought to be erased.[7]

Although the Zionists concentrated on securing Senate action only, they received help from another quarter as well. On 4 April, Represen-tative Hamilton Fish, Jr, apparently on his own initiative, presented a draft resolution of sympathy in the House, which called the 'recreating' of a 'national home' for the Jews in Palestine 'historic justice'.[8]

The difference in the text of the draft resolutions stemmed from more than just a difference of sponsorship. The Fish resolution would have merely put Congress on record as recommending an 'undertaking' while acceptance of the Senate resolution would have involved Congres-sional approval of the 'establishment of a national home', a distinction recognized by the Zionists.[9]

During the hearings on the resolution, Representative Fish, in search of a formula acceptable to the House, introduced a modification of his earlier resolution. On 30 June 1922, the resolution was passed without a roll-call vote, with no opposition mentioned.[10] The Zionists had done their work well. Whatever opposition might have surfaced in Washington was buried under a barrage of pro-Zionist telegrams and letters from all over the country, from non-Jews as well as Jews.[11] In this connection, the Zionists utilized the Society of Friends of a Jewish Palestine, an organization of Christians they had sponsored to draw sympathy among the general population.[12] The adoption of a text acceptable to both Houses was finally accomplished on 11 September. In this form, the joint resolution went to the President, and after receiving the reluctant sanction of the State Department, Harding signed it.[13] The Zionists had scored a major victory. The final resolution read as follows:

> Resolved by the Senate and House of Representatives of the United States of America in Congress assembled, that the United States of America favors the establishment in Palestine of a national home for the Jewish people, it being clearly understood that nothing shall be done which may prejudice the civil and religious rights of Christian and all other non-Jewish communities in Palestine and that the holy places and religious buildings and sites in Palestine shall be adequately protected.[14]

For whatever it might be worth, Zionists could now approach other governments waving the resolution aloft. The resolution not only, then, fulfilled one of the very aims of its sponsors, it strengthened the Zionists' position abroad.

To what exactly had the US committed itself by the adoption of the resolution? Certainly no legal commitment was involved. The intent of the Congress clearly was to avoid any specific political commitment as well. What it was, therefore, was an expression of sympathy with the Zionist movement and support for the Balfour Declaration. Congress had clearly entrusted its implementation to its architects, the British. But the resolution has also been interpreted as committing the United States not only to the protection of the holy places, but also to the national home itself, should the British move out for any reason.

Political developments in the 1930s caused a great deal of concern and fear for the Zionists, most significantly the Palestinian rebellion of 1936 and its repercussions in Palestine and outside. The rebellion prompted the British government to issue the 1939 White Paper, which limited Jewish immigration into Palestine to 75,000 in the following five years and forbade Jewish immigration after that time without 'acquiescence of the Arabs in Palestine'. The Palestinians were given promises of increased self-government also, although the sincerity of these promises could be questioned.[15]

The Zionists reacted to the White Paper in three ways: (1) they strengthened their military force in Palestine; (2) they switched their base of political operations from London to Washington; and (3) they intensified their efforts to obtain a firm political commitment from the United States.

American Zionists gathered in 1942 at the Biltmore Hotel to repudiate the British White Paper and to reaffirm their commitment to a national Jewish home in Palestine. After this conference the American Zionist movement emerged more united. The American Zionist Emergency Council was reorganized, Rabbi Abba Hillel Silver, chairman of the Executive Committee, was placed in charge of political and public relations work in the US and the scope of their efforts was broadened. The Emergency Council laid the groundwork for the introduction into both Houses of Congress of resolutions designed to put the legislature on record as favouring the creation of a Jewish state. They formed a systematic campaign of lobbying in Washington and at the local level to obtain the support of majority and minority leaders in Congress and a strong public backing.

The resolutions, introduced in the House by Representative James A. Wright (Dem., Penn.) and in the Senate by Senators Taft and Wagner, were identical and read as follows:

> Whereas, the 67th Congress of the United States on June 30, 1922, unanimously resolved that: 'the United States of America favors the establishment in Palestine of a national home for the Jewish people, it being clearly understood that nothing shall be done which may prejudice the civil and religious rights of Christian and all other non-Jewish communities in Palestine, and that the holy places and religious buildings and sites in Palestine shall be adequately protected', and
> Whereas, the ruthless persecution of the Jewish people in Europe has clearly demonstrated the need for a Jewish homeland as a haven for the large numbers who have become homeless as the result of this persecution; therefore, be it
> Resolved, that the United States shall use its good offices and take appropriate measures to the end that the doors of Palestine shall be open for the free entry of Jews into that country, and that there shall be full opportunity for colonization so that the Jewish people

may ultimately reconstitute Palestine as a free and democratic Jewish Commonwealth.[16]

The House Committee on Foreign Affairs held public hearings on the resolution in February of 1944, during which the Zionist, anti-Zionist and Arab nationalist views were presented.[17] Internationally, the resolution drew very strong reactions from the Arab world, particularly at a time when America needed the co-operation of the Arabs in its war efforts. Secretary of State Hull and Secretary of War Stimson urged postponement of the issue and warned Congress of the possible harm it would cause to America's interests in the Middle East at that time. The resolutions, whose passage had been virtually assumed, were shelved; the American commitment to the idea of a Jewish state was not to be forthcoming at this time.

President Roosevelt and Palestine

Roosevelt was the first American President since Wilson who was faced with the dilemma of making hard decisions for the United States with regard to Palestine. However, the conflict between the seemingly military, strategic and economic necessity to pacify the Arab world, and the apparently 'humanitarian' claims of the Zionists, fortified by considerable economic and political pressure, was never solved by the Roosevelt administration. Beset by the overriding consideration of winning the war, neither the State Department nor the White House was able to formulate a realistic policy on the Middle East as a whole.

Throughout 1943, it was evident that the US was still searching for a formula. In the spring and summer of that year, the State Department and the British Foreign Office discussed a suggestion that the UN declare no decision be taken on Palestine until after the war, and then only with full consultation with Jews and Arabs. Both Roosevelt and the British approved the text, but on the objection of the War Department, perhaps afraid that any statement at all might offend the Arabs, the declaration was not issued.[18] At their conference in Quebec in August, Churchill and Roosevelt resolved to review the Palestine situation from month to month.[19]

In the meantime the President was toying with another scheme. On 27 September 1943 he told Hopkins that he was impressed with the idea of a broader trusteeship for Palestine, with a Jew, a Christian and a Moslem as the three responsible trustees.[20] The State Department apparently took this plan under consideration but the problem was allowed to drift; the department felt that it was unlikely that Jews and Arabs could be brought together on friendly ground at that time, and that it would be wise to avoid stirring up trouble by 'prematurely' trying to settle the question.[21]

This policy of postponement and hope that the Arabs and Jews might come to terms helps to explain events in Washington as the White Paper deadline for an end to Jewish immigration drew near. Congressman Samuel Weiss requested President Roosevelt to intercede with the British for the abrogation of the White Paper. In his reply, drafted by the State Department, Roosevelt said that the matter was being given 'careful thought' but that many 'difficulties' and 'conflicts and problems' arose in connection with it. Similarly, the President refused to approve an Anglo-American statement on Palestine drawn up early in 1944, and presented to him by Under-Secretary of State Edward Stettinius.[22] This declaration would have:

1. Promised full consultation with Arabs and Jews before any decision was made.
2. Welcomed an agreement before the end of the war.
3. Pledged a review of the Palestine situation after the war to establish a 'just and definite solution equitable to all parties concerned'.
4. Involved a warning by the British that they would not permit the use of force to change the status in the meantime.[23]

Just why Roosevelt refused to sanction the issue of such a declaration is not clear. Its first three points were merely restatements of his own position, while there could hardly have been objection to the fourth. Stettinius was convinced that such a joint statement was needed to 'clarify' the situation, and advised Roosevelt to talk with Hopkins.[24] Stettinius and, with him, the State Department were anxious to counteract the effects on the Arab world of the pro-Zionist resolutions then before Congress.

However, when the time came for Congress to consider the pro-Zionist resolutions, the Department of State took a resolute stand against their passage. Hull wrote:

At the State Department, we felt the passage of these resolutions, although not binding on the Executive, might precipitate conflict in Palestine and other parts of the Arab world, endangering American troops and requiring the diversion of forces from Europe and other combat areas.[25]

As a result, Assistant Secretary Long communicated these fears to a group of senators and a memorandum was drafted to be sent to Congress by the President, if Roosevelt's personal influence was necessary to halt passage of the resolutions. As things developed, this was not needed, for the combined opposition of the State and War Departments succeeded in stopping any further action in both Houses. Indeed, the opposition in the Middle East was vocal enough. Protests had been received from Iraq, Egypt, Lebanon, Syria, Trans-Jordan, Yemen and Saudi Arabia. The Department assured these uneasy governments that, even if the resolutions were approved, they would not be binding on the Executive; President Roosevelt followed this up with personal assurances.[26] To Ibn Sa'ud, on 13 March, and to Abdullah of Trans-Jordan, on 17 March, the President replied that no 'decision altering the basic situation in Palestine would be reached without full consultations with both Arabs and Jews'.[27] Similar expressions appeared in the messages sent to Egypt and Yemen. At the same time, the President of the Chamber of Deputies and of the Senate of Iraq wrote to Speaker Sam Rayburn vigorously citing the danger to American interests in the Arab world if the resolutions were approved. On 7 March, Rayburn said: 'It will really lead to danger, I believe, if we are not careful. I think we have it in hand in the House.' The President's reply to Rayburn on 9 March was interesting. The messages from Iraq, Roosevelt wrote, were only part of a 'volume of protests . . . It merely illustrates what happens if delicate international situations get into party politics.' He was also 'glad' that the resolutions were under control in the House.[28]

But if Roosevelt was here the international strategist, concerned with power politics, domestic politics clearly influenced his announcement to the rabbis. Not only was the Democratic Party concerned with the coming elections, but the President and Rabbi Wise had been friends for years, since Roosevelt's term as Governor of New York (1929-33).[29] Perhaps this may explain why the President identified himself as a Zionist during his meeting with Stalin at Yalta:

Marshal Stalin said the Jewish problem was a very difficult one — that they had tried to establish a national home for the Jews in Virovidzhan, but that they had only stayed there two or three years and then scattered to the cities. He said the Jews were natural traders, but much had been accomplished by putting small groups in some agricultural areas.

The President said he was a Zionist and asked if Marshal Stalin was one.

Marshal Stalin said he was one in principle, but he recognized the difficulty.[30]

Wise actively supported the President in all his campaigns for office, speaking throughout the country on the latter's behalf.[31] Wise also acted as a gad-fly and a consultant on problems affecting the Jews and Palestine.[32] The President could be counted on to listen sympathetically, but he did not always satisfy Wise.

One would suspect that Wise may have overlooked one of the most significant American decisions on Palestine which was made by Roosevelt on behalf of the Zionists in 1943, when he urged the British government, then the authority in Palestine, to permit the entry of 100,000 Jewish refugees to Palestine, the very same refugees who had been denied entry into the United States. By this decision Roosevelt linked the fate of the European Jewish refugees to the future of Palestine, and thus validated the Zionist claim that Palestine must be reserved as the ultimate refuge of the world's Jews.

By the time he died, Roosevelt had discovered that any compromise solution between the Arabs and the Zionists would be far from easy. His hope to bring about negotiation between the two parties never materialized. Welles wrote that the President once remarked that if direct negotiations between Jews and Arabs failed, the United Nations Organization would have to create a Jewish Commonwealth and protect it by an international police force until it could protect itself.[33] Possibly this was the trend of Roosevelt's thinking at the time of his death. On the other hand, there is no direct evidence from any other source that this was a seriously considered, well thought-out policy. President Roosevelt's commitment to the creation of a Jewish Commonwealth was never abandoned; but it was his successor, Harry Truman, who had to make the most crucial decisions to ensure the realization of that goal.

President Truman and Palestine

Eight days after Roosevelt's death, American Zionists sought assurances from his successor that there would be no departure from the policies made by the Democratic Party and the late President. President Truman was much more squarely faced than his predecessor with the economic, political and strategic implications of the post-war Middle East situation. On 20 April 1945 Truman received Rabbi Stephen Wise, who pleaded with the President concerning the plight of the Jewish victims of Nazi persecution. He also stressed the need for a Jewish state.

Anticipating Zionist leaders' calls on President Truman, Secretary of State Stettinius briefed the President on Zionist goals and strategies. The Secretary pointed out that in dealing with the Palestine question the long-range interests of the country must be kept in mind. Accordingly, Stettinius attempted to draw a distinction between traditional American sympathy for the oppressed Jews and the problem of settlement in Palestine, which, he said, 'involves questions that go far beyond the plight of the Jews in Europe'.[34] The Secretary's expression of concern was shortly bolstered by Acting Secretary of State, Joseph Drew, who sent favoured information to the President two weeks later. The late President, said Drew, despite his expressions of sympathy for certain Zionist aims, had also given assurances to the Arabs which were regarded by them as 'definite commitments'.[35] Accompanying Drew's memorandum was the text of Roosevelt's last letter to Ibn Sa'ud written one week before his death. Also enclosed was a summary of the late President's conversation with the King, 'the original of which', said Drew, 'is presumably with Roosevelt's papers'.[36]

Truman was fully aware of Arab hostility to Jewish settlement. Like many other Americans, he was 'troubled by the plight of the Jewish people in Europe'.[37] Taking the words of the Balfour Declaration concerning a 'national home' for the Jews in Palestine, Truman somehow imagined that Wilson's principle of self-determination was linked to the Balfour document. Though self-determination was intended to apply to the Jewish immigrants to Palestine, it apparently ignored the Arab majority in Palestine. Moreover, Truman's basic outlook on the situation was coloured by his own deep sympathy for the survivors of Hitler's racism and his very 'legalistic' approach to the Balfour Declaration. He expressed no doubt as to either the content or the circumstances of that document and assumed that its existence involved a 'solemn promise . . . which should be kept, just as all promises made by responsible, civilized governments should be kept'.[38]

In these circumstances, Truman did not find it hard to reassure Rabbi Wise. He told the Zionist leader that he was in agreement with the expressed policy of Roosevelt's administration on Palestine and promised to do everything possible to carry it out.[39] Truman saw no collision between American interests and Jewish interests in Palestine when he said:

> It was my feeling that it would be possible for us to watch out for the long-range interests of our country while, at the same time, helping these unfortunate victims of persecution to find a home. And before Rabbi Wise left, I believe I made this clear to him.[40]

Therefore, from the outset of his administration, Truman made it clear that he intended to continue the same policy as previous American Presidents towards Palestine.

The Partition of Palestine

On 2 April 1947, the British delegation to the United Nations requested the Secretary-General to place the Palestine question on the agenda of the fall session of the General Assembly. In preparation for consideration of the issue at that time, Britain asked that he 'summon, as soon as possible, a special session of the General Assembly for the purpose of constituting and instructing a special committee' to report in the fall.[41]

An eleven-nation United Nations Special Committee on Palestine (UNSCOP) was formed. The committee visited Palestine, and on 31 August 1947 submitted a report to the General Assembly. The majority of UNSCOP favoured the partition of Palestine into separate Arab and Jewish states with an internationalized Jerusalem.[42]

The stage was set for the acrimonious partition debate in the United Nations, with the United States strongly backing partition. Commenting on Zionist pressures brought to bear upon the White House, Truman said, 'I do not think I ever had as much pressure and propaganda aimed at the White House as I had in this instance.'[43]

Under-Secretary Robert Lovett also reported that 'he had never in his life been subject to as much pressure as he had been in the three days beginning Thursday morning and ending Saturday night'.[44]

Sumner Welles claimed that the White House was directly involved in the matter:

> By direct order of the White House every form of pressure, direct or indirect, was brought to bear by American officials upon those countries outside of the Moslem world that were known to be either uncertain or opposed to partition. Representatives of intermediaries

were employed by the White House to make sure that the necessary majority would at length be secured.[45]

Some of the countries which were chosen as targets were the six nations which had opposed partition, namely, Haiti, the Philippines, Liberia, Nationalist China, Greece and Ethiopia. The Firestone Tire and Rubber Company, which has a concession in Liberia, reported that it had been telephoned and asked to transmit a message to its representative in Liberia directing him to bring pressure on the Liberian government to vote in favour of the partition.[46] An ex-governor, a prominent Democrat with White House connections, personally telephoned Haiti urging that its delegation be instructed to change its vote.[47]

Both Haiti and Liberia reversed their stand and voted for partition. So did the Philippines and Ethiopia, while China abstained from voting. Of those six chosen as targets, only Greece held fast to its earlier convictions. The final result was the approval of partition by the United Nations on 29 November 1947.

Further evidence of the political nature of the United States government stand on Palestine was furnished by Colonel Eddy, who described the recall to Washington of four American diplomats stationed in the Middle East: the United States ambassadors in Egypt, Lebanon and Syria (the joint post) and Saudi Arabia and the Counsel General to Mandated Palestine. The purpose was to give President Truman the diplomats' view of the effects of American policy in Palestine. The spokesman for the group was George Wadsworth, who spoke for about twenty minutes stressing the harm that would be inflicted on American economic interests if the United States government persisted in its anti-Arab policy in Palestine. When he had finished, Colonel Eddy wrote, 'Mr. Truman summed up his position with the utmost candor: I am sorry, gentlemen, but I have to answer to hundreds of thousands who are anxious for the success of Zionism; I do not have hundreds of thousands of Arabs among my constituents.'[48]

According to President Truman, Jewish pressure on the White House did not diminish in the days following the adoption of the resolution. Individuals and groups asked him, 'usually in rather quarrelsome and emotional ways to stop the Arabs, to keep the British from supporting the Arabs, to furnish American soldiers'.[49] The confusion and bloodshed in Palestine which followed upon the United Nations vote made it clear that partition could be effective only through the use of force, a stand taken by F.D. Roosevelt, Jr, Sumner Welles, Herbert Lehman, and other Zionist supporters.

The military, however, foresaw that the presence of American troops in the area could only assist the Soviets. The appearance of American troops would put the United States in the position of supporting an anti-Arab programme. This would then allow the Soviet Union to appear as the only real friend of Arab nationalism should that country then elect to desert the Zionists.[50] For these and other strategic reasons, Secretary of Defense Forrestal became increasingly active in seeking to prevent that situation from materializing. On 13 December, Forrestal spoke to Governor Dewey about removing Palestine from the round of partisan politics. Governor Dewey said that, while agreeing with Forrestal in principle, he was sceptical that the Democrats would really abide by any such decision.[51] The Secretary's concern was heightened after hearing from Mr. Jennings of Socony Vacuum, on 6 January 1948, that various oil companies had decided to suspend work on the Arabian pipeline because of disturbed conditions in Palestine.[52] Forrestal's efforts met little success with the Republicans as well as with members of his own party. At the same time, Forrestal came to believe that the gravity of the situation demanded that the Secretary of State should attempt to secure bi-partisan agreement on this matter. A paper to this effect was drawn up and presented on 21 January to Under-Secretary Robert Lovett, who agreed, in general, with Forrestal's conclusions.

A visit from Franklin D. Roosevelt, Jr to Forrestal on 3 February 1948 was obviously aimed at turning down the latter's activities. But to Roosevelt's warning that failure to implement partition could only harm Democratic chances in certain key states, the Secretary characteristically remarked that he 'thought it was about time that somebody should pay some consideration as to whether we might not lose the United States'.[53] Forrestal also informed Roosevelt that the tactics by which the partition resolution had been secured bordered on scandal, but on this the young Congressman professed ignorance.[54]

Military and diplomatic arguments for a new approach to the Palestine problem were reinforced by the lobbying activities of the oil interests.[55] Their representatives pointed out that if the United States continued to press for partition, the oil of the Near East would not be available for military purposes nor amenable to the effort of containing Communism.[56]

Perhaps the first indication of a new American attitude came on 5 December 1947, when it was announced that 'for the present', no licenses for arms shipments to 'troubled areas' in the Middle East would be granted. This policy brought about strong Zionist agitation for repeal of the embargo,[57] which did not, in fact, prevent illegal ship-ments from American ports to Palestine. Barnett Litvinoff notes that an engineer named Slavine purchased war equipment worth 'many millions' for $800,000.[58] The United States had shifted its position from partition to trusteeship in Palestine. This shift was designed to allow for delay while a new effort at conciliation was attempted. This new trend away from partition to reconciliation was evident in the American attitude displayed at a series of meetings of the Security Council beginning on 8 March 1948, and attended by all the permanent members, except Britain. United States Ambassador to the United Nations Austin expressed the hope that agreement would be reached by the Arabs, Jews and Britain without outside interference. The Jews and Arabs were formally asked by the United States, China and France on 15 March to agree to a truce in Palestine, a step which, strictly speaking, had not been authorized by the Security Council. However, the opinions expressed by both parties indicated that agreement was as far away as ever. It therefore seemed that force alone would effect partition. Having been brought to the crucial issue, the US thereupon refused to recommend to the Security Council that a threat to peace and security existed in Palestine.

With the trend of American policy away from the enforcement of partition, the Jewish Agency sought to reach the President of the United States secretly. In what was clearly a Zionist strategy to over-come this American reluctance, Eddie Jacobson, a member of B'nai B'rith and a friend of both Truman and Weizmann, was received by the President on 14 March, in spite of the former's decision to avoid further approaches by the Zionists. Weizmann then requested an interview with President Truman, which was granted. After a conversation lasting almost three quarters of an hour, Truman seemed convinced that the Zionist leader 'had reached a full understanding' of his policy.[59]

The day after the President's interview with Weizmann, events at the United Nations reached a new stage. On 19 March, Austin asserted before the Security Council that the partition plan did not constitute an obligation for the United Nations or any of its members. The plan itself, said Austin, had been agreed to only on the presumption that all of its parts would be carried out together. Since this was now manifestly impossible, the job of the United Nations was to see to it that peace and order were restored. It was therefore proposed that a temporary trusteeship under the Trusteeship Council be established. Such a procedure, said Austin, would remove the threat of violence and would make it possible for Jews and Arabs to reach an agreement on the future government of the country. Trusteeship, it was said, would not prejudice the character of the eventual political settlement. The American delegate, accordingly, asked the Security Council to recommend the creation of such a trusteeship to the General Assembly and to Britain, the mandatary. Pending a special session, it was suggested the Palestine Committee suspend its efforts to implement partition.[60]

Following Austin's statements, supporters of the partition plan in the United States accused the government of abandoning the plan. In order to clarify the United States' stand, Truman announced on 25 March that trusteeship was not proposed as a substitute for partition, but was only an effort to fill the vacuum created by the termination of the mandate. He said:

> Unfortunately, it has become clear that the partition plan cannot be carried out by peaceful means. We could not undertake to impose this solution on the people of Palestine by the use of American troops, both on charter grounds and as a matter of national policy. The United Kingdom has announced its firm intention to abandon the mandate on Palestine on May 15. Unless emergency action is taken, there will be no public authority in Palestine on that date capable of preserving law and order. Violence and bloodshed will descend on the Holy Land. Large-scale fighting among the people of that country will be the inevitable result. Such fighting would infect the entire Middle East and could lead to consequences of the greatest sort involving the peace of the world.[61]

Accordingly, the United States introduced into the Security Council, on 30 March, two resolutions: one calling on Arabs and Jews to meet with the Security Council to arrange a truce, and the other requesting the Security Council to convene a special session of the General Assembly. Both resolutions were adopted by the Security Council within two days.[62] Subsequent attempts by the United States to draw up a trusteeship formula — while ruling out the intervention of American troops unless both Arabs and Jews should agree to a truce — failed to find support in the Assembly. Arabs and Jews drifted into a full-scale war and the attempt of the Security Council to secure a truce proved ineffectual.

American Recognition of Israel

As 15 May 1948 — the date set by Britain for termination of the mandate — approached, the Zionist leadership continued to plan for the proclamation of an independent state, refusing to acquiesce on the proposed trusteeship. The Jewish Agency decided to confront the world with 'facts'. On 15 May President Truman received a letter from Weizmann advising him that at midnight that same day the provisional government of the Jewish State would come into existence. It was suggested that the United States take the lead in recognizing the world's 'newest democracy'.[63] Within a few hours, the United States, the first government to do so, granted the new state *de facto* recognition.[64] There are two versions as to how this came about. One version has it that the President was apparently favourable to Weizmann's suggestion, but before acting upon it he consulted with Secretary of State Marshall, who expressed opposition. Marshall's advice weighed heavily with Truman and it took some persuasion from the White House advisers, including Clark Clifford and David Niles, before the President would agree to a conference to discuss the situation. Marshall, Lovett, Niles, Clifford and Truman, plus an expert from the State Department, attended. Clifford argued that Truman had already said that he supported a Jewish state and, since it now actually existed, it should be recognized. Marshall thought the matter should be decided on the basis of policy not politics. The meeting closed with Truman apparently on the side of the State Department. Nevertheless, the next day recognition was granted, presumably because of a policy decision made within the State Department to recognize Israel within a few days, and pressure by Clifford on Truman to grant the recognition, already decided upon, at once.[65] The other version, reported in *The Forrestal Diaries*, indicates that the decision was communicated to Marshall and Lovett at the White House conference, and, moreover, that it was reached on 12 or 13 May.[66]

Truman's role in the creation of the state of Israel did not come to an end with his recognition of the state. He further committed the United States to the survival and security of that state. That commitment has been reiterated by all American presidents.

Throughout this period we can conclude that there was *no* American policy towards the Palestinian people. The Palestinians were seen as a non-people; American policy dealt mainly with the Zionists and the Arab states. It dealt with Palestine and the schemes through which a Jewish homeland could be realized in that country without jeopardizing

American interests in the Arab world. The Palestinians were treated as obstacles in the path of a desired scheme outlined in the Balfour Declaration and reaffirmed in American Congressional resolutions. Palestinians were referred to simply as the 'non-Jewish' population at a time when they constituted ninety-five per cent of the country. America refused to recognize the Palestinian right to self-determination, a right that Wilson had advocated and defended so vigorously for all the peoples of the dissolved Austro-Hungarian and Ottoman Empires, of which the Palestinians were a part.

Notes

1. J.C. Hurewitz, *Middle East Dilemma* (New York: Harper and Brothers, 1953), p. 107.

2. Reuben Fink, *America and Palestine* (New York: American Zionist Emergency Council, 1944), p. 20.

3. Ibid., pp. 21-3.

4. M.E. Jansen, *The Three Basic American Decisions on Palestine* (Beirut: PLO Research Center, 1971), pp. 7-17.

5. Roscoe Baker, *The American Legion and American Foreign Policy* (New York: Bookman Associates, 1954), pp. 256 and 305.

6. S.J. Res. 191, 67th Congr. 2nd Session, *Congressional Record*, vol. LXII, Part 5, 5376. It was at once referred to the Committee on Foreign Relations.

7. Ibid., 7 May 1922, Section 2, p. 6. It is true that Lodge had difficulties in the campaign of 1922. His biographer has written: 'Lodge's power had indeed lessened in his home state. The Senatorial campaign was difficult for him. And on election day in November he received a popularity of only 7,154 votes, running 50,000 behind the Republican candidate for governor.' Karl Schriftgiesser, *The Gentleman from Massachusetts: Henry Cabot Lodge* (Boston: Little, Brown & Co., 1944), pp. 358-9.

8. Lipsky, in the conversation referred to, asserted that Fish adopted the idea of a resolution from Goldberg. In a letter of 26 June 1953 to the author, Fish stated that Judge Mack and Rabbi Wise helped draft the text of the resolution.

9. Some Jews objected to the resolution because of very slight change in wording. They preferred the exact wording of the Balfour Declaration.

10. *Congressional Record*, vol. LXII, part 10, p. 9799.

11. See *New Palestine*, II (1, 14 April 1922), pp. 280-1, 230.

12. Ibid., (14 April 1922), p. 280.

13. See letter from the Department to Duke Christianson, Harding's Secretary, National Archives, State Department file 867, N. 01/311 A. See ibid., file 867N. 01/199 for a memorandum of the Near Eastern Division pointing out that the Anglo-American Convention then under negotiation might be endangered in the Senate if the resolution was not signed.

14. The Statutes at Large of the United States of America, vol. LXII, part 1, (Washington, DC: US Govt. Printing Office, 1923), p. 1012.

15. *The American Zionist Emergency Council, A Report of Activities 1940-1946* (New York: 1946) pp. 11-12, and Elihu D. Stone, 'The Zionist Outlook in Washington', *New Palestine*, XXXIV (17 March 1944), p. 305.

16. H. Res. 418, 78th Cong., 2nd session, *Congressional Record*, vol. 10, part 1, p. 856. Representative Ranulf Compton, Republican of Connecticut, introduced

a resolution identical to the Wright: H. Res. 419, in ibid.; the Wagner-Taft Resolution was S. Res. 247.

17. US Congress, House Committee on Foreign Affairs, *Hearings* on H. Res. 418 and J. Res. 419, *Resolutions relative to the Jewish National Home in Palestine*, 78th Congress, 2nd session, (Washington: US Govt. Printing Office, 1944).

18. Cordell Hull, *Memoirs* (New York: The Macmillan Company, 1948), p. 1533.

19. *The New York Times*, 24 August 1943, p. 3.

20. Hull, *Memoirs*, pp. 1533-1534.

21. Ibid.

22. F.D.R. *Memoirs*, p. 900.

23. Text in ibid.

24. Stettinius to F.D.R., in ibid., 4 March 1944.

25. Hull, *Memoirs*, pp. 1534-1535.

26. Ibid., p. 1535.

27. Ibid.

28. Text of letters in *F.D.R. Memoirs*.

29. Stephen S. Wise, *Challenging Years* (New York: G.P. Putnam and Sons, 1949), pp. 216-32.

30. US Department of State, *Foreign Relations of the United States. The Conference at Malta and Yalta, 1945* (Washington: US Govt. Printing Office, 1955), p. 924.

31. Wise, *Challenging Years*, pp. 216-32.

32. Ibid.

33. Sumner Welles, *We Need not Fail* (Boston: Houghton Mifflin Company, 1948), p. 30.

34. Harry S. Truman, *Memoirs: Years of Trial and Hope, 1946-1952* (New York: New American Library, vol. 1, 1961), p. 69.

35. Ibid., vol. 2, p. 132.

36. Ibid.

37. Ibid., p. 133.

38. Ibid., p. 132.

39. Ibid., vol. 1, p. 67.

40. Ibid., p. 69.

41. United Nations General Assembly, *Official Records*, first special session, vol. 1, Doc. A-286, p. 183.

42. *U.N. Yearbook*, 1947-48, p. 230.

43. Truman, *Memoirs*, vol. 2, p. 346.

44. Walter Millis (ed.), *The Forrestal Diaries* (New York, The Viking Press, 1951), p. 346.

45. Welles, *We Need not Fail*, p. 63.

46. *Forrestal Diaries*, p. 346.

47. Kermit Roosevelt, 'The Partition of Palestine: A Lesson in Pressure Politics', *Middle East Journal* (Washington, DC: 1948), p. 15.

48. William A. Eddy, *F.D.R. Meets Ibn Sa'ud* (New York: American Friends of the Middle East, 1954), pp. 36-7.

49. Truman, *Memoirs*, vol. 2, p. 160.

50. C.F. Halford Hoskins, *The Middle East: Problem Area in World Politics* (New York: Macmillan Co., 1957), pp. 18-38, 232-54.

51. *The Forrestal Diaries*, p. 348.

52. Ibid., p. 356f.

53. Ibid., pp. 359-62.

54. Ibid., pp. 362-5.

55. American petroleum interests in the Middle East date back to the period preceding World War I, when the Ottoman government granted a concession to the Standard Oil Company of New York in southern Palestine. Serious American investment in Arabian oil was vigorously championed by the State Department from 1929.

By World War II, American companies had penetrated Saudi Arabia, Bahrain, Kuwait, and, to a lesser degree, Iraq. Saudi oil production increased from 15,000 to 58,000 barrels per day in three years. The possibilities for future development seemed enormous. Proved reserves in the Aramco concession (Standard Oil of California and Texaco exploitation of Arabian oil) were set at from six to seven billion barrels with potential reserves at more than fourteen billion. Since production in the Middle East cost less than in the United States and the rest of the Western hemisphere, the value of the petroleum in the postwar market was clear.

56. Welles, *We Need Not Fail*, pp. 81-2.

57. *The Forrestal Diaries*, p. 376.

58. Barnett Nitvinoff, *Ben Gurion of Israel* (London: Weidenfeld and Nicolson, 1954), p. 159.

59. Truman, *Memoirs*, vol. 2, pp. 160-1.

60. UN Security Council, Verbatim Record of the 271st meeting, 19 March 1948, Doc. S/PP. 2871.

61. Richard Stevens, *American Zionism and U.S. Foreign Policy 1942-1947* (New York: Pageant Press, 1962), pp. 202-3.

62. Ibid., p. 203.

63. Ibid., p. 204.

64. *New York Times*, 15 May 1948, p. 1.

65. Jonathan Daniel, *The Man From Independence* (New York and Philadelphia: J.P. Lippincott Co., 1950), pp. 319-20.

66. *The Forrestal Diaries*, pp. 440-1.

3 UNITED STATES POLICY TOWARDS PALESTINIAN REFUGEES

American involvement with the issue of the Palestinian refugees began immediately after the 1948 Israeli war, which precipitated the first large exodus of Palestinians from their homeland. American officials linked the refugee problem with the general problem of resolving differences between Israel and the Arab states. This perception was succinctly expressed by former Under-Secretary of State Walter Bedell Smith:

> The refugee problem is the principal unresolved issue between Israel and the Arabs. Outstanding issues generally listed are compensation to the refugees, repatriation of the refugees, adjustment of boundaries, and the status of Jerusalem and of the holy places. None of these issues can be separated from the refugee problem because that is the human problem.[1]

The American government's approach essentially operated upon two tiers: (1) it continued to support financially palliatives for the difficult living conditions of the refugees and (2) it repeatedly attempted to find a workable solution to the refugee problem and thereby a resolution of the issues between Israel and the Arab states. This approach, which was continued until 1967, was predicated on the idea that, once the problem of the refugees was solved, other issues would fall into place for a final settlement. This chapter will examine the problem of the Palestinian refugees, as well as America's efforts to resolve them.

Problem of the Palestinian Refugees

In December 1949, the United Nations Economic Survey Mission for the Middle East estimated the number of refugees at 726,000.[2] They had lost their homes, property, livelihood and country. They lived under wretched physical conditions in camps sponsored by the United Nations Relief and Works Agency (UNRWA). Their problems exist to this day.

43

Refugee Numbers

The Director of UNRWA in his interim report of 1955 noted that 'an accurate statement of the number of refugees resulting from the war in Palestine is unlikely to be provided now or in the future'.[3] From the 726,000 refugees reported in December 1949, the refugee population showed a steady increase.[4] Many came from the Beersheba area. Many of the Bedouin tribes moved to Jordan because there they found fewer restrictions on their mobility, an essential feature of their way of life. Many Palestinians experienced being made refugees twice in their lifetimes, first as a result of the 1948 war and again as a consequence of the 1967 Arab-Israeli war.[5]

The latest available UNRWA report shows that the number of refugees registered with the agency as of 30 June 1977 was 1,706,486.[6] The refugees were distributed as follows:

Lebanon	201,171
Syria	192,915
West Bank	302,620
East Jordan	663,773
Gaza Strip	346,007
Total	1,706,486[7]

These figures do not include Palestinians who have lost their means of livelihood but not their homes, for as such they do not qualify for relief under the United Nations definition of refugees;[8] for example, many of the Palestinians living in the war front-line villages or along the 1949 cease-fire lines who lost all or most of their land but not their homes are not included in the UNRWA records. The figures also exclude those who re-established themselves in the surrounding Arab countries and are therefore not in need of relief, nor do they include Palestinians now scattered throughout the rest of the world.

Status of Refugees in the 'Host' Countries

The majority of Palestinian Arab refugees shared with the population of the neighbouring Arab countries common religion, language, historical outlook, and traditions. One might expect that the refugees would be well received. However, for many the welcome was short-lived. The influx of tens of thousands of mostly unskilled penniless refugees and the lack of hope of their repatriation raised many problems. The refugees constituted a serious economic liability in the countries already over-burdened with their own surplus unskilled population. In addition, they constituted a destabilizing political element. The refugees' status, and particularly their rights and obligations, differed from country to country.

Jordan. The largest number of Palestinian refugees were in areas controlled by Jordan before 1967. The 918,779 refugees made up over one-third of the population.[9] King Abdullah, the grandfather of King Hussein of Jordan, was eager to make his artificially created desert kingdom a viable one; so he annexed the Palestinian territories remaining in the hands of the Arab Legion after the conclusion of the armistice agreement in Rhodes.[10] Abdullah viewed the annexation of these areas, which became known as the West Bank, as a step towards 'unification'. This policy brought him into direct conflict with other Arab states, and, most importantly, with the majority of Palestinians. He was very active in promoting the annexation at the local level through the use of political stimuli, promises, intimidation and coercion.[11] He also worked on the international level from 1949 to April 1950 when the annexation was officially declared.[12]

The government took steps to integrate the Palestinian population into Jordan.[13] Palestinian refugees and non-refugees, together forming about 71 per cent of the population of the country, were granted the right to acquire Jordanian citizenship in accordance with Article 3 of the Jordanian nationality law. The article provided them with the full rights and obligations of Jordanian citizenship.[14]

Although Jordan attempted to integrate the refugees politically, the task was impossible. The refugees numbered over one-third of the population of Jordan and the country simply did not have the means to effect their economic absorption. Furthermore, the refugees preferred repatriation to their homes in Palestine. The Hashemite dynasty in Jordan came to doubt the prudence of annexing part of Palestine and its population. By this policy the monarchy unwittingly sowed the seeds of the Kingdom's own destruction. Already by the early 1950s there arose a strong current of resentment among the Palestinians living in Jordan. They suspected the Hashemite monarchy of collaboration in the Zionist conquest of Palestine. In 1951 a teenage Palestinian assassinated King Abdullah. A number of subsequent assassination attempts were carried out by Palestinians. Palestinian resentment of the Jordanian monarchy intensified in the aftermath of the 1970 Jordanian civil war, in which the Palestinian *fedayeen* suffered a major setback at the hands of the royalists.[15] King Hussein never trusted the Palestinian segment of his population and therefore entrusted the sensitive positions in the government and army to the loyal Bedouin and minorities.[16] Even in the less important positions Palestinians were treated as second-class citizens.

Syria. Syria's treatment of the Palestinians fluctuated according to its internal political situation and the general Arab policy toward Israel. Unlike Jordan, Syria did not offer the Palestinian refugees citizenship. However, their position was no worse than in Jordan. Specific amendments gave them the right to work, move, and engage in trade even though restrictions on the purchase of land were not completely removed.[17] Syrian law was amended sufficiently to facilitate their economic integration but not their total absorption — obviously for political reasons. The number of refugees was small. Of the slightly less than 200,000 Palestinian refugees in Syria, 53,175 lived in camps.[18] The total number of Palestinians in Syria, which comprised about three per cent of Syria's population, worked no economic hardship on Syria. The area in which Palestinians in Syria fared best was in education; Palestinian youths took full advantage of the free university education offered them, and this enabled them to get better jobs and thus move out of the refugee camps.

Egypt and the Gaza Strip. Only a small number of refugees fled to Egypt proper. There they were allowed to work, to travel freely in the country, and to have access to all courts of law. They were subject to taxation but were not granted Egyptian citizenship. In fact, they had virtually no political rights, nor were they obligated to serve in the army. Many of the refugees living in Egypt were from well-to-do Palestinian families who did not need any UNRWA aid.

The situation in the Gaza Strip was quite different. From the time the area fell under Egyptian rule in 1948, it was treated as occupied territory under military rule. The Military Governor of Gaza was appointed by the Egyptian War Department. The army had full control of the area and local government authority was virtually non-existent.[19]

The refugees of the Gaza Strip enjoyed the same rights and were subject to the same regulations as the local residents. Freedom of association and movement within the area were curtailed, allegedly for security reasons. Outside travel was restricted.[20] Gaza residents were isolated from the rest of the world and confined to a reservation locked between Israel on the north and east, the Mediterranean sea on the west, and the Sinai desert on the south-west. The Gaza Strip is an area of less than 150 square miles and, as of 1950, its population was about 270,000, of whom 190,000 were refugees.[21] Though the refugees have been allowed to seek employment, opportunities for work are very limited. Income taxes are paid by inhabitants and refugees alike. The unavailability of jobs, the high population density and the isolation all intensified their resentment of Israel and its allies.

Lebanon. The flight of Palestinians to Lebanon in 1948 increased that country's population by about ten per cent, comparable perhaps to the arrival in the United States of over twenty million refugees from Vietnam at a time of more than ten per cent unemployment. The economic impact of refugee migration in Lebanon was less acute than in Jordan or Gaza, but the political and social repercussions were no less severe. An estimated 90 per cent of the refugees were Muslim; their presence embarrassed the Lebanese government, which was based on a delicate balance between Muslim and Christian minorities.[22] No population census had been taken since 1932 for fear of undermining the supposed Christian plurality of one to three per cent. Lebanese society and politics were based on a quota system of approximately five Muslims for every six Christian inhabitants. Government posts from the Presidency down to clerkships and junior officer grades in the army and police force were allocated according to this ratio. The influx of tens of thousands of Sunni Muslim Palestinians threatened to shift the power balance from Christian to Muslim and jeopardize the communal life under which Lebanon operated.[23] Therefore, all groups rejoiced when the camps were placed under the constant surveillance of the Lebanese police, the Deuxième Bureau (Al Maktab Althani), to ensure their political neutrality. The Lebanese poor and unemployed saw a threat to their already miserable economic conditions in the influx of a new mass of unskilled and unemployed. The wealthy Lebanese had no desire to see the slums of Beirut extended to the outskirts of the city in the form of refugee camps and they feared instability. Police intimidation of Palestinians extended even outside the camps, only increasing Palestinian bitterness.[24]

Judicially the Palestinians were regarded as being in Lebanon 'on sufferance'. They were not granted residence visas and were not entitled to take advantage of the laws of citizenship. As a result, they had neither political rights nor military obligations. They were expected, however, to conform to the laws and regulations of the country, as well as to obey all measures taken for the maintenance of law and order to the same extent as foreigners; in addition, they were subject to certain restrictions which did not apply to other non-Lebanese.

The refugees were subject to taxation, but, since they were regarded as foreigners, they could acquire property only by permission of the President of the Republic. However, refugees found it difficult to obtain such permission.[25] Conditions of employment were not much better. As foreigners, the law required the refugees to obtain work permits.[26] (UNRWA employees were not required to secure permits.) In addition to those refugees who were able to obtain work permits, thousands worked without permits.[27] The government periodically took strict measures against them — most notably in early 1952 when the rate of unemployment among Lebanese workers rose to more than fifteen per cent.[28]

Unlike other non-Lebanese residents, Palestinian refugees were subject to restrictions based on the grounds of public order and security, as well as on the grounds of public policy. All refugees aged fifteen and above were required to carry identity cards; children under fifteen years were registered on the father's or mother's card.

The severely restricted status of Palestinian refugees in Lebanon helped sow the seeds of the present chaos which has overtaken that unhappy country.

United Nations Relief and Resettlement Efforts

In May 1948, the United Nations appointed Count Folke Bernadotte of the Swedish Red Cross to arrange a cease-fire between the Arabs and Israel and to look into the needs of the civilian population. By July 1948, thousands of Palestinians had reached neighbouring states; their initial welcome had worn thin and food supplies were running low. The threats of epidemic and starvation were real. The Arab League sought the aid of the International Refugee Organization, which expressed doubt as to its ability to help. Bernadotte then appealed to the United Nations Children's Emergency Fund, which provided more than four hundred thousand dollars in immediate relief. Thirteen nations also responded as did a number of private organizations, many of them American.[29]

On 11 September 1948, the United Nations Disaster Relief Project was established to co-ordinate emergency relief activities and the distribution of donations. It was succeeded by the United Nations Relief for Palestine Refugees. A continuing standing committee was set up in the United States in October 1948 to serve as a channel for private voluntary contributions. It was successful in raising about one million dollars in supplies and funds.[30]

In addition to the relief projects, Bernadotte tried throughout the summer to arrange for the refugees to return to Palestine. But the true dimensions of the problem were just beginning to appear. The Provisional Government of Israel refused to consider the refugee question except as part of a general peace settlement; the Arab states insisted that the refugees must be permitted to return before any direct negotiations could take place. These mutually exclusive positions have been maintained throughout the long conflict.

In support of Bernadotte, President Truman suggested on 6 September 1948 that 'the Provisional Government of Israel consider some constructive measures for the alleviation of Arab refugees' distress'. While the refugee problem attracted little public attention in Israel, the government was aware of the far-reaching implications. Nevertheless, the Israeli authorities were determined that this issue await a final peace settlement.[31] They disclaimed any responsibility for the exodus and said that only a limited number of carefully screened refugees could be repatriated. The best solution would be resettlement where the refugees could be integrated into the community. Even those who were repatriated would not be resettled in the area from which they had come.[32]

The Bernadotte Proposals. In his progress report on 16 September, one day before he was killed by Zionist terrorists in Jerusalem, Bernadotte wrote that there could be no just and complete settlement if the right of the Arab refugees to return home was not recognized. He stated that their exodus resulted from panic created by the fighting around them or by rumours of real or alleged terrorism; it also resulted from deliberate expulsion. It would be an offence against the principles of basic justice if they were denied the right to return while Jews were permitted — even encouraged — to immigrate into Palestine. He held that Israel should be responsible for restoring private property to the owners and for providing indemnity to those whose property was wantonly destroyed. He warned that establishing the right of return would not provide a solution, because many homes had already been destroyed and the refugees' return might present complex social and economic problems.[33] Nevertheless, like the Arabs, he thought that 'their unconditional right to make a free choice should be fully respected'.[34] In his conclusion to the report, the mediator wrote that:

> return at the earliest possible date should be affirmed by the United Nations, and their repatriation, resettlement and economic and social rehabilitation, and payment of adequate compensation for the property of those choosing not to return should be supervised and

assisted by the United Nations conciliation commission.[35]

Secretary of State Marshall called the report's conclusions 'a generally fair basis for settlement of the Palestine problem'. He strongly urged the parties concerned and the General Assembly 'to accept them in their entirety as the best possible basis for bringing peace'.[36] Two days later, in a speech to the General Assembly, Marshall said that the 'repatriation of refugees who wish to return and live in peace with their neighbours' should be sought in Palestine.[37]

These views by no means represented a consensus in the American government. Reflecting the sentiments of a large number of political figures, Representative Celler of New York contended that the Arab refugees 'deliberately uprooted themselves from their homes in Palestine'. He blamed their plight on Britain, 'who officered, supplied, and financed the Arab troops which invaded Palestine'. He said that any mass readmission of the Arabs would introduce 'a dangerous fifth column' in Israel and that Britain and the Arab states were responsible for their well-being. Relief should come from the national voluntary organizations. 'Humane repatriation is fine and high-sounding, but the Israelis cannot at present disregard the military effect. The return of these Arabs would put the Israelis at a decided military disadvantage.' He regarded the refugees as only one facet of the problem and said that the American delegate to the United Nations should refuse to discuss them as a separate issue. Their return should be conditional upon the economic stability and military security of Israel, the establishment of a long-range peace among the parties, a guarantee of security for Jewish minorities in Middle Eastern countries, and reparations for 'Arab-British aggression'.[38]

The major party platforms in that presidential election year expressed a similar concern for the well-being of Israel but made no mention of the Arabs in any context. A Democratic plank pledged full recognition of Israel and took pride in the role that the Truman administration had played in the partition resolution. It approved the boundary claims set forth in the resolution and stipulated that any modifications should first gain Israel's approval. It favoured a revision of the arms embargo to give Israel the right of self-defence and supported the internationalization of Jerusalem and protection of the holy places. The Republican party platform simply welcomed Israel into the family of nations and pledged full recognition of the state with its boundaries as sanctioned by the United Nations. It also promised aid to develop the economy.[39] These pledges were reaffirmed by the candidates during the presidential campaign.

United Nations Resolution. In the General Assembly in the autumn of 1948, the United States supported relief for the refugees and urged all members to make voluntary contributions to meet the programme's need for forty million dollars, of which the United States would contribute one-half.[40] Stanton Griffin, US ambassador to Cairo, was appointed director of this new agency, which took over many of the activities of the United Nations Disaster Relief Project but tried to confine itself to administration, coordination and logistics. The actual distribution of supplies was handled by established relief organizations, such as the Red Cross and American Friends Service Committee.[41]

UNRWA has been said to be 'one of the prices and perhaps the least expensive the international community is paying for not having been able to solve with equity the political problem of the refugees'.[42] The agency, a subsidiary of the General Assembly, was established by Resolution 302 (IV) on 8 December 1949. The United States has been a pillar of support of UNRWA through its annual contributions; in fact, during its twenty-five years (1950-75), the United States contributed about 57 per cent of the entire cost of UNRWA's operations. The Soviet Union has contributed nothing.[43] (See Appendix J). UNRWA's task is two-fold: to provide short-term relief for registered refugees in need and to provide the refugees with a range of technical services for their health, welfare, education and vocational training. During this time, the United States continued officially to favour at least partial repatriation. The American delegate to the General Assembly affirmed that the Palestine refugees 'should be permitted to return to their homes and that adequate compensation should be arranged for the property of those who choose not to return'.[44]

The United States also played a leading role in the final drafting of Resolution 194 (III) of 11 December 1948, the basis for all subsequent resolutions dealing with the Palestine refugees. Although this resolution grew out of Bernadotte's report, in its final form it was considerably altered. An early version, submitted by the United Kingdom, stated that the General Assembly

resolves that the Arab refugees should be permitted to return to their homes at the earliest possible date and that adequate compensation should be paid for the property which has been lost as a result of pillage, confiscations or of destruction.

Under American sponsorship, this paragraph went through several revisions to soften the language and add qualifications. In its final form, paragraph 11 of Resolution 194 (III) reads:

> The General Assembly
> Resolves that the refugees wishing to return to their homes and live in peace with their neighbors should be permitted to do so at the earliest practicable date, and that compensation should be paid for the property of those choosing not to return and for loss of or damage to property which, under principles of international law or in equity, shall be made good by the Governments or authorities responsible.[45]

Among the significant changes was the assertion of an earliest 'practicable' instead of 'possible' date for return. The final form also introduced the principle of repatriation 'or', instead of 'and', compensation and the phrase 'live in peace with their neighbors' in reference to the refugees, thus putting a subjective condition on their return. When the final vote was taken, the Soviet bloc and all the Arab states then members of the United Nations opposed this measure.[46]

The Role of the United Nations Conciliation Commission for Palestine: A Political Solution. Resolution 194 (III) established the United Nations Conciliation Commission for Palestine 'to facilitate the repatriation, resettlement, and economic and social rehabilitation of the refugees and the payment of compensation'. It was formed of representatives of France, Turkey and the United States. The Conciliation Commission arranged a meeting of the Arab states in March 1949 in Beirut to discuss the refugee situation. The Arabs insisted upon absolute priority for this question, as stipulated in paragraph 11 of Resolution 194 (III). Even at this early stage, the commission was doubtful about the refugees' supposed free choice between repatriation and compensation, since Israel would certainly oppose a mass return. It thought that the Arab states should agree in principle to resettle those who might not choose to return home and that they should be fully informed of the conditions under which they would return.

Following the Beirut conference, the commission proceeded to Tel Aviv, where Prime Minister Ben Gurion stressed that the refugees would have to 'live in peace with their neighbors' and that repatriation would depend on a final settlement; Israel considered resettlement in the Arab states a far more promising solution. The talks ended in a stalemate and the commission returned to the neutral environment at Lausanne.

There the Arab states accepted the territorial provisions of the UN partition plan in principle by signing the Lausanne Protocol on 12 May, thus recognizing some Jewish autonomy in Palestine. Israel signed the protocol separately. Then the two began submitting mutually unacceptable proposals. The State Department intervened through the Ambassador to Tel Aviv and the Chairman of the Conciliation Commission and urged Israel to permit two hundred thousand refugees to return. On 29 May, Ambassador James G. McDonald received a note from President Truman for Prime Minister Ben Gurion. It expressed deep disappointment at the failure of Walter Eytan, the Director-General of the Israeli Ministry of Foreign Affairs and the head of the Israeli delegation at Lausanne, to make any of the desired concessions on refugees or boundaries; found Israel's attitude to be dangerous to peace, and in violation of UN General Assembly resolutions on partition and refugees; and insisted that 'territorial compensations should be made for territory taken in excess of the November 27, 1947, UN division plan and that tangible refugee compensation should be made now an essential preliminary to any prospect for general settlement'.[47] In the operative part of the note was an implied threat that the United States would reconsider its attitude toward Israel.[48]

The Israeli reply was a clear rejection. Israel refused even to discuss the return of the refugees before peace and it elaborated on the problems of security. It also rejected the American appeal to humanitarian considerations, reasoning that the refugees' homes had either been destroyed or were now occupied by Jewish settlers and that there was no means of economic sustenance. Humanitarian considerations would argue in favour of no return.[49]

According to the Ambassador, it was 'a brilliant restatement' of the Israeli case, ending with a reassertion of its regard for the government and people of the United States and a hope that this reply would restore the sympathetic understanding of the American government for Israel's problems and anxieties. The American reply took a long time. Ambassador McDonald speculated that there was 'apparently indecision and much heart searching in Washington. Cool heads won the day.' The next note

abandoned completely the stern tone of its predecessor . . . The next few months marked a steady retreat from the intransigence of the United States' May note. More and more, Washington appraised the situation in realistic terms and . . . ceased to lay down the law to Tel Aviv. Thereafter, it declined the responsibility of suggesting specific solutions to either side.[50]

Early in June, Israel submitted a proposal to repatriate all the Palestinians in the Gaza Strip (about 270,000) in exchange for fixed international borders and the annexation of Gaza. The Arab states rejected this plan because it would concede more territory and repatriate only a third of the refugees. Furthermore, the refugees repatriated would not necessarily be returned to their homes or villages. After a change in both the American and Israeli representations in July, the Israelis put forth another proposal, this time offering to repatriate a hundred thousand Palestinians without asking for additional territory. The Palestinians would be settled in areas specified by the government in keeping with its plans for economic development. Neither the United States nor the Conciliation Commission thought this proposal adequate. The Arab states again refused to consider the plan because they regarded it as inconsistent with Resolution 194 (III).[51] Israel later withdrew the offer. After several weeks of futile talks, the United States decided to drop the political approach and concentrate on an economic solution. The Conciliation Commission had been unable to get the two sides together on a workable political formula.

Part of the difficulty lay in the commission itself, whose members took instructions from their respective governments, not from the United Nations. Pablo de Azcarate, Principal Secretary of the commission and a somewhat harsh critic of the United States, thought that the commission fell into a morass, partly because of the constant instability and vacillation of American policy. The first American representative, Mark Ethridge, publisher of the Louisville *Courier Journal*, displayed impatience and irritation at the slow and tortuous pace of the negotiations. He seemed surprised that rapidity in negotiation depended upon a clear and precise notion of the goals sought. Such agreement did not exist. Neither the American government nor its representatives had a clear idea how to approach the Conciliation Commission's mission.

Ethridge resigned after four months and was replaced by Paul Porter, a Washington lawyer, who stayed two months. Porter also expected to complete his task in a short time and was equally disappointed. An official of the State Department, Raymond Hare, whom de Azcarate described as 'a model of good sense, objectivity, and deliberation', stepped in temporarily until a permanent member, Ely

Palmer, assumed the position. Palmer's tendency was to consider questions from the human and personal standpoint rather than from the general political view. This, along with the inconsistency of American policy, left the commission without the political support indispensable to its proper functioning.[52]

De Azcarate felt that the member governments had no intention of putting such pressures on the parties as would have enabled them to achieve results. Each, especially the United States, had interests of their own in the Middle East and were not prepared to waste influence by supporting a cause which could only indirectly affect their immediate, concrete and tangible interests. During the last few weeks of the Lausanne talks, the commission adopted a firmer attitude and turned its attention to the more substantive aspects of the refugee problem,[53] but unfortunately that attitude was not sustained and the commission fell back into a state of torpor. Over the years, it was able to bring about the release of some funds from Arab refugee accounts frozen in Israeli banks and the reunion of some refugees with their families in Israel. This was but a small contribution towards solving the problem. The commission sank into obscurity after the June war. Its successes and failures were closely related to the rise and fall of United States concerns about the refugees and its inability or unwillingness to pressure Israel into accepting UN Resolution 194 (III). Although it had executive, mediatory, and conciliatory functions, it failed in its mission to implement the terms of the resolution, because it could not surmount the political obstacles in its path.[54] Its membership was too narrow and the Arab leaders either could not or would not accept the bona fides of the Western powers on the matter of refugees.[55]

US Efforts for Refugee Resettlement

Although the United States clearly expressed its humanitarian concern for the plight of the Palestinians, its overriding concern was political — to stabilize the Middle East. The interests of the United States government in the Middle East, as related to the refugee question, are as the Senate Foreign Relations Committee stated in 1953:

> The United States has an interest in doing what it can to help solve the refugee problem because of its direct relationship to the economic and political stability and the security of the Near East. The United States does not wish to see the internal order and the inde-

pendence of the countries of the Near East threatened by economic chaos, communist penetration, or military hostilities. Disorder with a resultant possibility of the renewal of hostilities in this part of the world would threaten the security interest of the United States and the free world generally.[56]

The United States sought to diffuse the threat of instability by attempting to pacify the refugees through material aid while finding a workable solution to the problem.[57] It attempted to achieve this through economic proposals and plans, as well as by political efforts. The successive unproductive plans and proposals demonstrated the centrality of the refugee issue to American policy in the Middle East. Each plan illustrated further the frustration of Congress and the administration at the continuation of financial support to UN refugee programmes and the absence of progress towards a final solution of the issue. Yet the urgency of the issue compelled fresh efforts to solve it. The initial approach emphasized repatriation. A shift towards resettlement outside of Palestine occurred with each new economic proposal and political effort. The shifts accommodated the desires of Israel and its allies in Congress rather than the wishes and aspirations of the refugees.

Economic Proposals

Economic proposals responded to the immediate need for relief. Congress approved $16 million for the United Nations Relief for Palestine Refugees in March 1949. Despite warnings that the refugees would not abandon the goal of repatriation, some House members were optimistic that the $16 million would create goodwill.[58] Representative Javits of New York described it as 'an elementary humanitarian measure to help these innocent victims of War . . . who', he said 'left their homes because of the hostilities and the urging of misguided leaders'. He felt that the entire Middle East would appreciate the American co-operation. No one expected the problem to last long.[59]

The McGhee Plan. In June 1949, Assistant Secretary of State George McGhee went to Beirut to introduce a plan for general economic development in the Middle East. All the countries in the area were to receive financial aid and technical assistance from an agency run by the United States, France, and Great Britain. Implicit in this was an assumption that many of the refugees would be resettled in the Arab states and not repatriated. The plan recognized that Egypt was already overcrowded and that neither Lebanon, because of the delicate sectarian balance, nor

Saudi Arabia, because of its vast desert area, could handle more than a few refugees. Although some would be settled in Arab Palestine and Jordan, many would go to Syria and Iraq, and these states would get financial assistance.[60] The Arab states rejected this plan as incompatable with Resolution 194 (III) since it denied the refugees the free choice to repatriate. The United States continued to hold out hope for an economic solution if the political approach proved inadequate.

The Economic Survey Mission. By August 1949, it was apparent that pressure on Israel to admit refugees would not work. Assistant Secretary McGhee said that the United States would not insist that Israel accept a 'specific' number nor that there be any 'specific' territorial settlement in Palestine.[61] The American representative on the Conciliation Commission for Palestine suggested that the Commission appoint an economic survey team under American chairmanship to draw up a comprehensive plan for the economic development of the Middle East. It would 'facilitate the repatriation, resettlement and economic and social rehabilitation of the refugees and the payment of compensation', pursuant to paragraph 11 of Resolution 194 (III) '. . . in order to reintegrate the refugees into the economic life of the area on a self-sustaining basis, within a minimum period of time'.[62] To succeed, this would require the Arab states to consider the refugees' final settlement in their territories as a means of helping solve the refugee problem.

The Conciliation Commission adopted the American proposal without discussion and on 26 August 1949, Gordon Clapp, Chairman of the Tennessee Valley Authority, was appointed to head the Economic Survey Mission to the Middle East. Other members came from France, Great Britain and Turkey. The Economic Mission worked independently of the Conciliation Commission.[63] As it was preparing to depart, President Truman said he was 'convinced that, if the Near Eastern nations affected by the recent hostilities will put aside their differences and bend their energies to constructive cooperation, they can find a basis on which to build permanent peace and stability'.[64]

The mission assembled at Lausanne on 8 September for preliminary meetings and then proceeded to Beirut. The group included experts in refugee matters and in developmental assistance. Throughout the autumn they met with officials in Egypt, Lebanon, Israel, Jordan, Syria and Iraq to discuss the prospects for economic aid as a means of stimulating growth in the region.

An interim report was issued to the General Assembly on 17 November 1949. It recognized the plight of the refugees as both a symptom and a cause of grave economic instability in the region and recommended a programme of useful public works to employ able-bodied refugees as a move towards their rehabilitation. It also recommended the continuation of relief. It acknowledged that development alone would not bring peace and warned that if the refugees were left forgotten and desolate, peace would recede yet further.[65] Contrary to earlier optimism the mission found that the outstanding political stalemate precluded any early solution by repatriation or large-scale resettlement.[66] It recommended a gradual reduction in emergency relief as men became employed, a program of public works, such relief as was needed as an integrated operation with the governments of the region, and the establishment of an agency to direct the relief and public works programme after 1 April 1950. The General Assembly adopted these recommendations.[67]

The total number of refugees was estimated at 774,000, of whom about 147,000 were self-supporting or provided for. Roughly 527,000 were dependent on the United Nations Relief, while another 25,000 lived in their own homes in Arab territory but were deprived of access to their lands. The greatest concentration of refugees was in the Gaza Strip and on the West Bank.[68] Those who fled brought assets with them but these were soon used up. The host countries helped as best they could during the first few months; in addition the Arab states contributed $6 million of the $32 million donated to the United Nations Relief for Palestine Refugees.

The report of the Economic Survey Mission stated that the refugees 'believed as a matter of right and justice they should be permitted to return to their homes, their farms and villages'.[69] It regretted that large development projects could not immediately proceed: 'The region is not ready, the projects are not ready, the people and Governments are not ready for large-scale development of the region's basic river systems or major underdeveloped land areas.'[70]

Water resources were international. In the absence of a peace settlement 'it is unrealistic to suppose that agreement on the complex question of the national water rights could be negotiated among the parties' . . . 'Whatever the full development of the Jordan river system holds for improving the economic life of the area, this must await mutual desire to create and share benefits from a better use of waters now denied to all parties.' The mission recommended instead 'pilot demonstration projects' to provide practical experience for the larger, as yet unattainable, tasks.[71] Despite all these warnings, the Western powers continued to encourage wholesale adoption of large-scale development projects in order to end the refugee problem speedily and effectively.

The mission's reports avoided the political and psychological aspects of repatriation and resettlement and left the ultimate fate of the Arabs unresolved. It apparently viewed resettlement as a more realistic solution, although it was aware that repatriation was still the basic Arab issue.

In February 1950 the House Committee on Foreign Affairs held hearings on the Palestine refugees and the Economic Survey's report. Chairman Kee of Virginia expressed confidence that practically all of the refugees would find jobs by the end of the year and that by that time there would be no need for direct relief. Assistant Secretary of State McGhee told the committee of US humanitarian concern at the Palestinians' plight and the danger it posed to the delicate equilibrium of the armistice. The issue delayed the conclusion of a peace settlement, perpetuated a major source of friction between the parties, and gave the Communists a natural focal point for exploitation. Direct relief would only prolong an already bad situation; therefore, the State Department chose to disassociate the economic from the political problem.[72] Responses to McGhee's remarks and to the mission report itself indicated the Congressional dissatisfaction. One member wanted to know how long the United States would have to continue supporting the refugees before they could be 'absorbed' in the Arab countries.[73] Gordon Clapp, the mission's head, appeared before the committee in the hope of opening up new farming areas in eastern Syria and creating new acreage in Iraq, thereby providing a place for the refugees 'to settle permanently.' He described the difficulties the mission had experienced in the Arab countries which feared plans to establish the refugees among them. Only Jordan was willing to discuss the matter, for it was the only Arab country in which the refugees would not constitute a serious social, political or economic liability.[74] Clapp stressed that the Arab governments were ill-equipped to feed the people and warned of starvation and epidemics, as well as serious political disruption unless the United States acted. He warned that if large-scale schemes were tied to specific proposals to settle the refugees away from their homes permanently, the political stalemate would simply continue. Even if the Arab states earmarked their total budgets for refugee relief, it would still not be enough. According to Clapp, the refugees were becoming more and more dominated by a sense of hopelessness and the longer this continued, the more bitter they would become.[75] Despite that warning, the United States continued to hold out hope that vast development schemes could provide a way out of this intractable problem.

Establishment of UNRWA. The third recommendation of the Clapp report was the establishment of an agency to organize and direct relief and public works programmes, later implemented in General Assembly Resolution 302 (IV) on 8 December 1949. The resolution was introduced by the four countries whose representatives had served on the mission and was passed with the Soviet bloc and Arab states abstaining. It reaffirmed paragraph 11 of Resolution 194 (III) and established the United Nations Relief and Works Agency for Palestine Refugees, authorizing it to spend up to $54 million on relief and public works during an eighteen-month period beginning 1 April 1950.[76] It was directed to absorb the responsibilities of the United Nations Relief for Palestine Refugees and consult with the Conciliation Commission about refugees who desired repatriation, to terminate relief no later than the end of 1950, and to consult with the governments about preparing for the time when international assistance was no longer available. Emphasis was shifted from relief to rehabilitation.[77]

UNRWA began its life under a cloud of Arab suspicion that it was a creation and a tool of Western imperialism. The Arabs felt that finding work for the Palestinians was only the first step in integration into the various countries to which they had fled.[78] The State Department, on the other hand, considered the agency a worthwhile forward movement. The new relief and works programme would give reasonable assurance that the dangerous situation would not deteriorate further.[79] It would improve the morale of the refugees, restore self-respect and make them less likely 'to follow the political agitator'. The department concluded that 'by changing men's attitudes and by fostering and strengthening local governmental institutions, the program will help to bring about the peace settlement which the United Nations is so actively seeking and which all men of goodwill so earnestly desire'.[80] This optimistic assessment was shortly to change.

UNRWA began work on 1 May 1950. The Arab League advised host governments to co-operate provided the work did not prejudice refugee rights. In the United Nations Palestine Refugee Act of 1950, Congress appropriated $27.4 million, half of the UNRWA's operating budget from 1 May 1950 to 30 June 1951. Congress also provided that the President could reallocate part of the money to any agency of the government to further the purpose of the act; such reallocation would still constitute contributions to UNRWA.[81]

By June 1950, Congress was concerned that American efforts would be obscured in a programme operated by a UN agency. In hearings before the Senate Committee on Appropriations Deputy Assistant Secretary of State Hare warned that taking too much credit and acting on its own would make the United States appear to be assuming responsibility for the situation. He assured them that the refugees understood how much the United States was contributing and that they appreciated American assistance on their behalf.[82]

Further Economic Plans. Since it was clear that UNRWA could not end relief operations by 31 December 1950, as recommended in the Clapp report, the United States, Great Britain, France and Turkey introduced a joint draft resolution in the United Nations calling for 'the reintegration of the refugees into the economic life of the Near East, either by repatriation or resettlement' and setting up $40 million as a reintegration fund. This was later incorporated into Resolution 393 (V) of 12 December 1950, 'without prejudice to the provisions of paragraph 11 of Resolution 194 (III)', although developmental plans were perceived as more likely being about resettlement than repatriation.

President Truman's message to Congress in May 1951 stressed 'the orderly settlement of homeless refugees.' The programme for assisting the Palestinian Arab refugees had the threefold purpose of 'assisting the settlement of refugees, of strengthening those states wherein they settle, and assisting both Israel and the Arab states by removing this threat to the peace of this area'.[83]

In July 1951, Assistant Secretary of State McGhee admitted that little progress had been made on the Palestine question, because the future of the refugees had not been decided.[84] Representative Cooley of North Carolina criticized American policy in Palestine. He felt it was not so much the conflict itself which had adversely affected America's relationship with the Arab states, but its policy, attitude and conduct resulted in a loss of prestige and friendship. Even though the Jews had endured great suffering in concentration camps, liberation had renewed them, but the Arabs in refugee camps had no hope. He said that this country had given Israel generous amounts of aid and had provided some relief for the Arab refugees, 'but the program here contemplated for the resettlement and rehabilitation of refugees certainly is not equal or impartial'.[85] For example, many Arabs were to be settled in Sinai, with two hundred dollars allotted to each person. Yet for the resettlement and rehabilitation of each Jewish refugee, $2,500 was needed, according to figures supplied by State Department 'experts'.

The latter estimate was challenged by House members. Representative Cooley called for elimination of the amount for the Jewish refugees. This measure was defeated after a long debate, although others also thought the aid inequitable.[86] The final amount for the fiscal year 1952 was $50 million for the Arab refugees. The bill retained the Presidential proviso of the previous Mutual Security Act, which implied that Congress had some reservations about the ability of UNRWA to resettle and reintegrate the refugees.[87]

The State Department persuaded the Conciliation Commission to make one more effort to solve the refugee problem by convening a conference of the Arab states and Israel in Paris in September 1951. Among the proposals was one which urged Israel to accept 'repatriation of a specified number of Arab refugees' in categories which could be integrated into Israel's economy, to be chosen from among those willing to return and live in peace. The commission thought it important that the Jewish state have a definite figure for purposes of economic planning and that the refugees be fully informed about the actual conditions under which they would be repatriated, since these conditions had changed radically since 1948. The Israelis rejected the proposal for military, political and security reasons, while the Arabs said that it violated the terms of paragraph 11 of Resolution 194 (III).[88]

The Blandford Plan. Meanwhile an American, John B. Blandford, Jr, had replaced the Canadian Howard Kennedy as director of UNRWA. On 28 November 1951, he asked that the General Assembly seek $250 million for a programme of assistance to Near East governments 'for the relief and reintegration of Palestine refugees'. This programme would be carried out over a three-year period and would consist of $50 million for relief and $200 million for integration. Local governments would assume maximum possible administrative responsibility.[89]

In the report accompanying the request, Blandford said that reintegration could be 'broadly interpreted as the building of homes in areas which would permit the refugees to become self-supporting, without prejudicing their rights to repatriation or compensation in accordance with other General Assembly resolutions.' The report stated that the purpose of the findings and recommendations was to agree on a formula which would promise the refugees an end to camp life and ration lines, promise the governments a termination of social and economic dislocations, and promise contributors a definite time when large relief expenditures would stop.

The American representative on the United Nations *Ad Hoc* Refugee

Committee, Philip C. Jessup, explained that the refugees who co-operated in the plan would not forfeit their freedom of action, but at the end of the period would retain their freedom of choice as to whether to stay where they were or to settle elsewhere according to the possibilities open. Meanwhile, they would have had an opportunity to acquire more varied skills and the capital needed for choice of action.[90] The Blandford Plan was approved and incorporated into General Assembly Resolution 513 (V) on 26 January 1952 without prejudice to the provisions of paragraph 11 of Resolution 194 (III) or paragraph 4 of Resolution 393 (V) of 2 December 1950. The resolution instructed the relief agency to 'explore with the governments concerned arrangements looking toward their assuming administration of reintegration projects at the earliest possible date'.[91]

Although there were several subsequent attempts to initiate development projects under this plan, the Arab states refused to accept any scheme which they thought might lead to a permanent resettlement of the refugees. Despite protestations and assurances to the contrary, the projects proposed, largely at the instigation of the United States, carried a strong implication that resettlement would be the end result.

The Johnston Mission. The Eisenhower administration took office in January 1953, and with it came further efforts and new enthusiasm for solving the refugee problem. A few months after taking office, Secretary of State John Foster Dulles travelled to the Middle East. He concluded that some of the refugees could be settled on Israeli-controlled territory, but most 'could more readily be integrated into the lives of the neighbouring Arab communities'.[92] This resettlement, however, would have to await irrigation projects.

The Mutual Security Act of 1953 included $194 million for integrating the refugees and promoting economic stability.[93] To this end, President Eisenhower sent Eric Johnston of the Technical Cooperation Administration to the Middle East with the rank of Ambassador. Congressional pressure was for an economic approach to the refugee problem that would conveniently bypass a political solution. The waters of the Jordan river would be tapped for irrigation and electrical power to provide employment for refugees who would be tempted to resettle. The plan had economic merit and promised political dividends. 'It is my conviction that acceptance of a comprehensive plan for the development of the Jordan Valley would contribute greatly to stability in the Near East' said President Eisenhower.[94] Even though there were early indications from the Arab states that it would not be acceptable, Johnston was generally optimistic about the plan. It would allot a substantial area of the irrigated lands in Jordan to the refugees and provide for about one-third of the total number of refugees.[95]

Despite the economic advantages of the Johnston plan for both Israel and the Arab states, they did not outweigh the political drawbacks. After two years and five trips to the Middle East, Eric Johnston was unable to convince the two sides of the utility and long-term benefits of his plan. His failure did not alter the United States' feeling that the solution of the refugee problem lay in economic development.

The Smith-Prouty Study Report. Early in 1954, the House Foreign Affairs Committee sent their own special study mission to the Middle East. The members, Representatives Lawrence Smith and Prouty of Vermont, issued a report late in February 1954, which stated that little progress had been made in the official United Nations programme for resettlement because of the 'persistent refusal of Arab leaders to consider any proposal than that the refugees should be allowed to return to their former homes'. Any Arab leader who suggested an alternative to repatriation ran the risk of losing not only his office but his life. It was thought that the five-year period of waiting had made some of the refugees and the Arab governments realize that holding out on all UN proposals would not necessarily result in repatriation. Because over half of the refugees were under 15 years of age with little recollection of Palestine, it was felt that 'time is working in the direction of resettlement'.

The Congressional Mission recommended increased pressure on the Arab states to open their doors to the refugees. It wanted UN aid cut off after a certain date. The United States would then provide aid to the countries which provided homes for refugees and gave them citizenship. The mission thought that if it were made clear to the Arabs that the refugees' former homes could not be restored and that their future was 'inevitably' in the Arab countries, the process of resettlement would be greatly facilitated. It agreed with UNRWA that administration of the refugee camps should be turned over to the Arab governments. 'The Arab states will object but it is essential that they realize that the refugees are people who are with them to stay.' As usual, the commission's conclusions were based on its own assessments of the refugees' best interests rather than on input from the refugees.

In order to improve Arab-Israeli attitudes, the mission recommended that the United States serve notice that it would not support the return of the Arab refugees to their former homes within the boundaries of Israel under existing conditions and that it press Israel to compensate the refugees for real and personal property lost.[96]

In the United Nations as well, the US representative anticipated a cut-off of UNRWA funds unless resettlement projects in the Sinai and the Jordan Valley got underway.[97] Arab countries should agree on the Johnston plan. In a subsequent discussion of refugee rights, the United States significantly took the position that Israel ought to provide repatriation or compensation. The refugees must understand 'that the true destiny of most of them lies in the Arab world'.[98] A 1955 House study mission to the Middle East under Representative Vorys concluded that, while the United States should help to ameliorate refugee suffering, it should not assume responsibility for repatriation or resettlement, indicating congressional impatience with the intractable problem. 'Where it is in our interest to help these refugees, our help should be directed toward permanent solutions.'[99] The Senate, as well, complained of lack of progress. Of the $54 million authorized for UNRWA, $16.5 million was for relief and $37.5 million for rehabilitation. A permanent solution could only be found through rehabilitation and resettlement, it said.[100]

The 1955 Dulles Proposal. The failure of the Johnston plan was not sufficient to bring about a shift in US policy towards the refugees, and throughout 1955 Dulles emphasized resettlement through water development and de-emphasized the repatriation demanded by the refugees and the Arab governments.[101] Dulles said repatriation would be done to 'such an extent as it may be feasible'.[102] The United States was willing to lend Israel funds to pay compensation. The plan was designed to promote the primary American objectives of securing stability in the Middle East. Economic development would lead to prosperity and stability. It would also assist in the resettlement of the refugees. Dulles sought to advance his plans through the United Nations with congressional support. In the General Assembly sessions in the autumn of 1955, the US delegate again urged co-operation among the Arab states on development of agricultural lands for the refugees and warned that the United States would not extend payments indefinitely.[103]

Congressional initiatives in 1956 only restated the Dulles proposal. Representative Anfuso of New York limited repatriation in accordance with Israeli security regulations, which he thought could all be carried out by the United States.[104] A letter from forty members of the House to Secretary Dulles in early February 1956 omitted any mention of repatriation.[105]

Representative Hunter of California blamed the Arab leaders for continuously obstructing plans to find permanent quarters for the refugees. He said they had no intention of relieving the situation because this would remove 'most of the emotionalism from the Arabs' campaign against Israel'. He noted that less than two thousand refugees had applied for visas to enter the United States under the refugee relief programme and said that if Arab leaders were really sincere in their protestations of sympathy, there would have been more applications. He was convinced that the leaders had no interest in resettling the refugees and intended to exploit the situation for incursions into Israel.[106]

Former Ambassador James McDonald expressed the view that the Johnston plan was the only realistic way to solve the refugee problem, because it took into account 'the psychology of the Arab people and the pride which they take in their newly won sovereignty and dignity'. He thought that they could be resettled in Iraq, Syria and Jordan, if the Arabs themselves controlled it and set up a corporation to take charge. This would also bring economic gain to the countries and the people.[107]

The House sent another study mission under Representative Zablocki of Wisconsin to the Middle East about this time. In its report, issued in the spring of 1956, it recognized the refugees' strong attachment to the land and the sense of injustice at having lost it. It noted that the refugees did not accept the improvements in camp life as an answer to their problems; a camp mentality, compounded of frustration and bitterness, was developing. According to the House report, 'None [of the refugees] expressed even a modicum of gratitude for United States' assistance. On the contrary, they held the United States responsible for their plight.' Not only had the United States given assistance to the state which had seized their property, it had failed to help them recover it. The study mission recommended that 'serious consideration be given to the United Nations' termination of all assistance to the refugees within about two years'. The mission also recommended resettlement and compensation for lost property, as well as having local governments take over the financing of the refugees' problem.[108]

Altogether, the situation remained much as it had been since the 1948 war, with the exception of considerable improvement in the camp facilities and training opportunities afforded under UNRWA. Materially, the refugees were far better off than many of the other Arabs, but psychologically they were unprepared to accept anything less than their original repatriation demands. The Eisenhower administration remained under considerable pressure from Congress to promote measures to make the Palestinians self-supporting and Congress itself continued to pass appropriations in the Mutual Security Acts of 1957 and 1960 containing strong statements of support for bringing the refugee problem to an end.

The Humphrey Report. The 1956 Suez war obscured the refugee issue for a time, while Congress and the White House turned their attention to getting the Israelis to withdraw from the Sinai and the Arabs to accept the newly proposed Eisenhower Doctrine. Nevertheless, resettlement and economic development remained the most acceptable means of solution in the view of American policy-makers, although the United States was careful to point out that 'reintegration' and 'rehabilitation' should not prejudice the refugees' right of repatriation or compensation.

Senator Hubert Humphrey made a trip to the Middle East in the spring of 1957, visiting some of the refugee camps, which he described as 'appalling' and 'a ready-made situation for Communist agitation'. He said there was no easy solution 'to this bitter problem, but it seems that the right of repatriation should be established as should the right of compensation'. Once this was done 'it should become possible to begin some major public works to make possible the resettlement of refugees in some of the Arab states surrounding Israel'. He thought it 'most unfortunate and unwise' that the Arab states had thus far refused to co-operate with these plans.[109]

In his report to the Foreign Relations Committee upon his return, Humphrey only restated previous American positions. He said that the young, who constituted half the refugees, had no roots in Palestine at all, despite the clamour of leaders for a return. To return them to an alien society they had been taught to hate would be self-defeating:

> The destiny of these young Arabs clearly lies in an opportunity for a productive and self-reliant life in an Arab environment and culture . . . The facts of the situation themselves point to the only possible solution — the provision for the vast majority of permanent homes and tolerable livelihoods in the Arab states and a commitment by Israel to accept a limited number of token recipients.

He remarked that Iraq desperately needed people and that 'the entire refugee population could readily be absorbed in that country alone with benefit to the indigenous population'. He also said that if the Arab states would accept the Johnston plan two hundred thousand could be settled in the Jordan Valley. Significantly, he described repatriation of a large number of refugees as 'no longer possible', since it would only establish a fifth column and would result in bitter disillusionment among the refugees living in an alien country. He concluded that resettlement with compensation and a programme for economic development was the only effective and realistic way of solving the Palestinian refugee problem. [110]

Further Congressional hearings, studies and reports reflected increased disillusionment with UNRWA and impatience with the lack of progress towards refugee settlement. Congress urged substantial reduction in American financial contributions to UNRWA, but the State Department could find 'no acceptable alternative to the extension of UNRWA', because its disappearance would result in 'serious internal security problems for all the Arab host countries'. [111]

After a dozen years of American involvement with the Palestinian refugees, the early optimism about an economic solution gave way to frustration and disillusionment. While American financial help continued to flow to the refugees through UNRWA, American policymakers focused new attention on finding a political solution.

US Political Proposals

Simultaneously with attempts to improve refugee living conditions and to seek an economic solution to the Palestine problem, there were also political efforts made to resolve this issue. The main thrust of these efforts was towards achieving a compromise between Israel's resistance to any return of a large number of Palestinian refugees and Arab opposition to resettlement outside Palestine. During the first decade after the 1948 war, the preferred vehicle remained the UN-sponsored Conciliation Committee for Palestine. Then came the election of John F. Kennedy.

The Kennedy Initiative. The brief years of Kennedy's administration were encouraging to the Arabs. They believed that he understood the complexity of the Middle East question and had genuine intentions of tackling the issue even-handedly. One of the first gestures Kennedy made was to send a letter to the leaders of the United Arab Republic, Iraq, Jordan, Lebanon and Saudi Arabia, informing them of his administration's intention to work fairly and seriously to resolve the refugee problem and the Arab-Israeli conflict. He wrote:

We are willing to help resolve the tragic Palestine refugee problem on the basis of the principle of repatriation and compensation for

property, to assist them in finding an equitable answer to the question of the Jordan River water-resource developments and to be
helpful in making progress on other aspects of this complex problem.[112]

Although Kennedy took no significant action to solve the refugee
problem his emphasis on American impartial support for UN resolutions, and the use of American influence for a just and peaceful solution raised Arab hopes and began to reconcile much of the antagonism
between the United States and the Arab world.

Congress, traditionally more supportive of Israel's position, did not
share President Kennedy's views, and Senator Javits took issue with his
omission of the word 'resettlement' which he said 'could lead to distor-
tion and false illusions about a softening of US policy'. That policy
should continue to emphasize resettlement and rehabilitation. Israel
might repatriate a fair number of refugees, but if they were used by
Arab 'demagogues and agitators to inundate Israel, this would run
contrary to American policy'.[113] Similarly, Senator Scott of Pennsylvania
described repatriation as 'a mortal threat to a friendly power yielding
to a persistent blackmail' and was 'repugnant morally' as it had proved
to be futile politically. 'The Arab refugees must be resettled in Arab
countries. There is no other valid alternative.'[114] House sentiment
stressed also the threat to security. In reply, the administration replied
that the United States still supported 'some reasonable' implementation
of paragraph 11 of Resolution 194 (III), but agreed that any repatriation would 'have to be implemented so as to take fully into account
Israel's legitimate security and economic requirements'.[115] In the same
vein, Representative James Roosevelt of California denounced 'lip
service to dead resolutions'. Keeping alive the hope of repatriation
would serve only to prolong displacement of refugees.[116]

In a report of his trip to the Middle East during August 1961,
Representative Lindsay of New York said that the general view of
American officials and others was that no solution could be achieved
without a final political settlement between the Arabs and Israelis.
According to Lindsay, the result of this view was that 'the interrelated-
ness of the political and the human aspects is thus cited for a policy or
non-policy of resigned action'. For the immediate future, American
policy should focus on sustaining and expanding the work of UNRWA.

There was some diversity of views. During his trip to the Middle East,
Representative Lindsay of New York talked with Palestinian refugees.
He related his encounters in this way:

In every camp I visited in company with UNRWA personnel, we met with the Arab elders to listen to their complaints and suggestions . . . And we were admonished not to believe that the passing of the present generation of displaced Arabs would cause the problem to disappear. "Tell your governments" they would state "that we are teaching our children that the injustice is permanent and that their right to Palestine is the only legacy which their fathers will leave them.

The refugees' warnings made an impression. The solution to the Arab problem would seem to 'lie in some combination of integration, resettlement and a measure of repatriation in Israel', he said. The Congressman felt that possibilities for homes and jobs in Syria, Iraq and the Sinai Peninsula were reasonably good and suggested Australia, Canada and Latin America as other possibilities. As for the United States, Lindsay said: 'We are under an obligation, in advancing an overall plan, to offer homes within our own country to at least a reasonable number of refugees.' He felt the admission of 100,000 to 200,000 Palestinian refugees would be beneficial to both the United States and the refugees; furthermore, it would demonstrate to both Arabs and Israelis that the United States was trying to solve the problem in good faith.[117]

The Johnson Mission. Outside the US government, others sought various positions between the poles of repatriation and resettlement. In August 1961, the Conciliation Commission sent Joseph Johnson, President of the Carnegie Endowment for International Peace, to the Middle East, as a special representative 'to explore with the host governments and with Israel some practical means of seeking progress on the Palestine-Arab refugee problem'. Johnson found that, despite the signs of intransigence, responsible statesmen on both sides wanted peace in a general way and as a long-term goal, but they were not ready to make the necessary adjustments. Johnson observed 'a consistency of obdurate determination on both sides and time only seemed to harden attitudes'.

Johnson's report stated that both sides tended to view the refugee problem as an inextricable part of the Palestine question as a whole. Yet both sides had also expressed a grudging willingness to consider a step-by-step process. All had expressed humanitarian concern, and, while this did not imply a willingness to surrender national interests, it did indicate a conscious desire to harmonize the two. Johnson anticipated that there would be Palestine refugees for at least another decade. Many would need training and all had to be helped to be effectively integrated into society wherever they might settle. Probably no progress could be made on the question apart from an overall settlement. Yet Johnson believed he had found enough willingness among the parties to make it worthwhile to continue the effort towards a settlement.[119]

Johnson began a second tour of the region on 15 April 1962, still confident that the parties were ready to move towards settlement, however slowly. Late in the summer, his new set of proposals became known, although they were never published officially because of strong opposition to them. One proposal was to enable the refugees to express their preference for a return to their homes or to new sites in Israel or resettlement in Arab lands or elsewhere. These preferences were to be made privately with the provision that the refugees could change their minds later. Israel could reject individual security risks. With outside help, Israel would be expected to compensate the refugees for lost property. A special United Nations fund would be set up from voluntary contributions from governments and other sources. The United Nations would also assist in the resettlement operation. A new administration and staff would pursue this effort and a council of advisers would include representatives from Israel and the host countries. Refugees would not necessarily get their first choice and the United Nations would be responsible for giving them full information on their selection.[120]

Neither the Arabs nor the Israelis would compromise their position, and both rejected the Johnson proposals. The Arabs felt that they stressed resettlement over repatriation; Israel again opposed repatriation and said that the refugee problem would have to await a final peace settlement. Afterwards the United States carried on months of quiet talks through normal diplomatic channels in an attempt to break the deadlock, but all negotiations were unsuccessful.[121]

The Johnson Mission drew strong backing from the State Department, but support from other quarters was less forthcoming.[122] The American public showed little interest. President Kennedy devoted limited time and resources to this complex problem. Israeli opposition to the proposals raised the domestic political costs of supporting them. As long as the proposals seemed alive, the administration tried to reduce domestic opposition, and it requested the Israelis to temper the opposition of their American supporters. Still, the Johnson initiative was a political liability for the Kennedy administration. With the approach of Congressional elections in the autumn of 1962, enthusiasm for the plan died down. Kennedy and the Democratic Party were worried that large campaign contributions from active sympathizers of

Israel would be withheld.[123] Discouraged, Johnson resigned at the end of January 1963, warning that the refugee matter still called for urgent attention.[124] Meanwhile, the United States continued its support of UNRWA, though it made it clear in the General Assembly that emphasis must be shifted from relief to training, especially teacher and vocational training; it called upon the host governments to adopt a more co-operative attitude to make certain that aid went to bona fide refugees only.[125]

Rise of Palestinian Resistance

In all of the American plans, the Palestinian refugees remained a passive entity. In 1965 and 1966, however, the Palestine liberation movement developed sufficiently to carry out military operations against Israel and became a formidable political force. The Palestinian refugee camps soon became the main centres of freedom fighter recruitment. Congress and the administration acted with anger and disappointment.

Such irritation was evident in Representative Roosevelt's complaint in 1965 that the refugees were being manipulated as pawns in a campaign against Israel. He decried the terror and sabotage of *fedayeen* groups, and he blamed the Arab states for prolonging the plight of the refugees. Roosevelt lashed out at the 'fraudulent' claims of refugee status, 'misuse' of ration cards, and the permanent status of UNRWA.[126] He saw no justification for continuing American support of UNRWA at the rate of 70 per cent of the budget, and he proposed that the refugees be resettled and that UNRWA activities be transferred to Arab governments.[127]

By the spring of 1966, Congress reacted strongly to the growing Palestinian resistance, particularly after Ahmad Shukairy's statements that the People's Republic of China was arming and training Palestinian refugees.[128] In the summer of 1966, House members demanded that UNRWA cut off funds to refugees serving in the Palestine Liberation Army. Hence, American aid to Palestinian refugees became conditional on their passive existence. Congressmen who were traditional supporters of Israel and those opposed in principle to liberation movements spoke out on this issue. Several objected to contributing aid to UNRWA schools which used textbooks denouncing the United States and Israel. Representative Halpern of California suggested that Israel be provided with more arms on a grant basis in view of reports that the People's Republic of China was encouraging an Arab war of liberation to divert attention from South-East Asia. He noted that friendly relations existed between certain Arab states and the North Vietnamese and the fact that some Palestinians had gone to Peking for training.[129]

In a report to the Senate Foreign Relations Committee in April 1967, Senator Joseph of Pennsylvania suggested that the United States urge the United Nations to break up the camps gradually through international subsidies paid to the Jordanian government to transfer families to stable land or into communities where there were employment opportunities. Such actions along with improved economic conditions would reduce the possibilities of refugee participation in the Palestine Liberation Army or other 'subversive' organizations. This same 'subversion', however, prompted the Senate for the first time to call for diplomatic pressure on Israel to repatriate a substantial number of refugees who might be willing to return to their villages inside Israel.[130]

The 1967 war marked the nineteenth year of the refugee problem. During these nineteen years American contributions to UNRWA totalled $411 million or 65 per cent of its budget. As far as US policy was concerned, the Palestinian people existed only as 'refugees' whose immediate material needs must be met. Thus pacified, the Palestinians would stay obligingly out of view. For nearly two decades, the Palestinians sought to create a common Arab front. After 1965, this exploded into armed struggle.

The June War and President Johnson's Five Principles

Added to the new Palestinian militance, the June war of 1967 altered greatly the dimensions and the nature of the Palestine refugee problem. In addition to the more than one million Palestinians already classified as refugees, hundreds of thousands more were displaced by the war. This time the Palestinians were not the only refugees; there were about half a million Syrian and Egyptian refugees from the Syrian and Egyptian territories captured by Israel in the war. About 250,000 Palestinians fled from the West Bank and Gaza; some of them were selectively expelled or pressured to leave. However, the vast majority fled in fear because their homes were in the areas of fighting. Some left because they wanted to join family or relatives elsewhere. Egyptian and Syrian refugees were cared for by their respective governments; Palestinian refugees were mostly destitute. However, American aid soon came to the refugees. During Congressional appropriations of the emergency aid, the familiar dual themes appeared: blaming the Arab states for their failure to solve the Arab refugee problem and praising Israel for its outstanding development. Representative Herbert Tenzer of New York introduced his own proposal for solving the refugee problem with the comment that the efforts to meet the situation over the past twenty years had been 'unimaginative'.[131]

During the UN Security Council debate, US Ambassador Arthur Goldberg urged that the displaced civilians be allowed and encouraged to return and that they be given adequate assurance of safety in the locations in which they resided before the hostilities. He urged all concerned, and 'particularly the government of Israel, to exert every possible effort toward this end'.[132] The United States voted for a Security Council resolution to this effect. Under pressure from the United States, Israel allowed relatively small numbers of Palestinian refugees to return to the West Bank and Gaza; while over 100,000 refugees petitioned Israel to allow them to return home, less than 20,000 petitions were approved.[133] The Palestinian territory that Israel captured in 1967 (the West Bank and Gaza) included 271,977 refugees living in camps.[134] This group represented only a portion of the refugees that had lost their former homes in Haifa, Jaffa, Lod, Falujeh and other locations. With all of Palestine now under Israeli control, they thought access to their former homes would be facilitated. However, the Israeli military authorities refused to allow them to return home, reinforcing the Arab concern that Israel's major objective was territorial aggrandizement rather than co-existence in equality. The American administration felt that the problem would be solved within the framework of an overall Arab-Israeli settlement.

On 19 June 1967, shortly after the ceasefire, President Lyndon Johnson announced five principles of peace in the Middle East, two of which were related to the refugees. First:

Every nation living in the area has a fundamental right to live and to have this right respected by its neighbor . . . (No) nation would be true to the United Nations Charter or to its own true interests if it should permit military successes to blind it to the fact that its neighbors have rights and interests of their own.

Second, President Johnson called for:

justice for the refugees. A new conflict brought new homelessness. The nations of the Middle East must at last address themselves to the plight of those who have been displaced by wars. In the past both sides have resisted the best efforts of outside mediators to restore the victims of conflict to their homes or to find another proper place to live and work. There will be no peace for any party in the Middle East unless the problem is attacked with new energy

by all and, certainly, primarily by those who are immediately concerned.[135]

On 20 June 1967, Ambassador Goldberg repeated the proposals to the
United Nations. The emphasis was on the right of national life and
territorial integrity of the existing states in the region and not of
peoples as such. Therefore, at that time, in the perception of the
American policy-makers, the Palestinians did not qualify as a nation or
state in the generally accepted sense of the term and were still referred
to as 'refugees'.[136]

The Security Council passed Resolution 242 on 22 November 1967
(see text in Appendix B), recognizing the centrality of the refugee issue
to the Arab-Israeli dispute. Among other provisions, Resolution 242
affirmed the 'necessity . . . for achieving a just settlement of the refugee
problem' to make possible 'a just and lasting peace in the Middle East'.[137]
This was patterned after President Johnson's five principles of 19 June,
although no attempt was made to define what constituted a 'just settlement'. Ambassador Goldberg had earlier stated that the problem called
for a permanent and human solution which 'must be a part of the
framework of the peace settlement'. Linking it to the total conflict,
Goldberg said that 'the needs of the refugees and the needs of peace
in the Middle East are not in conflict, they are inseparable. They must
be attended to together.'[138]

Despite the centrality of the Palestinian question to American
policy-makers' approach during this period, the problem of the Palestinians remained one of resettlement and integration. Indeed, the various
plans proposed by the United States remained unavailing because they
still approached a primarily political problem through economic means.
Nevertheless, President Johnson's five principles marked a shift in US
policy. Until this time, the American approach centred on settlement of
the refugee problem mainly through resettlement and integration into
neighbouring Arab countries. US policy-makers assumed that the
resettlement of the refugees would then facilitate the solution of all
other issues. The new emphasis now became 'justice for the refugees',
which would be accorded within the framework of an overall Arab-
Israeli settlement.

The search for a political settlement now moved to the fore, and the
United States finally abandoned the quest for a facile technical solution
to the agony of a nation in exile.

Notes

1. US *Department of State Bulletin*, 9 June 1953, p. 823.
2. UN Document A/AC. 25/6 Part 1, 1949, p. 22. The Israeli Government estimated the number of Arab refugees at 400,000. See *The Arab Refugees: Arab Statements and the Facts* (Jerusalem: 1961).
3. Interim Report of the Director General of UNRWA, A/1451, 1955, pp. 9-10.
4. UN Doc. A/AC. 25/6 Part 1, 1949, p. 22.
5. For further information see Appendix I.
6. Report of the Commissioner General of UNRWA for Palestine refugees in the Near East, July 1974-June 1975, Supplement No. 13 (A/10013) p. 66.
7. Ibid.
8. A working definition of a refugee was adopted by UNRWA. It read as follows: 'A person eligible for relief . . . is one whose normal residence was in Palestine for a minimum period of two years preceding the outbreak of the conflict in 1948 and who, as a result of this conflict, has lost both his house and his means of livelihood.' See UN Document A/1451, p. 10 and A/2717 of 1955, pp. 2 and 19.
9. See Appendix I.
10. The annexed territory was 21,165 square miles. Jordan was created by the British at the end of World War I as a political pay-off to Prince Abdullah. It became known as Trans-Jordan. It was sparsely populated. The whole of Trans-Jordan was then about 34,500 square miles, of which 30,700 square miles was desert. After the annexation, the country became known as the Hashemite Kingdom of Jordan. See Royal Institute of International Affairs, *The Middle East: a Political Study* (London: 1954), p. 345.
11. The pro-Hashemite elements among the Palestinian population were encouraged by being given administrative appointments in the government, while those who showed opposition were barred. Various daily newspapers, including some very important ones, were stopped. Thus at the end of May 1949 the refugee leaders in Ramallah were detained after a demonstration against Trans-Jordan which took place in that city (see *Al-Ba'th*, 4.6.49) on 14.6.49. The editor of the opposition newspaper, *Al-Jil Al Jadid*, published in Ramallah, was arrested and the newspaper was closed down. On 1.8.49 Abdullah Rimawi, the editor of the well known newspaper *Filastin*, published in the Arab part of Jerusalem, was arrested and sent to a detention camp in Ba'ir. (See *Al-Yawm* 15.8.49 and *Filastin* of 17.8.49.) Abdullah appointed Raghib El Nashashibi, the well-known pro-Hashemite Palestine politician, Minister of the newly-established Ministry for Refugee Affairs (on 14.8.49), and two days later General Governor of the Arab part of Palestine under control of the Arab Legion – (*Hamezrah Ha'Hadash*, vol. I, no. 1, pp. 62-4). In the meantime, the government took steps to eliminate all limitation of movements between West and East Jordan (radio Ramallah 14.11.49) and decided to stop charging any customs duties on goods crossing the Jordan either way (*Al-Difa'*, 21.11.49). Finally it was decided to dissolve the Parliament (on 1.1.50) and to call upon the population in West and East Jordan to elect a new Parliament (*Difa'* and *Filastin* 3.1.50). On 11.4.50 the election took place and 40 representatives were elected: 20 from West Jordan (the Arab part of Palestine) and 20 from East Jordan (the former Kingdom of Jordan). On 17.4.50 King Abdullah appointed the members of the Senate: 12 from Trans-Jordan and 8 from the Arab part of Palestine. *The New East*, vol. I, no. 4, pp. 302-303. (*idem*, Rony E. Gabbay, *A Political Study of the Arab Jewish Conflict. The Arab Refugee Problem* (Geneva: Librairie E. Droz, 1959), p. 203.
12. The resolution concerning the annexation and the establishment of the

kingdom was decided upon by the first meeting of the House of Representatives and the Senate. It should be kept in mind that these two houses have always been a rubber stamp for the monarch. Whenever the parliament opposed the king, it was dissolved and a new, more obedient one was elected. The Jordanian cabinet has always included at least four to five Palestinians out of 11 to 13 members.

13. See P.C. Phillips, *Hashemite Kingdom of Jordan: Prolegomena to a Technical Assistance Programme* (NY: 1954), p. 68.

14. The Government of Jordan: *Al-Jarridah Al-Rasmiyah*, No. 1171 of 12 February 1954, cited Gabbay, *A Political Study*, p. 204.

15. Naser Aruri, 'Palestinians in Jordan: Two Nations One State', paper presented at the American Political Science Association meeting, 1973, pp. 44-7.

16. Ibid., pp. 43-5.

17. Gabbay, *A Political Study*, pp. 211-13.

18. UN Doc. No. 13 (A/10013), p. 66.

19. However, since February 1958, following the formation of the United Arab Republic, there were some considerations of joining the Gaza Strip as an entity-part of Palestine with the Union.

20. Don Peretz, *Israel and the Palestine Arabs* (Washington, DC: The Middle East Institute, 1958), p. 23.

21. Arif Al Arif', *Torith Ghazzah* (The History of Gaza) (Jerusalem: Dor Al Teba'h, 1953), p. 60. (in Arabic).

22. Lebanon is a country of minorities. The political set-up in that country is based on a balance of interests between the different minorities. By 1952 the breakdown of groups and subgrouping was as follows:

Christian Groups	Number	Muslim Groups	Number
Maronite	377,544	Sunni	273,125
Greek Orthodox	130,858	Shi'ite	237,107
Armenian Orthodox	67,139	Druze	79,651
Catholic (Greek)	31,764		
Protestants	12,641		

Thus, in 1952 the Christian population totalled 53.6 per cent and the Muslim 45.5 per cent of the total population. Thus, by convention, the President of the Republic must be Maronite, the Prime Minister a Suni, and the speaker of the Chamber of Representatives, a Shi'ite. The Parliamentary seats are divided among fixed groups according to set quotas. For further details see Hussein Kanaan, *Confessionalism as a Matrix of Lebanese Domestic and Foreign Policy*, unpublished thesis (George Washington University, 1969). Also see Royal Institute of International Affairs, *The Middle East*, p. 478.

23. Leila Mao, *Lebanon, the Improbable Nation* (Bloomington: Indiana University Press, 1965), pp. 9-15.

24. In the pre-1967 period, Palestinians in Lebanon, particularly those living in the refugee camps, endured a great deal of abuse. In the street language, to refer to someone as a Palestinian was an abuse. They were the 'niggers' of Lebanon. However, after the defeat of the Arab armies by Israel in 1967, they were able to carry arms. Subsequently, they gained control of the camps by ousting the Deuxième Bureau. They formed their local administration and prohibited outsiders from entering the camps without permits. In essence, each camp constituted a quasi autonomous municipality. This condition was resented by many Lebanese rightists and created special problems for the government. The Palestinians' refusal to hand over the administration of the camps to the Lebanese government springs from their bitter experiences in the pre-1967 period.

25. UN Doc. A/2171. (Annual report of the Director for the period 1 July 1950 to 30 July 1952), p. 45.

26. Ibid., p. 46.

27. Ibid., p. 45.

28. See discussions of the House of Representatives of 27 December 1951 cited in Gabbay, *A Political Study*, p. 209.

29. Gabbay, *A Political Study*, pp. 115-18.

30. Ibid., pp. 119-20.

31. James G. McDonald, *My Mission in Israel* (New York: Simon and Schuster, 1951), pp. 53-4.

32. J.C. Hurewitz, *The Struggle for Palestine* (New York: W.W. Norton Company, 1950), p. 321.

33. Michael E. Jansen, *The United States and the Palestinian People* (Beirut: The Institute of Palestine Studies, 1970), pp. 72-3; UN Doc. A/648, 16 September 1948.

34. Folke Bernadotte, *To Jerusalem* (London: Hodder and Stoughton, 1951), pp. 20-1; UN Doc. A/648, 16 September 1948.

35. 'Conclusions from Progress Report of the UN Mediator on Palestine', excerpts from UN Doc. A/648, 16 September 1948; *Department of State Bulletin*, XIX, 483 (3 October 1948), pp. 438-440.

36. Press Release, *Department of State Bulletin*, XIX, 483 (3 October 1948), p. 436.

37. 'No Compromise on Essential Freedoms', Address by Secretary of State Marshall on 23 September 1948, *Department of State Bulletin*, XIX, 483 (3 October 1948), p. 434.

38. US, *Congressional Record*, 80th Cong. 2nd Sess. (1948), XCIV, (7 October 1948), A4997.

39. Kirk H. Porter and Donald Bruce Johnson, *National Party Platforms, 1840-1960* (Urbana: University of Illinois Press, 1961), pp. 432, 453.

40. UN Res. 212 (III), 19 November 1948, UN Doc. A/810. 'Progress Report on Conditions of Refugees in Near East', *Department of State Bulletin*, XIX, 490 (21 November 1948), pp. 434, 436.

41. Gabbay, *A Political Study*, p. 131.

42. Fred Khouri, *The Arab-Israel Dilemma*, (Syracuse: Syracuse University Press, 1968), p. 147.

43. UN Doc. Supplement No. 13 (A/10013), *Official Records of the General Assembly*: 13th session, 1 July 1974-30 June 1975, United Nations, New York 1975.

44. 'Discussion of the Palestine Situation in Committee I', statement by Philip C. Jessup, US Delegate to the General Assembly on 20 November 1948, *Department of State Bulletin*, XIX, (21 November 1948), p. 659.

45. UN Doc. A/810, *Official Records of the General Assembly*, 3rd session, pp. 21-5. See also George Tomeh (ed.), *United Nations Resolutions on Palestine 1947-1974* (Beirut: Institute for Palestine Studies, 1976), p. 41. For detailed discussion of the drafting of this resolution see Jansen, *US and Palestinian People*, pp. 83-95.

46. Peretz, *Israel and Palestine*, pp. 39-41.

47. Walter Eytan, Director-General of the Israeli Ministry of Foreign Affairs and head of the Israeli delegation at Lausanne.

48. McDonald, *My Mission*, p. 181.

49. Peretz, *Israel and Palestine*, p. 42.

50. McDonald, *My Mission*, pp. 183-4.

51. Jansen, *US and Palestinian People*, pp. 109-12.

52. Pablo de Azcarate, *Mission in Palestine, 1948-1952* (Washington, DC: The Middle East Institute, 1966), pp. 136-8.

53. Ibid., pp. 145-6, 154.

54. Fuad S. Hamzeh, *United Nations Conciliation Commission for Palestine,*

1949-1967 (Beirut: Institute for Palestine Studies, 1968), p. 59.

55. US Congress, Senate Committee on Foreign Relations, *United States Foreign Policy, Middle East*, Staff Study, 86th Cong., 2nd sess. 9 June 1960, (Washington: Government Printing Office, 1960), p. 40.

56. *US Dept. of State Bulletin*, 18 January 1954, p. 97.

57. Kermit Roosevelt, Letter to the editor, *New York Times*, 11 February 1949, p. 22.

58. *US Congressional Record*, 81st Cong. 1st sess. (1949) XCV, 16 March 1949, pp. 2647-8.

59. Ibid., p. 2653.

60. *New York Times*, 12 June 1949, p. 16.

61. Ibid., 23 August 1949, p. 17.

62. de Azcarate, *Mission*, pp. 1954-6.

63. Ibid.

64. Benjamin Shwadran, 'Assistance to Arab Refugees', *Middle Eastern Affairs* I, (1 January 1950), p. 3.

65. United Nations General Assembly, *First Interim Report of the United Nations Economic Survey Mission of the Middle East*, 4th sess., UN Doc. A/1106 (17 November 1949), p. 3.

66. Ibid., pp. 8-9.

67. Ibid., p. 10.

68. Ibid., p. 14.

69. Ibid., pp. 15-19.

70. United Nations Conciliation Commission for Palestine, *Final Report of the United Nations Economic Survey Mission for the Middle East*, UN Doc. A/AC. 25/6 (Lake Success: United Nations, 1949), p. 3.

71. Ibid., pp. 4-5.

72. US Congress, House Committee on Foreign Affairs, *Palestine Refugees*, Hearings, 81st Cong., 2nd sess., 16-17 February 1950, (Washington: Government Printing Office, 1950), pp. 1, 9, 15, 18.

73. Ibid., pp. 27-31.

74. Ibid., pp. 39-41, 43.

75. Ibid., pp. 52, 54-5.

76. US Congress, Senate Committee on Foreign Relations, *United States Foreign Policy, Middle East*, p. 130.

77. J.C. Hurewitz, *Middle East Dilemma* (New York: Harper and Brothers, 1953), p. 143.

78. Gabbay, *A Political Study*, p. 387.

79. US Department of State, Division of Publications, Office of Public Affairs, *The Palestine Refugee Program*, Pub. 3757, Near and Middle East Series, (Washington: n.n., 1950), pp. 32-3.

80. Ibid.

81. Jansen, *US and Palestinian People*, p. 142.

82. US Senate, Committee on Appropriations, *Foreign Aid Appropriations for 1951*, Hearings, 81st Cong., 2nd sess., 13 June 1950 (Washington: Government Printing Office, 1951), pp. 353-4.

83. *New York Times*, 25 May 1951, p. 4.

84. 'Bolstering the Near East and Africa as a Barrier to Aggression', statement by Assistant Secretary of State George McGhee on 20 July 1951, *Department of State Bulletin*, XXV (6 August 1951), p. 219.

85. *US Congressional Record*, 82nd Cong., 1st sess., (1951) XCVII, 17 August 1951, p. 10265.

86. Ibid., pp. 10265-66.

87. Hansen, *US and Palestinian People*, p. 142.

88. Peretz, *Israel and Palestine*, pp. 75-6.

89. Harry N. Howard, 'The Development of United States Policy in the Near East, South Asia, and Africa, 1951-52', *Department of State Bulletin*, XXVII, 702 (8 December 1952), p. 896. See also UN Doc. A/1905/Add I.

90. 'US Urges Support for New Plan of Assistance to Palestine Refugees', Statement by Philip C. Jessup in the *ad hoc* Political Committee on 17 January 1952, *Department of State Bulletin*, XXVI (11 February 1952), pp. 225-6.

91. Ibid., p. 226.

92. Jansen, *US and Palestinian People*, pp. 143-4. Also see *US Department of State Bulletin*, vol. XXVIII (15 June 1953), pp. 831-4.

93. Ibid., p. 145. Public Law 118, 83rd Cong., H.R. 5710, p. 2.

94. 'Press Release', statement by President Eisenhower on 16 October 1953, *Department of State Bulletin*, XXIX (26 October 1953), p. 553.

95. Eric Johnston, 'Mission to the Middle East', *Department of State Bulletin*, XXX (22 February 1954), 282-4.

96. US Congress, House Committee on Foreign Affairs, *The Arab Refugees and Other Problems in the Near East, Report of the Special Study Mission to the Near East*, 83rd Cong., 2nd sess., 24 February 1954 (Washington: Government Printing Office, 1954), pp. 2-9.

97. 'U.S. Extends Mandate of Relief Agency for Palestine Refugees', statement by James J. Wadsworth in the *ad hoc* Political Committee on 19 November 1954, *Department of State Bulletin*, XXXII, 810 (3 January 1955), p. 24.

98. Ibid., pp. 25-6.

99. US Congress, House Committee on Foreign Affairs, *Report of Survey Mission to the Far East, South Asia, and the Middle East*. 84th Cong., 1st sess., 24 March 1955 (Washington: Government Printing Office, 1955), p. 8.

100. US *Congressional Record*, 84th Cong., 1st sess., (1955), CI, 1 June, 1955, 3767.

101. 'The Middle East', speech by John Foster Dulles on 26 August 1955 *Department of State Bulletin*, XXXIII, 845 (5 September 1955), p. 379.

102. Ibid.

103. *New York Times*, 30 November 1955, p. 17.

104. US *Congressional Record*, 84th Cong. 2nd sess., (1956), CII, 26 January 1956, p. 1427.

105. 'Members of the House of Representatives to Secretary Dulles', Letter dated 3 February 1956, *Department of State Bulletin*, XXXIV 20 February 1956, p. 287.

106. US *Congressional Record*, 84th Cong., 2nd sess., (1956), CII, 7 March 1956, p. 4243.

107. Letter to the Editor, *New York Times*, 4 March 1956, Sec. IV, p. 10.

108. US Congress, House Committee on Foreign Affairs, *Report of the Special Study Mission to the Middle East, South and Southeast Asia, and the Western Pacific*, 84th Cong., 2nd sess., 10 May 1956 (Washington: Government Printing Office, 1956), pp. 43-4.

109. US *Congressional Record*, 85th Cong., 1st sess., (1956), CIII, 27 May 1957, p. 7715.

110. US Congress, Senate Committee on Foreign Relations, *The Middle East and Southern Europe Report of Sen. Hubert Humphrey on a Study Mission*. 85th Cong., 1st sess., July 1957 (Washington: Government Printing Office, 1960).

111. Fred J. Khouri, *The Arab-Israeli Dilemma* (Syracuse: Syracuse University Press, 1968), p. 144.

112. *New York Times*, 26 June 1961, p. 2.

113. US *Congressional Record*, 87th Cong., 1st sess., (1961) CVII, 20 July 1961, pp. 13009-10.

114. Ibid., pp. 13028-9.

115. Ibid., 3 August 1961, pp. 15214-15.

116. Ibid., 17 August 1961, pp. 16191-2.

117. Ibid., 20 August 1961, pp. 16754-5.

118. *New York Times*, 25 August 1961, p. 3.

119. Ibid., 26 November 1961, p. 20; UN Doc. A/14921/Add 1, 24 November 1961.

120. *New York Times*, 3 October 1962, p. 5.

121. Khouri, *Arab-Israeli Dilemma*, pp. 146-7.

122. William B. Quandt, *United States Policy in the Middle East: Constraints and Choices* (Santa Monica: The Rand Corporation, 1970), p. 34.

123. Ibid., pp. 34-6.

124. *New York Times*, 1 February 1963, p. 7; 2 February 1963, p. 5.

125. *New York Times*, 21 December 1962, p. 2.

126. US Contribution to UNRWA in 1964 and 1965 constituted about 70 per cent of the total budget (See UN Document no. 13 A/8013, 1969).

127. US *Congressional Record*, 89th Cong., 1st sess., (1965) CXI, 24 August 1965, pp. 21618-22.

128. US *Congressional Record*, 89th Cong., 2nd sess., CXII, 25 May 1966, p. 02423.

129. Ibid., 27 September 1966, pp. 24054-5.

130. US Congress, Committee on Foreign Relations, *War or Peace in the Middle East*, Report, 90th Cong., 1st sess., 10 April 1967 (Washington DC: Government Printing Office, 1967), p. 13.

131. US *Congressional Record*, 90th Cong., 1st sess., 1967, p. 15647.

132. 'U.N. Security Council Continues Debate on Near East', US *Department of State Bulletin*, LVII, p. 1462, (3 July 1967).

133. Harry Howard, 'The Problem of the Arab Refugees', in Majid Khadduri (ed.), *Arab-Israeli Impasse* (Washington, DC: Robert B. Luce, Inc., 1968), p. 175.

134. *Report of the Commissioner-General of the United Nations Relief and Works Agency for Palestine Refugees in the Near East*, General Assembly Official Records, 25th Session, Supplement No. 13 (A/8013).

135. *Department of State Bulletin*, (10 July 1967), pp. 33-4.

136. George Lenczowski (ed.), *United States Interests in the Middle East* (Washington: American Enterprise Institute for Public Policy Research, 1968), p. 119; 'Principles of Peace in the Middle East', statement by President Johnson on 19 June 1967, *Department of State Bulletin*, LVIII, 1463 (10 July 1967), pp. 33, 69.

137. UN Doc. S/Res/242 (1967).

138. 'Security Council Affirms Principles for Peace in the Middle East', statement by Arthur Goldberg on 15 November 1967, *Department of State Bulletin*, 18 December 1967, p. 840.

4   UNITED STATES POLICY TOWARDS A PALESTINIAN ENTITY 1967-1976

In the aftermath of the 1967 war, the United States shifted its emphasis to reconciliation of Israel and the Arab states. While the Palestinian issue was broadened after the 1967 war to include the question of terrorism and the beginnings of an awareness of a Palestinian entity, the main US focus moved from the refugee problem to the search for a settlement between the Arab states and Israel.

The US approach evolved in the post-1967 war period from President Johnson's 'five principles' to support of the UN Security Council Resolution 242 on 22 November 1967 and, subsequently, encouragement of the efforts of UN Special Representative Gunnar Jarring.[1] Resolution 242 was designed to settle the conflict among the Arab states and Israel and addressed the Palestinian refugee problem as merely one of several issues. The terms of the resolution called for 'a just and lasting peace', including freedom of navigation through international waterways, a just settlement of the refugee problem, secure and recognized boundaries in the area, withdrawal from occupied territories, and an end to all claims and states of belligerence.[2] Not surprisingly, differences with regard to this resolution arose among the antagonists.

In a vain attempt to resolve the differences, Dr. Jarring shuttled between Cairo, Amman, Beirut and Tel-Aviv until at the end of 1968 France and the Soviet Union suggested four-power talks at the United Nations. Preoccupied in Indochina, the United States did not play a leading role. Following a French proposal, the Soviet Union took the first initiative by circulating, on 2 January 1969, detailed proposals for the implementation of UN Security Council Resolution 242 to the governments of Britain, France and the United States. (See text in Appendix B). On 17 January, the French Government proposed that the 'big four' meet to discuss peace efforts in the Middle East. The four-power talks did not start until early April 1969. Egypt and Jordan welcomed the new effort; Israel opposed it. The Israeli government said the four-power talks were weighted against it and that direct Arab-Israeli talks should take place instead.[3]

In this unpromising environment the four-power representatives held fifteen meetings in thirteen weeks and adjourned on 1 July 1969, *sine die*. The prospects for agreement were as remote as ever. Meanwhile, bilateral discussions between the Soviet Union and the United States continued in Washington.

The Rogers Plan

Although the Nixon administration had participated in the four-power talks, its first major initiative was what became known as the Rogers Plan. On 28 October, Secretary of State Rogers submitted a plan to the Soviet Union consisting of a short preamble calling for the conclusion of a final and reciprocally binding accord between Egypt and Israel, followed by ten main points made public in a speech by Rogers on 9 December 1969.[4] The speech emphasized four main issues: peace, security, withdrawal, and territory. Rogers said: that peace rested with the parties to the conflict and that the major powers could act as catalysts; that a durable peace must meet the legitimate concerns of both sides; that the only framework for a negotiated settlement was one in accordance with the entire text of Resolution 242; and that a 'protracted period of war, no peace, recurrent violence, and spreading chaos would serve the interests of no nation in or out of the Middle East'. He maintained that the United States' policy in the Middle East 'is and will continue to be a balanced one'.[5] The United States would not support Israel in seeking any major changes from the pre-1967 war boundaries.[6]

On the Palestinian refugees, Rogers recognized that:

> There can be no lasting peace without a just settlement of those Palestinians whom the wars of 1948 and 1967 have made homeless . . . The problem posed by the refugees will become increasingly serious if their future is not resolved. There is a new consciousness among the young Palestinians who have grown up since 1948 which needs to be channeled away from bitterness and frustration toward hope and justice.[7]

This was the first official American recognition of Palestinian consciousness. Rogers did not refer to Palestinian rights, only to the interests and 'legitimate concerns' of governments in the area.

He proposed as well a Jordan-Israeli settlement with many of the same points as the Egyptian-Israeli plan, adding or modifying some points fitting special circumstances on the Jordanian front:

(1) The parties would establish a timetable for the withdrawal of Israeli troops from substantially all of Jordan's West Bank occupied in the June 1967 war.

(2) Each country would accept the obligations of a state of peace between them, including the prohibition of any acts of violence from its territory against the other. The point would commit Jordan to preventing commando raids by Palestine 'irregulars'.

(3) The two countries would agree upon a permanent frontier between them, approximating in the armistice the demarcation line that existed before the 1967 war, but allowing for alterations based on practical security requirements and 'administrative or economic convenience'.

(4) Israel and Jordan together would settle the problem of ultimate control over Jerusalem, recognizing that the city should be unified, with free traffic through all parts of it. Both countries would share in the civic and economic responsibilities of city government.

(5) Jordan and Israel would participate in working out final arrangements for the administration of the Gaza Strip on the basis of a parallel accord to be reached by Israel and the United Arab Republic.

(6) The two countries would negotiate practical security arrangements, including the delineation of demilitarized zones on Jordan's West Bank to take effect with the Israeli withdrawal.

(7) Jordan would open the Straits of Tiran and the Gulf of Aqaba to shipping of all countries, including Israel.

(8) The Arab refugees from the 1948 Palestine war would be given the choice of repatriation to Israel or resettlement in Arab countries with compensation from Israel. It would be up to Israeli and Jordanian negotiators to agree upon a figure of refugees to be permitted repatriation annually, but the first refugees should arrive in Israel no more than three months after the conclusion of a negotiated settlement. Dr. Jarring could establish an international commission to determine the choice of each refugee.

(9) The two countries would enter into mutual agreement formally recognizing each other's sovereignty, territorial integrity, political independence and right to live in peace.

(10) The total accord would be recorded in a signed document to be deposited with the United Nations. From then on any breach in any provision could entitle the other country to suspend its obligations until the situation had been corrected.

(11) The completed accord would be 'endorsed' by the Security Council, and Britain, France, the USA and the USSR would 'concert

their future efforts' to help all parties to abide by the provisions of the peace.[8]

The US proposal linked its implementation with the simultaneous accord planned for Israel and the United Arab Republic. It was reported that King Hussein was pleased with the American proposal. By stipulating that each state would prohibit acts of violence from its territory against the other, it was clearly the responsibility of Jordan to control the activities of the Palestinian commandoes and halt their attacks upon Israel. In his press conference on 23 December 1969, Secretary Rogers rejected the possibility of dealing directly with any of the Palestinian guerrilla groups. He insisted that the problem of the refugees should be settled between the 'parties', meaning Egypt, Jordan and Israel.[9] The Arabs viewed the American proposals as positive. Israel's supporters in the United States registered their strong opposition to the Rogers proposals. Rabbi Israel Miller, chairman of the American Zionist Council, scorned Rogers's stand.[10] Hubert Humphrey charged that the 'Nixon Administration's Middle East proposals would promote American-Soviet relations at the expense of our Israeli friends', and that they 'raised grave doubts among all people concerned for the continued independence and security of Israel'.[11]

The Soviet Union rejected the Rogers Plan on the basis that it was unbalanced and biased towards Israel.[12] Israel's reaction was even stronger, charging that Israel was being sacrificed in the process, and it rejected any form of imposed settlement. An Israeli Cabinet statement on the subject charged further that 'the proposal by the U.S.A. cannot but be interpreted by the Arab parties as an attempt to appease them at the expense of Israel'.[13]

With the Soviet Union, Israel, and Israel's American supporters all opposed, and presidential support itself weak, the Rogers Plan was marked for oblivion. The demise of this plan ended the first major Middle East peace initiative of the Nixon administration and the last significant attempt to find a direct political solution to the Palestinian problem.

Revised and implemented by Henry Kissinger, the new American step-by-step approach avoided any Palestinian involvement in the negotiating process. Following a trend which had begun as early as 1967, only the Arab states and Israel were elements in the Kissinger equation for an Arab-Israeli settlement. The Palestinians were treated merely as an indirect, intervening variable that could affect progress towards a solution and were dealt with indirectly through the Arab states. Nevertheless, the growing prominence of the Palestinian national liberation movement in the Middle East and internationally slowly extracted an American recognition of the Palestinians.

Growing American Recognition of the Palestinians

The 1969-70 period marked the beginning of an increased awareness in the United States of the Palestinians as more than simply refugees. By the summer of 1970, the success of high-visibility guerrilla activities, such as the March 1968 Battle of Karameh, and the Palestinians' relative freedom of action in Lebanon and Jordan, brought their influence to a new high.[14]

One measure of the growing Palestinian influence was increased interest in Congress. In a Senate speech in July 1970, Senator George McGovern set forth peace proposals, adding, 'Should the Arab nations so desire, representatives of the Palestinian Arab organizations should be permitted to participate in the negotiations.'[15] Although McGovern conditioned Palestinian participation upon acceptance by the Arab governments, neither the Johnson nor the Nixon administration had advocated such participation in any overall peace settlement. At the same time McGovern considered that because Israel was created as a Jewish state, it could not accept a large, hostile, non-Jewish population in its midst. Since repatriation was not possible for the thousands of Palestinians who sincerely felt that they had been unjustly barred from their homes, reparations were necessary. Some Palestinians might be able to enter Israel, but most could find new homes in underpopulated Arab nations. In addition to the compensation to which Israel had already agreed, it might also allocate money for compensation and place it in an escrow account for the refugees, to cover losses in real property and 'indemnity for the psychological loss suffered by Arab people who have no prospect of ever returning to their homes'. Other nations, including the United States, could contribute to this account.

McGovern believed the feeling of the Palestinians that they had unjustly lost their homes and property was one of the greatest sources of tension in the area. A unilateral act of Israel recognizing this to be the case could be the greatest single step towards peace in the Middle East. He also said that because Israel wanted to maintain its integrity as a Jewish state, it could not continue to occupy vast territories in which a sizeable number of Arabs lived. With thousands of Arabs under Israeli jurisdiction as a result of the June 1967 conflict, 'Israel must be prepared to yield much of the territory gained in that war'.[16]

Senator Mark Hatfield then urged the Senate 'to undertake a better understanding of the problem of the Middle East than we have thus far exhibited in floor debate and public discussion'. He said the situation was filled with complexities, not only in the Arab world but in Israel, a democratic and Jewish state 'wherein people who are not Jews are not going to have the full rights of citizenship' and 'which still withholds from certain of its people who live within the border of Israel the full rights the Jews hold because they are Jews'.[17] He noted that the Palestinian factor was another complexity because those people owned and occupied the land for generations before the creation of Israel. Many were driven from their homes or had left out of fear and resignation. 'Whatever the case, we are dealing with human problems of a sense of injustice, human problems of a sense of fear, and they are not easy to resolve.'[18]

The House Foreign Affairs Committee held hearings on the Near East conflict in mid-July 1970, during which committee members heard a variety of views on the refugee situation. Dr Landrum Bolling, President of Earlham College, felt that the United States should make a declaration to the Palestinians of full support for their efforts to achieve self-determination, including their own state on the West Bank and in Gaza if they wished. He said that peace could not be purchased by offering a loan or grant for economic development apart from a political settlement.[19]

Professor Don Peretz suggested that prevailing attitudes and analysis in the US, reflected in the media, tended to oversimplify the issues and portray the conflict as a struggle between good and evil. There was a tendency to polarize all discussion, so that those who expressed some human concern for the Arab refugees were labelled anti-Israeli or even anti-Semitic. There should be, he felt, a sympathetic understanding of both peoples and their aspirations. He indicated that the issue was often obscured by talk of Soviet penetration and of Nasser, while the real issue was the Palestinians. Peretz quoted an Israeli political leader who said that

The Palestine Nation is identifiable as a national entity by a national consciousness, by continuous territory where most of the Palestinians live, a history of several decades replete with battles and wars, and a diaspora which maintains a link with the Palestinian homeland. At the same time it is conscious of a common national catastrophe, sacrifice, suffering, of its own heroes. It has dreams and the start of a national literature and poetry.

Peretz said that compensation for refugees' property was neither an Egyptian nor a Lebanese concern because it was not Egyptian or Lebanese property that had been lost. It was a Palestinian concern that could only be settled by negotiations between them and the Israelis. Peretz noted that, until recently, neither Israeli nor American policy had taken much cognizance of the importance of the Palestinians, though he cited Senator McGovern's speech the day before as a recent exception.

> Until there is a mutual recognition of rights, that is, Palestinian recognition of the right for an Israeli nation to exist and Israeli recognition of the right of a Palestinian nation to exist, until these two people who seem to be invisible to each other as far as national existence is concerned, until these two peoples become visible to each other, I think the conflict will continue.[20]

Dr Peretz said that a major breakthrough in the refugee problem could be achieved if there were official recognition of the Palestinians as a national entity, including recognition by the United States and Israel.[21]

Other witnesses testifying at the House Foreign Affairs Committee hearings included John Badeau, former US Ambassador to Egypt, Professor Harry Howard of the American University, and Dr John Davis, a former head of UNRWA. They expressed sympathy for the Palestinians and stressed the need for some kind of self-determination. However, I.L. Kenen, editor of the *Near East Report* and a registered lobbyist for the Israeli government, had differing views. He charged that the United States 'imprudently perpetuated the Arab refugee problem by urging unrealistic repatriation proposals and by failing to insist on resettlement', which he termed as 'the sensible and logical solution. Repatriation has never been a solution for refugee problems.'[22] He concluded by citing the findings and recommendations of numerous congressional study missions and the various party platforms, all of which called for resettlement rather than repatriation.

The majority of members remained supportive of Mr. Kenen's argument. Dissenting voices became more frequent, however. On 23 August 1970, Senator William Fulbright proposed a comprehensive solution for the Arab-Israeli conflict, urging the Palestinians to accept the existence of Israel and to cease their efforts to destroy it.

The Palestinians have been done a great historical injustice but it cannot now be undone in the way they would have it undone. Indeed, after twenty-two years of Israel's existence as an independent state, it would now be as great an injustice to disrupt that society as it was for the Jews to drive the Arabs from their land in the first place. A certain rough justice accrues to any existing state of affairs, insofar as it affects people's lives and homes; once people are established and living in a place — regardless of how they got there — it becomes an injustice, even if it were a practical possibility to disrupt and expel them. This must be a bitter pill for the Palestinian Arabs to swallow, but, myths and realities being what they are, they are going to have to do it if they want an end to futile guerrilla warfare.[23]

Fulbright was perhaps the first American official to express public recognition for some form of Palestinian self-determination, including the possibility of a Palestinian state in the West Bank and the Gaza Strip.

Whether, whenever, and however they do it, the Palestinians are entitled to some form of self-determination on the non-Israeli territory of Palestine. Whether they will wish to form an independent Palestinian state or rejoin the Kingdom of Jordan, or federate with it in some way, is beyond the reach of a foreigner's judgment, and perhaps beyond the feasible scope of any foreseeable peace settlement in the Middle East.[24]

Fulbright was followed by other prominent Americans voicing increased support for the Palestinians. In the aftermath of the September 1970 war between the Palestinian commandoes and King Hussein's forces, former American Ambassador-Designate to Egypt, Richard Nolte, called for American support for a sovereign Palestinian state in the West Bank, Gaza, and East Jerusalem. He said that the Palestinians had concluded that self-help was the only answer. They regarded themselves as 'victims of monstrous discrimination'. In the eyes of Western society, they felt that they were not considered worthy of equal consideration when the claims of others were involved. Nolte said 'it should not be surprising that such a denial of status and self-respect by those proclaiming inalienable rights, equality and self-determination for all people should result in a deadly resentment and a fanatical preoccupation with right and principle'. In an attempt to find peace, the first concern and the precondition of success 'must be to show the Palestinians they have at last gained the attention of the West, including Israel, and to assure them of that equal treatment which is the basis of status and self-respect'. He said that most Palestinians wanted only to live in peace on conditions satisfying the minimum requirements of security and self-respect. Were these provided them, the extremists would lose their mass support.[25]

In yet another statement in April 1971, Senator Hatfield expressed sympathy for the plight of the Palestinians and criticized American Middle East policy as self-defeating. Hatfield questioned a policy which he believed 'helped create and perpetuate the wrongs done to the Palestinians — to the people and their subsequent generations who lived in what is now Israel'. The policy had provided a national homeland for the Jews but had also inflamed Palestinian nationalism, brought forth the *fedayeen*, produced wars between Arabs and Israelis, generated two and a half million Palestinian refugees, spawned a civil war in Jordan and threatened a nuclear confrontation between the United States and the Soviet Union. He said that the United States bore a major responsibility for these events because of what he called 'its schizophrenic policy toward the Middle East for the past twenty-two years'. He pointed out that the real conflict was between the Palestinians and the Israelis rather than between the Arabs and the Israelis, and that unless this problem were resolved, 'peace will not be forthcoming in the Middle East'.[26] He added that the United States had failed to deal adequately with the Palestinian refugees living in camps 'which depress the human spirit and turn their inhabitants toward hatred and violence toward us, the Arabs and the Israelis'.[27]

Hatfield claimed that the essential American interests in the Middle East lay in humanitarian and moral considerations, which were the only feasible justification for the magnitude of American involvement in the Middle East since the end of World War II. While the goal had been a just peace, until recently American policy had not progressed towards it. He concluded by urging the United States to press for 'the inclusion of representatives of the Palestinians' as a full party to any peace talks if a long-term settlement were envisioned.[28]

Representative Lee Hamilton of Indiana sought to balance public debate over the Palestinians. He favoured self-determination for the Palestinians, warned of further fighting if an acceptable settlement were not achieved, urged greater US efforts to ensure against another generation of refugees in camps, and called the refugee problem the root of the whole Middle East dilemma. Treating other aspects of the situation without solving this problem would constitute a cosmetic palliative with little hope of lasting success, he said.

Two constants remained that should provide the basis for settlement, Hamilton went on. First, there should be an appreciation of Israel's concern that mass repatriation inside Israel could create a fifth column. Second, there must be political and humanitarian as well as economic justice for the refugees. This could mean some sort of compensation and the right of self-determination. The efforts of UNRWA must be continued and expanded, so that more refugees could make a choice between acquiring skills to improve their lot or remaining in the camps and turning to violence. The importance of the *fedayeen*, Hamilton considered, was not their capacity to act against Israel or the United States but their ability to veto moves toward peace, as well as to affect Arab politics and to destabilize the Jordanian and Lebanese regimes. He perceived hopeful signs in the strengthening of King Hussein's government against the commandoes, the curbs on inflammatory rhetoric, the moderating influence in Israel, and most importantly the growth of a moderate Palestinian political consciousness in the West Bank. Unlike the *fedayeen*, these moderates supported the Rogers peace plan and UN Security Council Resolution 242. The way to curb the guerrilla movement was to provide the Palestinians with political as well as economic alternatives.

Hamilton listed five elements of what he believed to be a just settlement. First, he limited repatriation of Palestinians, recognizing Israeli concerns that unlimited repatriation would create political problems and would weaken the Jewish character of the state. It would still be difficult to determine which refugees should be repatriated. Second, compensation must be made to all refugees, Jews and Arabs, for loss of property. The international community should help to pay the bill and determine the amount to be paid and which refugees should be paid. Third, education and health programmes for Palestinian refugees should be expanded and intensified. Fourth, a political alternative should be offered the Palestinians. Self-determination would help break the present impasse on one of the more troublesome areas. The international community should not try to impose the form it might take, be it an independent Palestine on the West Bank, a semi-autonomous status with some connection to Jordan or full union with Jordan. Hamilton felt that giving the Palestinians the right of self-determination would undercut the Palestinian guerrilla organizations. Fifth, the international community must take responsibility for the execution of these plans, despite all the problems and tensions.

Hamilton also felt that the international community should pay a good part of the costs, which were small in comparison to the potential human cost of another war.[29]

Although the increased recognition of the Palestinians by members of Congress and other prominent Americans and their interest in official recognition of Palestinian rights were not immediately reflected in administration policy, they were nonetheless indicative of significant changes in American perception of the Palestinian people. Even up to the present, however, no American administration has fully adopted Hamilton's proposal for the recognition of a Palestinian right to self-determination.

The Palestinians in US Middle East Policy: From 'Step-by-Step' to Disengagement, 1970-6

The Palestinian problem moved from centre stage after 1967 to become only one of several issues within a comprehensive settlement; similarly in the 1970-3 period the transition to a step-by-step approach pushed the Palestinian issue even further from the immediate focus of American efforts. Paradoxically, during this same period statements by officials of the Nixon administration demonstrated increased cognizance of the Palestinians as an entity.

In 1970 two parties were actively engaged in warfare with Israel: the Palestinian *fedayeen* organizations attacking Israel from the Jordanian front, and Egypt conducting a war of attrition across the Suez Canal against Israeli forces in Sinai.[30] Meanwhile, Israel heavily attacked Egyptian forces with deep air raids into Egypt against military and economic targets. Similar raids were conducted against Jordan, though on a much smaller scale. The United States, alarmed by the deteriorating situation on the Egyptian front, feared that further escalation would increase the chances of drawing in the two superpowers. The increased number of Soviet advisers and the use of Soviet pilots in air defence missions in the Egyptian army were viewed by the Nixon administration as perilous factors.[31] In a television interview on 1 July 1970 President Nixon expressed concern over the developments in the Middle East:

I think the Middle East now is terribly dangerous. It is like the Balkans before World War I — where the two superpowers, the United States and the Soviet Union, could be drawn into a confrontation that neither of them wants.[32]

Secretary of State Rogers sought to defuse the situation through a new diplomatic initiative. Rogers adopted the simple formula of 'stop shooting and start talking'. On 19 June 1970, he proposed a cease-fire of at least three months to facilitate peace talks.[33] Israel's immediate reaction was to reject the proposal. Egypt's answer was not forthcoming until after Nasser's visit to Moscow. Jordan could not afford to risk a unilateral acceptance of the appeal, particularly in light of the presence and strength of the Palestinian commandoes in Jordan. On 22 July 1970, President Nasser accepted the Rogers proposal. On 26 July Jordan followed suit. A combination of US pressure and promises of more military hardware enticed Israel to accept the initiative on 31 July. The cease-fire took effect on 7 August 1970.

An interesting aspect of the Rogers initiative was the inclusion of Jordan, particularly since Israel and Jordan still formally respected the 1967 cease-fire. It is likely that the United States wanted to ensure that both Jordan and Egypt would be committed to controlling the Palestinian *fedayeen* who were expected to oppose any political settlement based on the Rogers Plan or Resolution 242. In accepting the new cease-fire proposals, King Hussein clearly understood that he would be responsible for preventing all acts of force from his territory. Prior to announcing his acceptance of the cease-fire, the King informed his cabinet that further clashes with the *fedayeen* might be inevitable.[34]

Rogers's second initiative profoundly affected the Palestinians. Their feelings of betrayal engendered by Nasser's and King Hussein's acceptance of the cease-fire were manifested in a public, verbal campaign against both heads of state, accompanied by massive demonstrations in Jordan and Lebanon. Angered by this, Nasser closed the Palestinian-run radio programme, the 'Voice of Palestine', in Cairo and countered with his own attack on Palestinian guerrilla groups through the Egyptian media. King Hussein continued his preparation for the inevitable showdown with the *fedayeen* in Jordan.[35]

The Jordanian army defeated the *fedayeen* in a devastating ten-day war that lasted from 17 to 26 September 1970. Thousands of Palestinian civilians were killed as well. Palestinian armed resistance to Israeli occupation of the West Bank and Gaza was substantially weakened and *fedayeen* power and prestige in the Arab world suffered immensely.

The second Rogers initiative therefore succeeded in containing the Palestinian *fedayeen* activities. It also ended the active hostilities on the Egyptian-Israeli front, reducing substantially the possibility of American and Soviet involvement. Finally it revived the moribund peace mission of Gunnar Jarring.[36]

Following the failure of the second Jarring mission in February 1971, the United States took a new approach to the problem. It now sought to bring about an 'interim settlement' with a step-by-step approach. The starting point was to break the impasse between Egypt and Israel by arriving at a temporary agreement on reopening the Suez Canal, and, once that was achieved, to take further steps, as Secretary Rogers explained:

> Eventually we will have to get to the problems between Jordan and Israel, the problem of Jerusalem, the problems of refugees, but at the moment the impasse has to do with Israel and Egypt and I would hope that some method can be arrived at to break that impasse.[37]

The Secretary of State believed that 'if this process continues step-by-step' it would be possible to work out a peaceful settlement through the complete implementation of Resolution 242.[38]

The Suez interim agreement was to involve the withdrawal of Israeli troops from the canal area and, in return, the opening of the waterway to international shipping by Egypt. Soon Egypt and Israel were deadlocked. They disagreed about Israeli rights of free shipping and cargo passage, the distance of Israeli withdrawal from the canal, the period of the cease-fire, supervision of the agreement, and the deployment of Egyptian troops across the canal. Nevertheless, on 4 October 1971 Rogers made public his proposal for a 'major step' towards peace, namely an interim Suez Canal agreement.[39] It would comprise several detailed items to augment the existing cease-fire, to be followed by 'proximity talks' between Egypt and Israel.[40]

An interim agreement was highly desirable to the United States. It would separate the combatants, extend the cease-fire and further diminish the risk of superpower involvement. It would enhance America's role as peacemaker, lessening Egypt's dependence on the Soviet Union. And it might establish a momentum towards a more comprehensive settlement.

However, these proposals were not to be realized at that time. Following a memorandum of understanding between Israel and the United States on 2 February 1972, Israel accepted the American proposal for 'proximity talks', but Egypt's President Sadat rejected these talks, preferring a return to the Jarring mission.[41] The period of 1971-3 became one of standstill diplomacy, and the White House told the State

Department not to embark on any new initiatives until after the 1972 elections.[42] Israel was satisfied with this approach, since it felt that the status quo weighed in its favour. It now enjoyed relative calm in its border regions and American-Israeli relations were stronger than ever. Throughout the election year, Nixon portrayed his administration as a strong supporter of Israel. Rabin, Israel's Ambassador to the United States, reciprocated by trying to win American-Jewish support for Nixon. He spoke openly and positively about his admiration for the Nixon-Kissinger administration, and clearly expressed his fear of McGovern. Rabin helped swing many traditionally Democratic Jewish voters to the Republican column, winning 40 per cent of the Jewish vote for Nixon in 1972.[43]

Egypt and other Arab states were displeased and frustrated by the stalled American diplomacy. Sadat's 1971 'Year of Decision' came and went without any decision. Even after Sadat expelled Soviet military advisers from Egypt in the summer of 1972, the Nixon administration did not rush to reactivate diplomatic efforts in the Middle East.[44] In contrast, the Palestinians were not disturbed by the stalled diplomacy, particularly since they had anyway been assigned to the waiting room in the American Middle East diplomatic theatre. Many Palestinians, particularly the Palestine Liberation Movement, viewed American initiatives with apprehension and at times with outright hostility. They felt they were deliberately excluded and feared that the initiatives intended to reduce, or ultimately liquidate, their movement. At least on one occasion, 25 June 1970, Secretary Rogers attempted to reassure the Palestinians, when he indicated that a settlement would have to take into account 'all of the people in the area', including the Palestinians. He stated: 'We do recognize, and I think anybody has to recognize the fact that we have to consider the welfare of all the people in this area.'[45] However, Rogers's overtures failed to mollify Palestinian suspicions, particularly in the light of the defeats they suffered in their 1970-1 conflicts with Jordan's Hussein and the rumours of an invisible American role in these events.

The events of this 1970-3 period illustrate the new American step-by-step approach to resolution of the Middle East conflict, and the moving of the Palestinian issue to the side. At the same time, statements of Nixon administration officials revealed an increased cognizance of the Palestinians as a people with 'legitimate interests and aspirations'.[46]

It was only in the aftermath of the Jordanian crisis that the administration's acknowledgement of a Palestinian entity emerged in public statements. On 12 October 1970, in a background briefing to the press, Assistant Secretary of State Sisco addressed the question.

> More and more Palestinians are thinking in terms of a given entity, wherever that may be . . . So that if I were to look ahead over the next five years, assuming that we can stabilize this area, it would be on the basis of the Arabs having adopted a live and let live attitude; that is, willing to live along side of Israel; Israel meeting at least part of the Arab demands insofar as the occupied territories are concerned; and, lastly, giving expression to the Palestinian movement and very likely in the form of some entity.[47]

Three days later, Department of State spokesman John King at a press briefing answered questions on the concept of a Palestinian entity and the role of the Palestinians in the Middle East settlement:

> Their legitimate interests and aspirations will have to be considered in any such peace settlement. We have no preconceived ideas about what form Palestinian participation might take. We do note that more and more Palestinians seem to be talking about some entity. It is fair to say that we believe that most Palestinians want a political solution despite the fact that the militant *Fedayeen* refuse to accept the idea of peaceful co-existence with Israel.[48]

Mr King also indicated that the United States would not deal directly with the Palestinians; it would only deal with the established Arab governments. They and Israel, not the Palestinians, would determine through negotiations what might emerge for the Palestinians in any peaceful political settlement.[49]

During an appearance on ABC's 'Issues and Answers', Secretary Rogers expressed American willingness to provide aid for the Middle East, including the Palestinians. He was asked then if aid to the Palestinians included setting up a separate state for them. He replied that aid did not mean something specific. He repeated his earlier statements that the welfare of the Palestinians 'had to be taken into consideration'.[50]

Several weeks after Rogers's remarks on ABC, the US Ambassador to the United Nations, Charles W. Yost, expanded further on US policy. If there was to be peace in the area, 'the legitimate concerns and aspirations of the Palestinians' had to be recognized, he said. The United States had no preconceived ideas as to 'Palestinians' participation in a settlement nor was it clear what peaceful goals the Palestinians had set for themselves, who spoke for them, what their relationship was to established Arab governments', or if a consensus existed on the Palestinian role in a peaceful settlement. This statement clearly indicated that the United States did not recognize the Palestine Liberation Organization as a spokesman for the Palestinians or as a representative of their 'legitimate concerns and aspirations'. In concluding his remarks on the Palestinians, Yost asserted that the answer to these questions needed to be clarified and that this was primarily a matter for the Palestinians to work out in conjunction with established Arab governments.[51]

Yost's statement pointed to US recognition of the emergence of the Palestinians as a political force. First they should work out an agreement with the Arab governments on their role in a settlement. After that perhaps the United States could state its views on their perceived role. This was certainly a step forward from the earlier American acknowledgement of the Palestinians only as refugees. Secretary Rogers stated American cognizance of Palestinian consciousness as a people for the first time before the UN General Assembly on 25 September 1972: 'An overall settlement in accordance with Security Council Resolution 242 (1967) must meet the legitimate aspirations of the governments on both sides, as well as of the Palestinian people.'[52]

US Palestinian policy was in transition. It no longer treated Palestinians solely as Arab refugees or Palestinian refugees, it recognized the existence of a Palestinian entity as a people. It did not recognize their right to self-determination; the United States voted against all UN General Assembly resolutions recognizing the Palestinian right to self-determination.[53] A wait-and-see attitude prevailed in Washington, which watched among other things the ability of the Palestinian national consciousness to survive the devastating Palestinian-Jordanian 'Black September' of 1970. US policy-makers held back pending further indications of what the Palestinians would do, or what the Arabs would do to them or with them. During the early stage of step-by-step diplomacy (1970-3), these five patterns emerged:

(1) The United States would not deal directly with the Palestinians but only through Arab governments.

(2) The PLO was not acceptable as a partner to any negotiations of a settlement, because of its publicly avowed position to 'liberate all of Palestine', and its refusal to recognize Israel or accept Resolution 242.

(3) The United States would take a position with regard to the Palestinians only 'if and when the Palestinians decide what they want'.

Since the PLO had already declared what was acceptable to the Palestinians and since that was totally unacceptable to the US, this statement implied that the PLO had to modify substantially its position, or that an alternative moderate Palestinian leadership would have to emerge to be accommodated in the peace process.

(4) Official statements cited above indicate that the Palestinian case was no longer viewed simply as a refugee problem. The United States recognized the Palestinians as a people with legitimate aspirations and concerns that should be included in any peace settlement.

(5) The Palestinians were not included by direct participation in any peace initiative during the period of step-by-step diplomacy, an approach which would also characterize the second phase of American step-by-step diplomacy in the Middle East in 1973-6.

Disengagement and the Palestinians: 1973-6

When Henry Kissinger became Secretary of State in September 1973, the United States was still engaged in its preventive diplomacy, which extended from 1971 to 1973. This approach essentially attempted to contain the conflict and prevent an all-out war in the Middle East. The Nixon administration attained this goal by maintaining what it called a balance of power in the region, ensuring that Israel would possess more military power than all the combined Arab forces.[54] It was felt that only an insecure Israel, a desperate Israel, would strike preemptively against Arab forces. This argument further maintained that the Arabs would not strike against far superior Israeli forces, and, even if they struck first, Israel would have sufficient power to absorb the shock and regain the upper hand in the battle. It was also assumed that a more secure and strong Israel would be more forthcoming in the peace negotiations and more willing to make concessions. Furthermore, Arab recognition that they would not be able to regain their territory by military means would make them more flexible in negotiations and likewise more willing to make concessions.

Although there was no change in the disposition of either Israel or the Arab states towards serious negotiations, the American policy of conflict containment worked successfully for a period of three years. As American officials were fond of saying, peace had not broken out, but neither had war. A false sense of security prevailed in Washington. In his address before the national foreign policy conference for editors and broadcasters on 29 March 1973, Under-Secretary of State for Near

Eastern Affairs Joseph Sisco expressed his belief that the *status quo* in the Middle East 'has been very considerably improved'. He cited a number of reasons for this belief: continuation of the cease-fire between Egypt and Israel, a more stable situation in Jordan after the ejection of the *fedayeen*, reduction of the number of incidents on the Israeli-Lebanese and the Israeli-Syrian borders, and a sharp reduction of the possibility of American-Soviet confrontation.[55] Perhaps this may explain why Sadat's political moves, preparations, and threats of war were not given much credence but were perceived merely as 'sabre-rattling' for political effect.[56]

New conditions emerged within the Arab world: modified political alignments, the assumption by King Faisal of Saudi Arabia of a more prominent role in Arab affairs and his decision to use 'oil power' for political ends, and the determination by Egypt and Syria that a military gamble was preferable to going on with the 'intolerable' *status quo*. When Egypt and Syria went to war against Israel on 6 October 1973, the American preventive diplomacy collapsed.

The October War and its aftermath accelerated Kissinger's initiation into the problems of the Middle East — a place he earlier felt was 'not really ready' for him. Kissinger continued Rogers's step-by-step diplomacy without any definite end in sight. As a man who thrived on positive results, Kissinger was aware of his predecessors' failures, and he staked all of his resourcefulness, skills and ego on effecting a settlement. Now he felt the area was ready for him. As he remarked once: 'I never treat crises when they are cold, only when they're hot. This enables me to weigh the protagonists one against the other, not in terms of ten or two thousand years ago but in terms of what each of them merits at the moment.'[57] His principle faced a crucial test in the gruelling heat of the October War.

After the war broke out, Kissinger stated that the United States had set two principal objectives: one, to end the fighting as quickly as possible, and two, to end it in such a way that it would 'contribute to the maximum extent possible' to the promotion of a more lasting solution to the Middle East problem. This meant that as the war progressed, Israel should be prevented from gaining such a decisive military victory that it would humiliate the Arab leaders and their armies.[58] When the hostilities finally stopped, Kissinger seemed to have emerged as the only winner. He had the trust of both Israel and Egypt — an important factor in his ability to achieve results when he embarked on his disengagement diplomacy. Furthermore, once this process was in motion, he effectively eliminated any significant Soviet involvement in the peacemaking process.

The unfolding events of the Watergate saga impaired Nixon's ability to discharge fully his constitutional and political responsibilities, enhancing Kissinger's authority. On 22 October 1973, a fragile cease-fire was arranged for the Egyptian and Israeli troops in the Sinai after sixteen days of fighting. On 23 October, despite the cease-fire, Israeli trooped moved to encircle and thus threaten to annihilate the 20,000-man Egyptian Third Army. Early the next day, 24 October, American intelligence detected Soviet military movements which might have been indicative of Soviet intervention. Additionally, an urgent message from Brezhnev was received asking that joint American-Soviet action be taken. He stated that, failing that, the Soviet Union would take 'appropriate steps unilaterally'. Kissinger then informed Nixon of the Soviet threat and its possible consequences. At that point Nixon 'empowered Kissinger to take charge of the American response'. Kissinger quickly ordered a worldwide alert of US military forces. The following day, the Soviet Union and Egypt accepted a UN peace-keeping force. The Israelis were restrained and the immediate crisis passed.[59]

The October alert marked the beginning of Kissinger's dramatic and almost exclusive involvement in Middle East diplomacy over the next two years. During the first eight months, Kissinger managed to bring about a cease-fire stabilization agreement between Egypt and Israel, with subsequent meetings of Egyptian and Israeli military representatives. Kissinger arranged the convening of the Geneva conference on 21 December between Israel, Egypt and Jordan, and he also persuaded King Faisal of Saudi Arabia to lift the embargo imposed during the October War.[60] In January 1974, Kissinger worked for the disengagement of the Syrian and Israeli armies on the Golan Heights. His attempt at another Egyptian-Israeli disengagement in the Sinai failed in March 1975, then finally succeeded in August.[61]

One element of American strategy in the post-October War diplomacy was to avoid the most difficult problems and to deal with each Arab state separately, step-by-step, thus avoiding confrontation with a collective Arab position. A second element was to avoid linking diplomatic steps with the nature of a final peace agreement. A third key element was to avoid the Palestinian problem and the question of their involvement in the peace negotiation process. Two weeks prior to the convening of the Geneva peace conference, on 6 December 1973, Kissinger fielded questions about the role of the Palestinians. He alluded to the thorny problem of Palestinian representation at the conference and stated that the American position was that the conflict would be best settled by the parties to the conference, meaning Egypt, Israel and Jordan. Furthermore, he added, 'Some relationship will have to be found between the rights of the Palestinians, to which the United States has made reference in several international documents, and the limitations of absorption in the mandated territory of Palestine.'[62] This appeared to indicate American recognition that 'Palestinian rights' would have to be somehow reconciled with Israeli rights and objections. Indeed, Israel's objections had already thwarted Palestinian participation in the conference. Israel indicated earlier that if the PLO attended the conference Israel would not.

Kissinger was faced with the problem of Palestinian participation almost from the outset of preparation for the Geneva conference. During the first encounter with Sadat, the Egyptian urged a role for the Palestinians. Kissinger said that he would try to arrange some form of Palestinian participation.[63] On 7 December 1973, at a meeting at the Department of State with Israeli Defense Minister Moshe Dayan and Israeli ambassador to the United States Simcha Dinitz, Kissinger was pressured by the Israelis not to include the Palestinians:

> Dinitz spoke of the Israeli elections scheduled for late December — and the Palestinians:
>
> Dinitz: I have Golda's (Meir) instructions to get an understanding between the United States and Israel in Geneva.
>
> Kissinger: I will be in touch with you, especially on the problem of Palestinian participation.
>
> Dinitz: Golda cannot go into the elections if there is any doubt on the Palestinians at Geneva.[64]

Faced with Israel's refusal to go to Geneva if the Palestinians participated, Kissinger yielded. Subsequently, he informed Sadat that he did not favour Palestinian participation. Israel would not object to Palestinians within King Hussein's delegation, but would not tolerate a separate delegation dominated by the PLO. Jordan opposed PLO participation as well.[65] Furthermore, on 20 December 1973, the day preceding the convening of the Geneva conference, Kissinger passed to the Israelis a secret memorandum of understanding promising that no other parties would be invited to future meetings at Geneva 'without the consent of the initial participants'. This in essence meant an Israeli veto over PLO participation in any future peace conference.[66] Israel was adamant and unyielding about PLO participation. Kissinger also guessed correctly that, although the Arab states were opposed to such a move, they could be persuaded to go along with it. Sadat was displeased, but acquiesced, and Assad later suggested the inclusion of a Palestinian delegation within the Syrian delegation if the Geneva conference was to reconvene.

Kissinger's effort to keep the PLO out of the negotiations received a setback after the Arab leaders met in Algiers in February 1974 and agreed that there was a need to create a Palestinian state under the leadership of PLO chairman Yasser Arafat.[67] Pressures escalated for forming a Palestinian government-in-exile. At a meeting between Kissinger and King Hussein on 2 and 3 March, Hussein asked whether the United States would recognize such a government. Kissinger denied any such intention. The King reiterated his dissatisfaction with the Israeli offer of 'administrative disengagement on the Jordanian front', which meant that Israel should maintain military control of the West Bank while Hussein would administer the territory. Hussein indicated that in any agreement with Israel he would have to regain sovereignty over the West Bank and East Jerusalem. Kissinger urged Hussein to give the Israelis more time to come up with a more meaningful offer, and the two men agreed that the United States and Jordan should work to prevent the formation of a Palestinian government-in-exile.[68]

Kissinger's public position on the issue of accommodation of the Palestinians in the peace negotiations was often evasive. At his press conference on 6 June 1974, Kissinger was asked: 'Is the U.S. position for a role for the Palestinians as a separate delegation in the peace conference?' He replied that 'the issue of the Palestinians has not yet come to us. Our present position is that the delegations at the Geneva Peace Conference were established at the opening session.' He was questioned further as to whether the US would oppose a separate seating for a Palestinian delegation at Geneva. He answered that 'the issue has not yet arisen'. He also noted that there 'has been no contact between this country and the Palestinians'.[69]

Kissinger continued his unpublicized efforts to lock out the Palestinians from negotiations. He preferred that Hussein continue to represent the Palestinians, leaving open the option of returning the West Bank to Hashemite sovereignty. He pressed for Sadat's support for Hussein as spokesman for the Palestinians, a topic which then arose at the Arab summit conference in October 1974 at Rabat. The outcome of the conference dismayed and annoyed Kissinger, dealing serious setback to his disengagement strategy. It gave a clear endorsement to the PLO to act as the sole legitimate representative of the Palestinian people. Sadat's attempt to bring about a more ambiguous statement failed.[70] On 28

October 1974, the Rabat summit unanimously resolved:

> The conference again affirms the right of the Palestinian people to return to its homeland and to define its self-determination;
>
> Again affirms the right of the Palestinian people to establish an independent national authority under the leadership of the Palestine Liberation Organization (PLO) as the sole legitimate representative of the Palestinian people in all liberated Palestinian territory. The Arab states will support this authority upon its establishment, in all respects and degrees;
>
> Supports the Palestine Liberation Organization in carrying out its national and international responsibility within the framework of Arab obligations.[71]

In light of this resolution, Hussein had no more right to continue to negotiate for the West Bank and Gaza than any other leader. The PLO's claim to this responsibility had gained Arab recognition. The Rabat summit decision was particularly significant since the Arab states recognized, for the first time in thirty years, a Palestinian body to represent and speak for the Palestinians. Kissinger could no longer claim he did not know 'whom to talk to'. The Arabs had decided who spoke for the Palestinians and made it more difficult for him to evade this issue.

The Rabat summit was shortly followed by another major Palestinian milestone with significant international impact. On 13 November 1974, Yasser Arafat addressed the UN General Assembly. He was accorded the reception and courtesy of a head of state – a rare courtesy to be extended to a leader of a liberation movement and historic in the annals of the United Nations. In his UN speech, Arafat reiterated his call for the formation in Palestine of a secular democratic state,[72] a statement understood by the Palestinians to mean the 'de-Zionization' of Israel, the repatriation of the Palestinians to their homes, and the integration of Jews, Arabs, Muslims and Christians into one society. However, the United States perceived this as the destruction of Israel as a Jewish state.

Israel's refusal to negotiate with the PLO remained unwavering. The United States detected no signs of moderation in Arafat's speech nor in the position of the PLO towards Israel, and took no steps towards PLO involvement in the peace negotiations; it continued to avoid direct contact with the organization.

In late May 1974, in Damascus, the Syrians unsuccessfully attempted to persuade Kissinger to meet with Yasser Arafat. According to the Syrian version, Kissinger complained that he would not 'be able to return home' if he met with Arafat, and he explained the enormous domestic political problems the meeting would raise.[73] Kissinger clearly overstated his fears of the negative domestic reaction to the proposed meeting. His real concern, however, was the enormous difficulties he would have encountered with Israel in his quest for further disengagements. The Israelis, always very sensitive to any US gesture towards the PLO, would have certainly regarded a meeting with Arafat as a signal of a change in policy.

Kissinger felt the brunt of Israeli pressure again during the negotiations of the period leading up to the set of agreements known as Sinai II, the second phase of disengagement between Egypt and Israel. He yielded once more on the PLO issue when the United States agreed not to recognize or negotiate with the organization unless it recognized Israel and accepted Security Council Resolutions 242 and 338. The American-Israeli Memorandum of Agreement said:

> The [US] Government . . . will seek to prevent . . . proposals which it and Israel agree are detrimental to the interests of Israel. . . . The United States is resolved to . . . maintain Israel's defensive strength through the supply of advanced types of equipment, such as the F-16 aircraft [and] to undertake a joint study of high technology and sophisticated weapons, including the Pershing ground-to-ground missiles with conventional warheads with the view to giving a positive response . . .
>
> The United States will not recognize or negotiate with the Palestine Liberation Organization so long as the [PLO] does not recognize Israel's right to exist and does not accept Security Council Resolution 242 and 338. The [US] Government will consult fully and seek to concert its position and strategy at the Geneva Peace Conference with the Government of Israel.[74]

American commitments detailed in the memorandum were the price for Israeli acceptance of the Sinai II disengagement agreement with Egypt.[75] The memorandum meant further American intractability on the PLO and the Palestinian issue. However, Kissinger sought to reassure the Arabs when he promised Arab representatives at the United Nations on 29 September 1975 that he would begin to refine his thinking on how the legitimate interests of the Palestinian people could be met.[76]

On 12 November 1975, Deputy Assistant Secretary for Near Eastern

Affairs Harold Saunders gave a prepared policy statement on the Palestinians before a special House International Relations subcommittee, later known as the Saunders Document. Although the 1970-3 period had witnessed growing awareness of the Palestinians as more than refugees, this was the first statement by an administration official terming the Palestinians as a 'people [who] . . . desire a voice in determining their political status'. It was a question of how, not where, this could be accomplished. The document referred to the Palestinian issue as the 'heart of the Arab-Israeli conflict'. The Palestinian issue was no longer a refugee problem exclusively:

> we recognize that, in addition to meeting the human needs and responding to legitimate personal claims of the refugees, there is another interest that must be taken into account. It is a fact that many of the three million or so people who call themselves Palestinians today increasingly regard themselves as having their own identity as a people and desire a voice in determining their political status.
>
> As with any people in this situation, they have differences among themselves, but the Palestinians collectively are a political factor which must be dealt with if there is to be a peace between Israel and its neighbors . . .
>
> What is needed at first is a diplomatic process which will help bring reasonable definition of Palestinian interests — a position from which negotiations on a solution of the Palestinian aspects of the problem might begin. The issue is not whether Palestinian interests should be expressed in a final settlement, but how. There will be no peace unless an answer is found. We are prepared to consider any reasonable proposal from any quarter, and we will expect other parties to the negotiation to be equally broadminded.[77]

The statement was meant to demonstrate America's continuing willingness to work for a peace settlement. Although he later disowned it, Kissinger checked the wording of the draft carefully, and it was also reported that he cleared the statement with President Ford.[78] The document represented a significant landmark in terms of the public record in US Palestinian policy.

From this point forward throughout the remainder of the Ford administration, no significant progress towards a peace settlement was achieved. The 1976 presidential election activities and the civil war in Lebanon commanded the primary attention of the administration.

Throughout his tenure as Secretary of State, Henry Kissinger had successfully resisted pressure by the Arab governments to recognize and deal directly with the PLO or to include the Palestinian issue in the negotiating process. Kissinger preferred to deal with it at a later phase for several reasons:

(1) Since this issue was viewed as the most difficult, it seemed that a lack of progress would impede movement on other less problematic aspects in the negotiations.

(2) Some progress on the other issues which seemed possible would have contributed to the generation of trust, optimism, and relaxation of tension among the negotiating parties, and might reduce the chances of an explosion.

(3) Progress on the less difficult aspects might have provided a momentum towards an overall settlement.

Kissinger's attitude towards the Palestinians and the negotiating process was reflected in one of his remarks to an Israeli during negotiations for the Sinai II agreement when, at the time he was particularly annoyed at what he perceived as Israeli inflexibility, he said:

The Arab leaders who banked on the United States will be discredited . . . Step-by-step has been throttled, first for Jordan, then for Egypt. We're losing control. We'll now see the Arabs working on a united front. There will be more emphasis on the Palestinians, and there will be a linkage between moves in the Sinai and on Golan. The Soviets will step back onto the stage.[79]

Kissinger dealt with each Arab state separately; he felt it far easier to negotiate with each Arab head of state than with the group of the involved Arab parties. Anwar Sadat became the cornerstone of the new US 'Arab policy'. Kissinger's strategy and his artful negotiating techniques produced in this period a series of American successes: Egyptian, then Syrian, disengagement with Israel, and Sinai II. He achieved the disengagement of combatant forces on the Golan and in the Sinai, the reduction of Soviet involvement and influence in the region, a closer relationship with Egypt, and a long delay in dealing with the thorny Palestinian issue. In 1977 the unenviable task of matching Kissinger's resourcefulness and diplomatic success in the Middle East or in finding a new formula for the promised comprehensive settlement, including the Palestinian issue, devolved on the Carter administration.

Notes

1. In accordance with Article 3 of UN Security Council Resolution 242, the UN Secretary-General appointed Dr Gunnar Jarring, Swedish Ambassador to Moscow, an experienced diplomat and talented linguist, as his special representative.

2. Text of Resolution 242 in Appendix B, p. 202.

3. *The Daily Telegraph*, 31 March 1969, p. 4.

4. *Washington Post*, 1 December 1969, p. 1.

5. 'A Lasting Peace in the Middle East: An American View', address by Secretary Rogers on 9 December 1969, *Department of State Bulletin*, LXII, 1593 (5 January 1970), pp. 7-11.

6. Ibid., p. 9.

7. Ibid., pp. 9-10.

8. Ibid., pp. 7-11. For the full text of the plan see also Department of State Press Release No. 371, 9 December 1969.

9. *Department of State Bulletin*, LXII, 1594 (12 January 1970), p. 24.

10. *New York Times*, 13 December 1969, p. 34:3.

11. *The Washington Post*, 12 December 1969, p. a-22.

12. *New York Times*, 13 January 1970, p. 10.

13. *Arab Report and Record*, 16-31 December 1969, p. 549.

14. The Battle of Karameh occurred on 21 March 1968. It was the first major confrontation between the Israeli Army and the Palestinian guerrillas since the 1967 six-day war. For further details see *New York Times* 22 March 1968.

15. *U.S. Congressional Record*, 91st Cong., 2nd sess., (1970), CXVI, 20 July 1970, pp. 11714-15.

16. Ibid., p. 11715.

17. Ibid.

18. Ibid.

19. US Congress, House Committee on Foreign Affairs, Subcommittee on the Near East, *The Near East Conflict*, Hearings, 91st Cong., 2nd sess., 21-3, 28-30 July 1970 (Washington: Government Printing Office, 1970), pp. 17-18.

20. Ibid., pp. 20-3.

21. Ibid., p. 39.

22. Ibid., p. 68.

23. Text of statement by Senator J.W. Fulbright, Chairman, Committee on Foreign Relations, US Senate, 'Old Myths and New Realities . . . II: The Middle East.' No. 63 (23 August 1970), pp. 34-6.

24. Ibid.

25. *New York Times*, 5 October 1970, p. 43.

26. *US Congressional Record*, 92nd Cong. 1st sess., (1971), CXVII, 30 April 1971, pp. 5985-6.

27. Ibid., p. 5987.

28. Ibid.

29. Ibid., 7 July 1971, pp. 6431-4.

30. Following the Battle of Karameh, where the Israeli forces crossed the Jordan River on 21 March 1968 (*New York Times*, 22 March 1968) to destroy the guerrilla bases in the deserted Karameh refugee camp, the Palestinian *fedayeen* made a strong stand against the much larger and well-mechanised Israeli invading forces. The *fedayeen* suffered heavy losses and inflicted some casualties on the Israeli forces. This event became a landmark in the development of the Palestine Liberation movement. Consequently, the Palestinian *fedayeen* became the new heroes in the Arab world.

31. B. Reich, *Quest for Peace: United States-Israeli Relations and the Arab-*

Israeli Conflict (New Brunswick, New Jersey: Transaction Books, 1977), p. 123.

32. *Department of State Bulletin*, 27 July 1970, pp. 112-13.

33. Ibid., 10 August 1970, pp. 178-9.

34. William Quandt, *Decade of Decisions* (Berkeley, California: University of California Press, 1977), pp. 101-3.

35. Annoyed at what he considered to be lack of control over the *fedayeen*, Nasser sought to have some influence over them by maintaining a balance in Jordan between them and King Hussein. Therefore, three days prior to the show-down, King Hussein met with Nasser in Alexandria. Nasser acquiesced to a crackdown by the King. However, during the war, when Nasser saw that Hussein's intentions were not a reduction of the *fedayeen* power but its total destruction, he was angered and initiated combined Arab action to stop the fighting. It was after the conclusion of the Arab summit meeting about the Hussein-Palestinian conflict that Nasser died of a heart attack.

36. As the cease-fire held, it was extended by agreement for a final 30-day period to March 1971. It continued thereafter as a *de facto* truce observed by both sides. When the Jarring mission was finally reactivated in January 1971, the negotiations were short. The disagreemeent between Egypt and Israel over signing 'a peace agreement' and 'withdrawal' from all occupied territories sent the Jarring peace mission to a final rest. For further discussion see Reich, *Quest for Peace*, pp. 159-66, 172-80, 192-4, 203-4.

37. *Department of State Bulletin*, LXIV, 1666 (31 May 1971), pp. 689-91.

38. Ibid., p. 691.

39. *Department of State Bulletin*, vol. 65, 25 October 1971, pp. 442-3.

40. See Reich, *Quest for Peace*, pp. 186-91.

41. Bernard Reich, 'United States Policy in the Middle East', *Current History*, (January 1976), vol. 70, no. 412, p. 1. According to the Memorandum of Under-standing the United States agreed to sell Israel 42 F-4 and 82 A-4 aeroplanes over future years. (see *New York Times*, 3 February 1972). Furthermore, according to Yitzhak Rabin, as quoted in *Ma'ariv*, the Memorandum of Understanding acknowledged that Israel would not be expected to make a commitment on full withdrawal as part of an interim agreement (See Quandt, *Decade of Decisions*, pp. 146-7). Sadat initially accepted the American proposal for 'proximity talks'; however, after further discussion, he rejected it, because he insisted that any interim agreement must be tied into an Israeli commitment in principle to with-drawal from all occupied Arab territories.

42. John C. Campbell, 'American Efforts for Peace', in Malcolm Kerr (ed.), *The Elusive Peace in the Middle East* (State University of New York Press, 1975), pp. 298-9.

43. Bernard and Marvin Kalb, *Kissinger* (New York, NY: Dell Publishing Co., 1974), pp. 239-40.

44. President Sadat proclaimed 1971 as a 'year of decision', meaning that if no real progress towards a settlement was achieved, he would make a decision with regard to peace efforts or war with Israel. The year expired and apparently no decision was made during that period.

45. 'Secretary Rogers News Conference of June 25', *Department of State Bulletin*, LXIII, 1620 (13 July 1970), p. 32.

46. *International Herald Tribune*, 16 October 1970, p. 2.

47. Quoted in Quandt, *Decade of Decisions*, pp. 130-1.

48. *International Documents on Palestine*, 1968, (Beirut: Institute for Palestine Studies, 1971), p. 351. Quoted from *International Herald Tribune*, 16 October 1970, pp. 1, 2.

49. Ibid.

50. 'Secretary Rogers and Secretary Laird Interviewed on "Issues and Answers" ', *Department of State Bulletin*, LXIII, 1636 (2 November 1970), pp. 5469-553.

51. 'U.S. Gives Views on U.N. General Assembly Debate on the Situation in the Middle East', statement by Ambassador Yost on 4 November 1970, *Department of State Bulletin*, LXIII, 1639 (23 November 1970), p. 658.

52. 'A World Free of Violence', statement by Secretary Rogers before UN General Assembly on 25 September 1972, *Department of State Bulletin*, LXVII, 1738 (16 October 1972), p. 427.

53. From 30 November 1970 to 7 December 1973, the UN General Assembly passed seven resolutions, each one recognizing or affirming the rights of the Palestinians to self-determination. They were: Resolution no. 2649 of November 1970, no. 2672 of 8 December 1970, no. 2787 of 6 December 1971, no. 2792 of 6 December 1971, no. 2963 of 13 December 1972, no. 3070 of 30 November 1973, and no. 3089 of 7 December 1973. The US and Israel voted against all of the seven resolutions. See George T. Tomeh (ed.), *The United Nations Resolutions on Palestine and the Arab Israeli Conflict 1947-1974* (Beirut, Lebanon: The Institute of Palestine Studies, 1975), pp. 78-100.

54. The Nixon administration maintained the 'balance of power' in the Middle East by meeting most of Israel's requests for military equipment so it would offset the effects of all Soviet arms shipments to the Arab States. For further discussion see Reich, *Quest for Peace*, pp. 119-20, 169, 172, 174, 190-1, 378-83.

55. Joseph J. Sisco, 'The Current Situation in the Middle East', *Department of State Bulletin*, 1765, vol. LXVII, (23 April 1973), p. 434-6.

56. Reich, *Quest for Peace*, p. 202.

57. Quoted in Edward Sheehan, *The Arabs, Israelis, and Kissinger* (Readers' Digest Press distributed by Thomas Y. Crowell Co., New York, 1976), p. 40.

58. Reich, *Quest for Peace*, p. 251-3.

59. Roger Morris, *Uncertain Greatness: Henry Kissinger and American Foreign Policy* (New York: Harper and Row, Publishers, 1977), pp. 245-7.

60. At the end of the initial round, the conferees agreed to issue a joint communiqué in which they voted the establishment of a military working group to handle the disengagement of forces. Furthermore, another Geneva Conference at the foreign ministers level would convene when needed. See Reich, *Quest for Peace*, pp. 254-5.

61. For a complete discussion of these events see Reich, *Quest for Peace*, pp. 254-94.

62. *Department of State Bulletin*, 1800, LXIX (24 December 1973), pp. 756-8.

63. Edward Sheehan, 'Step by Step in the Middle East', *Foreign Policy* 22 (7 March 1976), p. 15.

64. Ibid., p. 24.

65. Ibid., p. 25.

66. Sheehan, *The Arabs, Israelis and Kissinger*, p. 108.

67. Quandt, *Decade of Decisions*, p. 234.

68. Jordan requested disengagement with Israel along the same lines as the Israeli-Egyptian agreement. Israel did not accept this proposal and instead offered 'administrative disengagement' with Hussein – an offer rejected by the King. See Quandt, *Decade of Decisions*, pp. 233-4.

69. *Department of State Bulletin*, 1826, LXX, (24 June 1974), pp. 702-7.

70. Reich, *Quest for Peace*, pp. 299-300 and Quandt, *Decade of Decisions*, pp. 256-7.

71. Quoted in Reich, *Quest for Peace*, p. 300.

72. Text in *New York Times*, 14 November 1974, pp. 22-3. More recently Arafat said that the 'secular democratic State of Palestine' he proposed was merely a 'dream', a 'vision' and that he should have the right to dream. In an interview with Anthony Lewis in the *New York Times* of 2 May 1978, Arafat indicated that he had abandoned his dream and would accept a Palestinian State

in the West Bank and Gaza, living peacefully with Israel.

73. Interview with official in PLO United Information Section in Beirut, Lebanon, 28 July 1974.

74. Sheehan, 'Step-by-Step', p. 63.

75. Sinai II provided among other things the withdrawal of Israeli troops in the Sinai to points beyond the Mitla and Giddi passes. For details see Reich, *Quest for Peace*, pp. 295-347.

76. Quoted in Quandt, *Decade of Decisions*, p. 276.

77. *Department of State Bulletin*, December 1975, pp. 797, 798. The statement and its timing (10 November 1975) was something of a puzzle to many observers, since it came only two days after the UN General Assembly passed its anti-Zionist resolution, defining Zionism 'as a form of racism and racial discrimination'; a resolution which the US rejected in light of Kissinger's later statements referring to the Saunders Document as 'a somewhat academic exercise explaining in a purely theoretical manner several aspects of the Palestine problem as Mr. Saunders saw them'. The emphasized that this did not indicate a change of policy. See Reich, *Quest for Peace*, pp. 415-16.

78. Quandt, *Decade of Decisions*, p. 278. The most plausible explanation is that Kissinger was eager to regain the confidence of the Syrian President, Hafez Assad, and persuade him to renew the mandate of UN forces on the Golan which was due to expire at the end of November.

79. Quoted in Quandt, *Decade of Decisions*, p. 266.

5 THE UNITED STATES AND PALESTINIAN REVOLUTIONARY VIOLENCE 1968-1980

Several books have recently appeared in the United States in which Palestinian revolutionary violence has been labelled 'terrorism'. Government agencies and private corporations gave research grants to academics presenting themselves as experts on terrorism. Such experts seldom recognize that terrorist operations form an essential part of legitimate revolutionary violence and, indeed, are only one aspect of the strategy for national liberation of the Palestinian people. Occasionally an academic or journalist will make a vague allusion to violence by invoking the aphorism, 'One man's terrorist is another's freedom fighter.' The general perception of Palestinian operations in the media, in academic literature and in the American government's official records remains that of 'terrorism', regardless of the objectives. Israeli violence, on the other hand, is labelled as 'retaliation' and the actors as 'commandos'.

Palestinians and most Arabs view these operations directed against Israel (and its allies) as revolutionary violence, an integral part of their struggle against Zionist settler colonialism. The Palestinians, as a colonized and exiled people, apprehend that their struggle is, in essence, similar to that of the Algerian and Vietnamese people for national liberation. This is not to say that they are unaware of the dangers and ramifications of this use of violence. Frantz Fanon, in the *Wretched of the Earth*, perhaps expresses best an important aspect of the necessity of such violence. He sees that the outcasts of society, who are beyond charity, but not beyond redemption, can be 'saved' by participation in revolutionary violence. Decolonization comes after a ' decisive and murderous confrontation of the two protagonists' which turns the colonized 'object' into a man. The deep self-destructive urge is worked out in action:

> Violence alone, violence committed by the people, violence educated and organized by its leaders makes it possible for the masses to understand social truths and gives the key to them . . . at the level of individuals violence is a cleansing force . . . [it] frees the native from his inferiority complex and from his despair and inaction; it makes him fearless and restores his self-respect.[1]

No doubt, Fanon would concur that Palestinian violence, organized and designed to achieve certain goals in the general strategy of the movement, can be classified as revolutionary. However, violence that lacks political objectives or contradicts the strategy of national liberation of the Palestinian people should be classified as terrorism. The distinction is elusive. Here we merely indicate the divergence of Palestinian and American perceptions of this issue and its effect on American policy behaviour.

Rise of Palestinian Violence

Palestinian resistance organizations consider America's special relationship with Israel as at least partially responsible for their continued loss of their homeland. Consequently, American citizens and property have been frequent targets of Palestinian operations. 23 July 1968 marked the first Palestinian international operation. The PFLP hijacked an El Al plane and commandeered it to Algeria. This initiated a new policy of striking at Israeli targets no matter where they were located. This new policy also included striking at targets of states considered supportive of Israel.

Following is a list of selected Palestinian commando operations. In each operation the actor is designated wherever possible. Question marks indicate acts which were never claimed by a group or in which a *nom de guerre* was used by the group. Abbreviations used are as follows:

Fateh	Palestine National Liberation Movement
PFLP	Popular Front for the Liberation of Palestine
PDFLP	Popular Democratic Front for the Liberation of Palestine
PSF	Popular Struggle Front (also known as PPSF)
BSO	Black September Organization
Red Army	Japan's United Red Army (Affiliated with PFLP)
PFLP-GC	Popular Front for the Liberation of Palestine – General Command (Ahmed Jabril)
ANY	Arab Nationalist Youth Organization for the Liberation of Palestine
OSOT	Organization of Sons of Occupied Territory
OVZO	Organization of Victims of Zionist Occupation
AOLP	Arab Organization for the Liberation of Palestine
Other	Individuals or small groups other than those listed above

**Table 5.1: Table of Palestinian Commando Operations,
July 1968-March 1978[2]**

Date	Actor	Target	Location
23 July 1968	PFLP (before PFLP-GC split)	El Al plane (Israel) hijack	Rome to Algeria
26 Dec. 1968	PFLP	El Al plane (Israel) grenade, shooting	Athens
18 Feb. 1969	PFLP	El Al plane (Israel) machine-gunned	Zurich
May, 1969	PFLP	Tapline bomb (US)	Golan
18 July 1969	PFLP	2 Jewish-owned stores (Zionism), fire, bomb	
25 Aug. 1969	PFLP	ZIM shipline (Israel) bomb	London
29 Aug. 1969	PFLP and Latin American	TWA (US) hijack damaged plane	Paris to Syria
9 Sept. 1969	PFLP	El Al office (Israel) bomb	Brussels
9 Sept. 1969	PFLP	Israeli Embassy bomb	Bonn
9 Sept. 1969	PFLP	Israeli Embassy bomb	The Hague
Oct. 1969	PFLP	Zahrani Tapline (US) rockets	Lebanon
27 Nov. 1969	PSF	El Al office (Israel) bomb	Athens
10 Feb. 1970	DPFLP (PFLP) AOLP (?)	El Al bus and lounge (Israel) grenade	Munich
20 Feb. 1970	PFLP-GC	Swissair (Switzerland, Israel) bomb in air	Zurich
20 Feb. 1970	PFLP-GC	American Air (Austria, Israel) bomb in air	Frankfurt
25 Apr. 1970	Other	El Al office (Israel) bomb	Istanbul
4 May 1970	Fateh	Israeli Embassy shooting	Paraguay
7 June 1970	Other	US (US official kidnapped, one day)	Amman
7 June 1970	Other	US official (attempted kidnapping)	Amman
9 June 1970	PFLP	Hotels (2) hostages	Amman
10 June 1970	Other	US official killed	Amman

Date	Actor	Target	Location
22 July 1970	PSF	Olympic Air (Greece) hijack	Beirut to Cairo
5 Sept. 1970	PFLP	Pan Am (US) hijack	Europe to Cairo
5 Sept. 1970	PFLP, Latin American	El Al (Israel) hijack	Amsterdam to London
5 Sept. 1970	PFLP	TWA (US) hijack	Frankfurt to Jordan
5 Sept. 1970	PFLP	Swissair (Switzer-land) hijack	Zurich to Jordan
9 Sept. 1970	PFLP	BOAC (Britain) hijack	Bahrain to Jordan
2 Apr. 1971	Other	Tapline (US, Jordan) bomb	Jordan
14 June 1971	PFLP	Liberian tanker (Israel/Iran & Saudi) rocket	Red Sea (South Yemen)
24 Aug. 1971	Fateh (not claimed)	Alia plane (Jordan) bomb	Madrid
8 Sept. 1971	Individual of Fateh	Alia plane (Jordan) hijack	to Libya
9 Sept. 1971	Other	Tapline (US, Saudi Arabia, Jordan) bomb	Jordan
15 Sept. 1971	Other	Tapline (US, Saudi Arabia, Jordan) bomb	Jordan
7 Oct. 1971	Other	Alia plane (Jordan) bomb, no damage, before loaded	Beirut
24 Oct. 1971	Other	Tapline (US, Jordan) bomb	Jordan
10 Nov. 1971	Other	Intercontinental Hotel (Jordan, US) 4 bombs	Amman
28 Nov. 1971	BSO	Wasfi al-Tal (Jordan) assassination	Cairo
15 Dec. 1971	BSO	Zaid ar-Rifai (Jordan) assassina-tion attempt, wounded by machine gun	London
16 Dec. 1971	BSO Jordanian National Liberation Movement	Jordanian Ambas-sador, bomb package, 3 wounded	Geneva

Date	Actor	Target	Location
8 Feb. 1972	BSO	Gas pumping station (Netherlands, Israel) sabotage	Netherlands
8 Feb. 1972	BSO	Gen. Elec. plant (Israel, Germany) sabotage	Hamburg
22 Feb. 1972	PFLP and OVZO	Lufthansa plane (Germany) attack	New Delhi to South Yemen
8 May 1972	BSO	SABENA plane (Israel) hijack	Vienna to Tel Aviv
30 May 1972	PFLP and Red Army	Airport (Israel) hijack	Tel Aviv
5 Aug. 1972	BSO	Oil storage ctrl (Germany, Austria, Israel) sabotage	Trieste, Italy
16 Aug. 1972	ANY (?), BSO (?)	El Al plane (Israel) sabotage, bomb	Rome
5 Sept. 1972	BSO	Israeli Olympic team (kidnap)	Munich
Sept.-Nov. 1972	BSO	Israeli officials and Jewish interests, letter bomb	London, Rome, Geneva, Paris (worldwide)
6 Oct. 1972	Other (Palestinian students)	German Embassy (Germany)	Algiers
29 Oct. 1972	ANY (?) BSO (?)	Lufthansa (Germany) hijack	Beirut to Yugoslavia to Libya
20 Dec. 1972	BSO (?)	US Embassy, rockets	Beirut
28 Dec. 1972	BSO/ALI Taha	Israeli Embassy, hostage	Bangkok
8 Jan. 1973	BSO	Jewish Immigration Agency (Zionist) bombing	Paris
21 Jan. 1973	Jordanian Rep. — army Punishment Forces	Tapline (Saudi Arabia, Jordan, US)	Saudi Arabia
1 Mar. 1973	BSO	Saudi Embassy & US/Belgian officials, hostage	Khartoum
4 Mar. 1973	BSO	Greek ship (Israel) tourism, bomb	Beirut
9 Apr. 1973	ANY	Israeli ambassador, El Al plane, bomb	Cyprus
14 Apr. 1973	Other	Tapline (US) bomb	Lebanon
16 Apr. 1973	Other	Tapline (US) bomb, no damage	Lebanon
2 May 1973	Other	US Ambassador's residence, rocket	Beirut

Date	Actor	Target	Location
19 July 1973	OVZO individual	El Al office (Israel) attack, failed; hotel, hostages	Athens
20 July 1973	OSOT (Mt. Carmel Martyrs) Red Army and Latin American (PFLP) (?) Haddzd (?)	Japan airlines, Japan hijack, plane destroyed	Netherlands to Dubai to Damascus to Syria
5 Aug. 1973	BSO (?) 7th Suicide Squad	Airport passengers Israeli tourism (TWA to Tel Aviv, attack)	Greece
5 Sept. 1973	Fateh and PFLP	Saudi Embassy (hostage) Saudi Arabia officials kidnap (Jordan, Saudi Arabia)	Paris Kuwait/ Riyadh
11 Sept. 1973	BSO (?)	Israel's booth at fair	West Berlin
28 Sept. 1973	Eagles of Palestinian Revolution	Train from Russia hostage (Israel, Austria)	Austria
25 Nov. 1973	(Sa'iqa) ANY	KLM (Holland, Israel) immigration, hijack	Beirut to Damascus to Cyprus to Libya, Malta to Dubai
17 Dec. 1973	Ghaffur's Group	Italy, US Peace Conference (Pan Am plane and passengers) fire bomb, machine gun	Rome
		Lufthansa (Greece) attack	Rome to Athens
1 Jan. 1974	PFLP	(British Zionists) attack	London
25 Jan. 1974	PFLP	Bank of Israel bomb	London
31 Jan. 1974	PFLP and Red Army and OSOT	Shell Refinery (Netherlands) bomb	Singapore
6 Feb. 1974	PFLP and Red Army and OSOT	Japan Embassy, hostages	Kuwait
3 Feb. 1974	Ghaffur's Group	Greek freighter (Greece) seajack, hostages	Pakistan
4 Mar. 1974	ANY	British plane (Britain and US) hijack	Beirut to Netherlands
11 Apr. 1974	PFLP-GC	Israel	Israel
15 May 1974	PDFLP	Israel	Israel
13 June 1974	PFLP-GC	Israel	Israel

Date	Actor	Target	Location
24 June 1974	Fateh	Israel	Israel
15 Sept. 1974	Not claimed	2 Parisians killed, 26 wounded, in drugstore	Paris
21 Nov. 1974	Pal. guerrillas	British plane from Dubai, hijack, 1 killed	Landed in Tripoli
23 Dec. 1974	Pal. guerrillas	Pilgrimage to Holy Land, 1 wounded	Al Ayzariyah tourist bus
6 Mar. 1975	Fateh	Savoy Hotel, 6 wounded, 18 killed	Tel Aviv
16 Sept. 1975	Pal. guerrillas	5 hostages taken to Algeria, released	Egyptian Embassy Madrid
2 Dec. 1975	Fateh	Kibbutz and officers' club, 30 hostages	near Tel Aviv
23 Aug. 1976	3 Arab guerrillas (Libyan leader)	Egypt. Boeing 737, 97 passengers, 6 crew	Cairo
28 June 1976	PFLP and German radicals	Air France Jet Liner, 257 hostages	Tel Aviv
12 Aug. 1976	PFLP	Israeli El Al Boeing 707	Istanbul
5 Sept. 1976	Pal. guerrillas	KLM, 82 passengers	Nice, Amsterdam
29 May 1977	Fateh	Bomb explosion	Jerusalem
9 July 1977	Others	Kuwait Airlines	Kuwait
15 Oct. 1977	PFLP	Lufthansa, Boeing 337	Turkey – Dubai
17 Feb. 1978	Others	Israeli oranges poisoned	Europe
19 Feb. 1978	Others	Yousef Al-Seba (Egyptian Editor)	Cyprus
12 Mar. 1978	Fateh	Israeli bus	Haifa-Tel Aviv Road
7 Apr. 1978	Fateh	Israel Army	South Lebanon
11 Apr. 1978	Fateh	Israeli installation	Tel Aviv
13 Apr. 1978	PLO	Israeli Army	South Lebanon
21 May 1978	Sons of Southern Lebanon	El Al flight	Paris Orly
3-4 June 1978	Fateh	Israeli bus	Jerusalem
13 June 1978	Fateh	Kibbutz	Jordan Valley
30 June 1978	Fateh	Israeli market	Jerusalem
4-5 Aug. 1978	PLO	Bus stop	Tel Aviv
22 Aug. 1978	PLO	El Al crew	London

Date	Actor	Target	Location
15 Jan. 1979	PLO	(Ramat), Ishkol Kibbutz	Jerusalem
29 Feb. 1979	PLO	Israeli tourists	Gaza strip
20 Mar. 1979	PDFLP	Hotel	Muzlot
1 Apr. 1979	PLO	US Embassy	Beirut
10 May 1979	PLO	Market	Tel Aviv
10 June 1979	PLO	Kibbutz	Menara Israel
15 June 1979	PLO	Tiberias	Israel
20 June 1979	Fateh	El Al Airlines	Brussels Airport
25 June 1979	PLO	Israeli settlers	Nahonya
1 July 1979	Sa'iqa	Egyptian Embassy	Ankara
15 Sept. 1979	Fateh	Israeli army	Jerusalem
1 Oct. 1979	Arab Youths	Israeli army	Hebron
15 Nov. 1979	PLO	Market	South Israel
16 Nov. 1979	Palestinian demonstrators	Israeli truck	Nablus

Note: Attacks inside Israel and the occupied lands increased after 1974. Only those designed to affect political activities outside Israel, such as peace negotiations, are included in this list. It is also quite discernable that operations decreased substantially in 1976 due to Palestinian involvement in the civil war in Lebanon.

Source: *Arab Report and Record*, 1968-1978; *New York Times* 1974-8; and Paul A. Jureidini and William E. Hazen, *The Palestinian Movement in Politics*, (Lexington, Mass.: Edward Heath and Company, 1975), pp. 77-81.

Graph Summary of Table 5.1

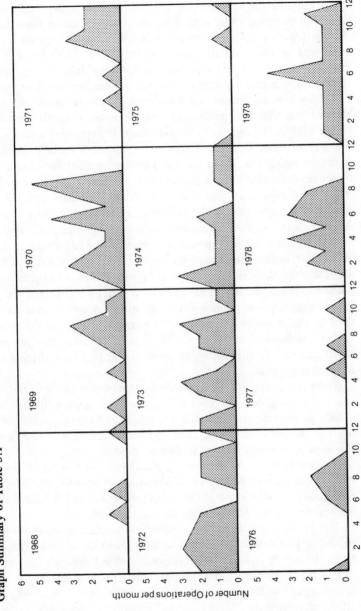

An examination of Table 5.1 and the graph summary indicates a pattern of increased violence in response to political circumstances and objectives, such as *actes de presence* to obtain recognition for the whole movement or for a specific group, such as PFLP, PDFLP and BSO. Increased activity of this type was notable from June to September 1970, responding to the Rogers cease-fire initiative on the Suez Canal. The Palestinian movement felt threatened by this isolation and they believed that the Arab governments had completely capitulated. The bizarre multiple hijacking of four aeroplanes in September ended with the war between *fedayeen* forces and those of Hussein in Jordan. Activities during this period could also be considered as part of another objective: defending the movement with activities which were undertaken to disrupt peace initiatives; the peace initiatives appeared to threaten the realization of the important Palestinian goal of true self-determination. A third objective was related to inter-group rivalry. Several smaller Palestinian groups were motivated to demonstrate their ability to translate into action their support for certain goals. Action also increased their visibility, legitimacy and efforts in recruiting new members. Many of the PFLP operations fall into this category. A fourth objective was punishment of countries, groups or persons for their hostile attitudes and policies. An example of this was the execution of Jordanian Prime Minister Wasfi Al-Tal in Cairo. This category could also include the mailing of letter-bombs to Israeli officials and supporters overseas.

There is a strong link between the pattern of commando operations and peace initiatives. The response to American peace initiatives was usually an increase in dramatic and violent acts. As the graph indicates, the US-initiated cease-fire of June 1970, the extension of the cease-fire a year later and interim settlement talks all prompted increased operations. Further, the increase in operations from July 1972 to May 1973 coincided with Sadat's expulsion of Soviet advisers, which led to speculation about the possibility of secret American-Egyptian agreements following the American presidential elections.

The 17 December 1973 fire-bombing and machine-gunning of a Pan American aeroplane at an airport in Rome, and the increased attacks from January to April 1974, corresponded with Kissinger's disengagement efforts. However, after Arafat ordered a moratorium on acts taking place outside occupied Palestine, the overall frequency of attacks decreased significantly. Arafat made that decision as a goodwill gesture by the PLO, and he hoped to receive an invitation to the Geneva peace conference. Still, Arafat approved the Palestinian hijacking of an

Israeli tourist bus on the Haifa-Tel Aviv highway in 1978, which resulted in the death of 36 Israelis and one American as well as providing a pretext for Israeli forces to invade southern Lebanon. Arafat did this to thwart and expose Sadat's peace initiative. Israel was the target of most terrorist acts that took place since 1968. Jordan was second and the United States third.

US Efforts to Counter Palestinian Violence

The United States viewed with much concern the rising level of terrorism and counter-terrorism that followed the 1967 Arab-Israeli war. The rise in terrorism made peace in the area extremely precarious. Secretary of State Dean Rusk in his press conference on 3 January 1969 recognized the dangers and urged restraint from both sides.

> We call upon the Arab governments to recognize that they must do their utmost to restrain terrorist activity. We call upon Israel to recognize that a policy of excessive retaliation will not produce the peace that Israel surely desires.[3]

The American's plea was not heeded. The first Palestinian hijacking of an El Al aeroplane on 23 July 1968 was soon followed by others. Some of these hijackings were of American aeroplanes and the attacks were on airports where American tourists are ever-present. The United States condemned aeroplane hijacking as illegal, and unacceptable terrorism. A period of confrontation between the United States and the PLO began. The US called the hijackers 'international outlaws'. It also joined in condemnation of Israeli terrorism termed as 'reprisals'. The first American aeroplane to be hijacked outside the western hemisphere was a TWA aeroplane commandeered by PFLP members on 29 August 1969. The aeroplane was bound for Tel Aviv with a stop in Athens. It was forced to land in Damascus where the commandos blew up the plane after the passengers were evacuated. Secretary Rogers termed this 'air piracy'.[4]

Reacting to attacks on American and Israeli targets by Palestinian groups, Congress attempted to cut off aid to UNRWA and put pressure on the refugees not to join the 'liberation struggle'. A section of the US Foreign Assistance Act of 1969 said:

> No part of the United States contribution to UNRWA shall be used

to furnish assistance to any refugee who is receiving military training as a member of the so-called Palestine Liberation Army or any other guerrilla-type organization or who has engaged in any act of terrorism . . . it is essential that continuous pressure be brought to bear on UN officials who maintain contact with that organization and those directly responsible for its operation to prevent the use of the Agency's funds to subsidize military or terrorist activities in any way.[5]

Though the amount of the United States' annual contribution to UNRWA was slightly reduced, the cut stemmed from the US belief that other countries should pay a more equitable share to UNRWA. This added section was never carried out, because the administration felt it would have the ultimate effect of destabilizing the situation and harming US interests.

The Palestine liberation groups perceived the United States as the main supporter of Israel, without whom Israel would not be able to continue the occupation of Arab lands and 'flagrant violations of Palestinian human and civil rights'. Therefore, they felt it was a legitimate target and directed more attacks at the United States and its interests. In March 1973, Black September guerrillas killed US Ambassador to Sudan, Cleo Noel, and his Charge d'Affaires Curtis Moore, after taking them hostage at a party at the Saudi embassy in Khartoum. The United States, acting through indirect channels, sent a stern warning to the PLO: 'Leave our diplomats alone, or else!' It threatened swift retaliation.[6]

The period following the American-sponsored cease-fire on the Egyptian-Israeli front in the summer of 1970 was a time of great US-Palestinian confrontation. The PFLP commandos decided to take drastic action, fearing that Palestine's future would be ignored in any peace settlement and that the movement would be crushed. They carried out four hijackings in early September 1970, at airfields in the Jordanian desert near Amman, taking several hundred hostages. These events demonstrated the destabilizing effect the PLO has had on the region, as well as the danger of drawing the big powers into the conflict. This drama took place only days before the outbreak of war between King Hussein and the Palestinians. That brief war was disastrous for the Palestinians. The guerrillas were ousted from the cities in an agreement between Hussein and the Arab governments, and thousands of Palestinians, mostly unarmed civilians, were killed by Hussein's loyal Bedouin troops.

The four hijackings from 5 to 9 September led to an outburst of anti-*fedayeen* sentiment in Congress. The hijackers were termed 'determined, demented men' and madmen who robbed language of all meaning by describing themselves as liberators. Their actions were characterized as 'inhuman and animal-like', although some of the hostages later described their captors as having conducted themselves in an admirable, civilized manner. Senator Russell Long of Louisiana said that if Jordan did not have a government, then other nations should move in and establish one for the people until they were able to establish one for themselves. Jordan should be told, the Senator insisted, to capture and punish the outlaws; if the terrorists killed anyone, then all of them should be killed 'and strung up by their heels'.[7]

In the period preceding and during the Jordanian civil war, there was great apprehension in Washington and Tel Aviv that King Hussein, a good friend of the United States and a moderate Arab leader, would be toppled and replaced by a radical regime allied with the Palestinians and other radical Arabs. A *New York Times* reporter revealed the extent of US-Israeli preparations for co-ordinated military action in the Jordanian crisis should King Hussein lose control. The plan envisioned an Israeli attack on Syrian forces that had entered Jordan in support of the Palestinians, should it appear that Hussein's army was incapable of handling them. The United States would use the Sixth Fleet and other units to safeguard Israel's rear from Egyptian or Soviet attacks from the Suez Canal area.

President Nixon assumed personal direction of the intense diplomatic and military activity as the crisis approached its climax. Plans for intervention in the event of serious Iraqi or Syrian penetration into Jordan never materialized. The 250 tanks of the Palestine Liberation Army, which Syria was controlling, were forced to withdraw under pressure from Hafez Assad, at the time Syrian Air Marshal and Defense Minister.[8] Nevertheless, Israeli forces moved close to the Syria-Jordan border and President Nixon placed units at Fort Bragg, in West Germany, and the Sixth Fleet on maximum alert. On 12 October 1970, PLO Executive Chairman Arafat displayed empty shells with Hebrew markings to newsmen in Amman. He made charges of American and Israeli involvement in the war which were, of course, denied.

The United States was most outraged and alarmed at the attack of the underground Black September guerrilla unit on the Olympic quarters of the Israeli athletes in Munich in 1972. The guerrillas demanded the release of two hundred Palestinian prisoners in Israeli jails in exchange for the eleven Israeli athletes. Israel rejected the demand.

Germany and Israel co-ordinated a plan to kill the guerrillas and free the hostages. The plan failed and the eleven athletes were killed along with five of the guerrillas.

Alarmed at the possibility of a similar occurrence in the United States, the Nixon administration created an anti-terrorist section in the State Department. It also launched counter-terrorist action on two fronts: (1) a programme of preventive measures inside the United States and (2) measures to prevent terrorism on an international level through co-operation with other nations.

Domestic Measures

In September 1972, President Nixon formed a cabinet committee to consider effective means for the prevention of terrorism at home and abroad. The committee was chaired by the Secretary of State and included several cabinet members in addition to the directors of the FBI and the CIA and the President's assistants for national security and domestic affairs. The committee subsequently developed preventive measures and improved procedures at home and abroad to deter terrorism. Nixon's executive order laid out five other anti-terrorist measures.

The first was ordering the CIA to carry out a security check on any Arab travelling to the United States. Secretary Rogers transmitted three cables to all American diplomatic posts in September 1972, detailing the security checks. The first cable, known by the code name 'Operation Boulder', went out three days after the Palestinian attack at the Olympic village in Munich. It instructed US embassies to screen all Arabs and others who might be associated with the terrorist organizations – nationals from France, Germany and Latin America. The second cable ordered the screening of every Arab alien applying for any type of visa anywhere in the world.

The security checks encountered immediate difficulties, however, because no one knew how to define an Arab. Latin America alone has some fifty thousand Spanish-speaking Arabs called Turcos, who were born or whose parents were born in Middle Eastern countries, but who now live in Mexico, Haiti, the Dominican Republic and Ecuador. To clear up the confusion, Rogers sent out a third cable defining an Arab as any ethnic Arab who was born or whose parents were born in the following countries, regardless of present nationality or country of residence: Algeria, Bahrain, Egypt, Iraq, Israel, Jordan, Kuwait, Lebanon, Libya, Mauritania, Morocco, Oman, Qatar, Saudi Arabia, Sudan, Syria, the Trucial States, Tunisia, Yemen and the United Arab Emirates.

Forcing all visitors to undergo a security check by Washington created another difficulty that led to weeks and months of delay for those seeking visas. An outcry arose from Arabs who were friendly to American interests or members of special groups or families. After a Saudi prince lodged a complaint with the State Department, Secretary Rogers dispatched a final cable early in October modifying Operation Boulder by authorizing US embassies to grant visas directly to applicants 'personally and favourably known' to them.[9]

Other anti-terrorist measures included special postal checks of mail from suspect areas, tightening of the anti-hijacking programme to include screening of all passengers and searches of all hand-carried luggage onto US aeroplanes, doubling of the number of wiretaps, and a nationwide surveillance and investigation campaign of politically active Arabs in general and Palestinians in particular. The FBI and immigration officials frequently abused, intimidated and harassed the individuals investigated. Agents usually threatened individuals with deportation or arrest if they failed to co-operate. Agents would arrive at the home of a person under investigation at any hour of the day or night, without advance notice. One agent told a Palestinian in the Washington area that he did this 'just to make sure you are at home'.

Sam Zutty, head of the New York Office of Immigration and Naturalization, told Dr. Sami Al-Banna, an engineering professor at Columbia University, that 'aliens are visitors and like children have no right to speak'. He went on,

> I would like to remind you that in certain countries of the world, when someone expresses a dissenting point of view, he is put to the wall and shot. In this country we don't do that. But if I have a naughty baby, I put him on my lap and spank him.[10]

In Brooklyn, federal agents burst into an Arab club and ripped Palestinian pictures off the walls. One agent warned the owner, 'We don't like to see those posters around.' Many other Arab community clubs felt similar pressure. People stopped coming and many clubs had to close.[11] During the first two months of this investigating campaign, 125 Arab students were deported, most of them without due process. About seventy students were arrested, but they were later released and acquitted of all charges.[12]

In 1974, an underground war of terrorism was raging in Europe and the Middle East between PLO agents and the Mosad (Israeli intelligence). The war included assassinations and a letter-bomb campaign.

The United States, fearful that the terror would spread there, carried out a second campaign of investigation of Palestinians. This time it was much more restrained and far less visible. The threat of violence that had prompted the executive order in 1972 had never materialized, and in the 1974 investigations, the FBI was ordered to carry out its responsibilities without violating the law. The United States did not become a battleground of Palestinian and Israeli terrorism and counter-terrorism, though the special anti-terrorist measures had little to do with that.

International Efforts

The United States initiated an effort at the United Nations for international action against terrorism. In September 1972, it circulated a draft convention consisting of sixteen articles and recommendations. The proposed draft required member states to prosecute or extradite anyone suspected of murder, causing serious bodily harm or kidnapping in a foreign state or against a foreign national with the intent to 'damage the interests of or obtain concessions from a State or an international organization'. These were the only offences that called for punishment or extradition. The rest of the draft dwelt upon the obligations each state bore to the others for the acts of its inhabitants. A member state would be required to: punish terrorist offences by severe penalties; seek out jurisdiction should the offence be committed or if an offender had fled; use preventive detention, if necessary, to insure the presence of the offender for prosecution or extradition; deny the use of its territory as sanctuaries; and take measures to prevent the commission of terrorist offences, including the exchange of information and data on the plans, activities, and movements of terrorists.[13]

In his speech before the General Assembly on 25 September 1972, Secretary of State Rogers called for UN action on several fronts to combat international terrorism. In addition to the draft treaty on punishment and prosecution, Secretary Rogers called for the enactment of another treaty on terrorism. This would provide for the suspension of all air services to countries which failed to punish or extradite hijackers or saboteurs of civilian aircraft.[14]

The Third World nations were disturbed at US initiatives against terrorism, feeling that it served those in power. They opposed the plan as likely to hamper wars of national liberation. Algeria submitted a substitute resolution calling for a study of terrorism and affirming the right of people to free themselves from foreign rule. Paragraph 3 of the substitute resolution read, '[the General Assembly] reaffirms the inalienable right of all peoples under colonial and racist regimes and other forms of alien domination and upholds the legitimacy of their struggle'.[15] This resolution was passed by the General Assembly, 76 votes to 34, with the United States opposed. The American delegation felt that it did not condemn terrorism and that action, not study, was needed.

Although the United States failed to gain General Assembly adoption of the proposed anti-terrorism convention in 1972, it won approval of a more modest measure the following year. The General Assembly adopted a convention for the protection of diplomats in December 1973, requiring extradition or prosecution of persons who attacked or kidnapped diplomats, or officials of foreign governments or international organizations.[16]

The American efforts to combat terrorism were not confined to PLO operations. The United States took the lead towards a global effort to limit terrorism. The United States is perhaps the most visible target for international terrorism. It has the largest number of diplomatic missions throughout the world, American corporations are active in numerous countries, and Americans travel abroad more than any others. Furthermore, the United States stands to suffer most from disruption of the current world order and it has a vested interest in the political stability of its friends and allies. The recent rise of European terrorism in Italy, Holland and Germany was a matter of grave concern for the American government.

The US government's policy is one of responding firmly to acts of terrorism. It does not pay ransom for kidnapping, resists all other forms of blackmail, and advocates the strongest possible measures against those who carry out acts of terrorism.[17] This response augments preventive measures taken to discourage terrorism. Preventive measures were the conclusion of bilateral and multilateral agreements such as the US-Cuban anti-hijacking agreement and the anti-hijacking agreement concluded on 17 July 1978 during the Bonn economic summit of the seven major non-communist, industrial nations (Britain, Canada, France, West Germany, Italy, Japan and the United States).[18]

The United States also has a working agreement with Israel to gather and exchange information on potential terrorists. Raphael Rothstein, author of *Fedayeen: Guerrillas Against Israel*, with close contacts with Israeli officials, reported in 1976 after returning from a visit to Israel, 'Mosad has the full co-operation of the CIA and the FBI.' Rothstein added that, according to the Israelis, 'The US has shown great initiative in relaying intelligence and coordinating anti-terrorist techniques.' Meanwhile, the FBI and possibly the CIA gets information from the

Israelis, as confirmed during recent Senate committee hearings, when Senator James Abourezk requested information from the FBI regarding reports that it gave Israel information about Sami Esmail's activities in the United States.[19] The FBI agent testified that they had received more information from the Israelis than the FBI had given them.[20]

By 1980 the United States had accepted the reality of Palestinian acts of violence against Israel and of Israeli retaliation, while seeking to contain it. The decade of Palestinian revolutionary violence had major effects on US Middle East policy. Indeed, ever since the 1950s American policy-makers had expressed their apprehension at the possible outbreak of Palestinian violence. They knew of the wretched conditions in the refugee camps and feared the impact of violence on the political and economic stability of the region. A report by the Subcommittee on the Near East and Africa of the Senate Foreign Relations Committee in 1953 expressed concern at the possible transformation of the Palestinian refugees into revolutionaries.

American refugee policy was primarily concerned to prevent the emergence of Palestinian revolutionary violence. The large US contributions to UNRWA over three decades only reflected this concern, as did the detailed proposals for refugee resettlement and integration reviewed in Chapter 3. When Palestinian revolutionary violence nevertheless emerged, the United States first developed a policy of confrontation. When this failed to stamp out the movement, the United States consequently turned to a policy of containment. Palestinian revolutionary violence generated myriad American concerns affecting policy considerations. The escalation of Palestinian revolutionary violence and Israeli attacks could draw Syria and possibly Iraq into the battle, thus increasing the likelihood of another Arab-Israeli war which could cause Soviet-American confrontation. Another concern was the arousal of the Arab masses in the struggle against Israel and its allies, which would hinder American settlement plans. Such arousal could further generate attacks on American interests in the Arab world, leading to the disruption of American commerce and of the flow of oil to the West. A third concern was the threat to Arab regimes friendly to the United States and susceptible to accommodation with Israel. For all of these reasons revolutionary violence threatened American interests and domination of the region.

While the goal of American Middle East policy remained the same, its tactics encompassed efforts to accommodate as well as to eradicate the source of revolutionary violence, the PLO. The eradication policy was clearly evident in the American role in the attempt to destroy the

Palestinian movement in Jordan in 1970 and in Lebanon in 1975-6.

During interviews, high-ranking State Department officials maintained that Palestinian violence had no direct or indirect effect whatsoever on US Middle East or Palestinian policy. But on the contrary, the facts suggest that Palestinian revolutionary violence has played a significant role in determining US policy. An examination of the graph of Palestinian operations shows a correlation between an increase of Palestinian revolutionary violence and changes in US policy during the last ten years. Revolutionary violence was not the only variable affecting the change, but it was an observable factor. In 1968, prior to the rise in Palestinian commando operations, the United States recognized the Palestinians simply as Arab refugees. After increased revolutionary violence in 1969 and 1970, the United States began to recognize the Palestinians as a political entity. In 1971-2 it began to talk of Palestinian interests; in 1973-4, legitimate interests; in 1975-6, rights; in 1977, a homeland. Every one of these terms has specific policy implications. Although the graph does not show an increase in Palestinian operations in 1975-7, the heightened Palestinian struggle in Lebanon during that period brought about yet another change in American policy.

Palestinian revolutionary violence also aroused the Palestinian and Arab people, particularly after the defeat of the Arab armies in the 1967 war. The *fedayeen* became the new symbol of Arab resilience, dignity and honour. The support of the Arab masses, in turn, created a reservoir of strength in the struggle for the liberation of Palestine. Arab governments, however unrepresentative in structure, had to reckon with popular sympathy toward the Palestinian cause. Events since 1967 intensified that sympathy, and revolutionary violence against the Zionist policy of occupation or against Israel's allies continued to receive Arab mass approval and support. The most dramatic or heroic attacks had the greatest popular impact. This mass support could not simply be taken for granted, however. Unless operations with the goal of drawing Arab mass support were followed by a political and educational campaign to raise consciousness and to cement relations with other Arab mass movements, guerrilla attacks would eventually lose their impact and might even backfire.

In any event, the pressure of popular sympathy for the Palestinians was reflected in Arab government policy, and this in turn influenced US Middle East policy. The strength of Arab government influence varied with the nature of the government's relationship with the United States as well as the extent to which it was willing to use its potential power or influence. In other words, revolutionary violence in conjunction with a political education programme directed at the Arab masses had a significant, if indirect, effect on US Middle East policy.

The argument was frequently made in the United States that Palestinian guerrilla attacks were counter-productive and greatly damaged the image of the Palestinians in the United States, as well as undermining public support for their cause. This was not entirely true. While violence did not gain any support or sympathy for the PLO or the Palestinian people, it did remind the public that something must be done to solve the Palestinian problem. The highly developed American commercial psychology has shown that the most effective advertising campaigns are those which either please people the most or those that make them the most angry. Despite the anger of the American public at Palestinian guerrilla attacks, they convincingly demonstrated that peace was not possible without the Palestinians.

US government officials insisted that 'terrorism' was completely 'unacceptable' and rejected it as a means to influence policy. They further argued that if the Palestinian leadership hoped to promote itself as 'responsible' it should halt these operations. In interviews, officials were asked, 'What would be the US response if the Palestinians stopped now all acts of force?' They answered that it would not change US policy. It would only improve the atmosphere and help the United States pressure Israel for 'concessions' on the Palestinian issue and in the autonomy negotiations. In other words, the United States would do nothing. American officials insisted that Palestinian attacks would never bring about American recognition of or dialogue with the PLO, whose acceptance of UN Resolution 242 was a precondition for direct talks with the United States. In themselves, such talks would produce nothing. But these same American officials argued that the halting of Palestinian operations, and recognition of Resolution 242, would bring considerable moral pressure to bear on Israel and would immensely improve the environment in favour of the Palestinians! Unfortunately, US Middle East policy has always been based not on moral principles but on political expediency and the protection of its vast interests. These interests will remain threatened so long as Palestinian *revolutionary* violence continues.

Notes

1. Frantz Fanon, *Wretched of the Earth*, trans. Farrington (Penguin, 1967), p. 74.
2. Paul A. Jureidini and William E. Hazen, *The Palestinian Movement in*

Politics (Lexington, Mass: Lexington Books, Edward Heath and Company, 1976), pp. 77-81; *Arab Report and Record*, 1968-1978; and *New York Times*, 1974-1978. Israeli counter-terrorism acts are at least twice as numerous as acts by Palestinians. The table includes all Palestinian attacks against Israel as of May 1974. That is when Fateh decided to end its international operations and increase attacks within Israel.

3. *US Department of State Bulletin*, LX, no. 1543 (20 January 1969) p. 24.

4. Ibid., Vol. LXI, No. 1577 (15 September 1969) p. 46.

5. 'House Version of Foreign Assistance Act of 1969', 6 November 1969 Section 4015, pp. 45-6.

6. Since that time, no American diplomat has been the subject of physical attack by the PLO. The assassination of US Ambassador Francis E. Meloy and US economic counsellor Robert O. Waring in Beirut, Lebanon, on 16 June 1976, in the midst of the Lebanese civil war was attributed to a small Lebanese radical faction. The PLO demonstrated a willingness to seek out and punish the assassins. See 'The Assassination of American Diplomats in Beirut, Lebanon', Hearing before the Subcommittee on Investigations of the Committee on International Relations, House of Representatives, 94th Cong. 2nd sess., 27 July 1976. (US Government Printing Office, Washington, DC, 1976).

7. *US Congressional Record*, 91st Cong. 2nd sess., 1970, XVI, 11 September 1970), p. 15224.

8. *New York Times*, 8 October 1970, p. 1.

9. Ralph L. Stavins, 'World-Wide Harassment of Palestinians' (Unpublished manuscript – Institute for Policy Studies, Washington, DC, May 1976), pp. 14-19.

10. Ibid., p. 24.

11. Ibid., p. 27. Included in the places closed across the country is 'Palestine House', an academic and cultural organization that was initially founded on George Washington University campus in 1970. The House membership was open to the public, and its activities were confined to lectures, seminars on the Middle East and some cultural functions. Many of the members were subjected to FBI harassment. On one occasion, during a visit to the House by FBI agents, Mr Anis Kassim, a co-founder of the House, explained to agents that the primary objective was to practice academic freedom. One agent by the name of Mr Grant replied: 'We are not interfering with academic freedom. We are simply concerned with the political dimensions of it.'

12. *Arab-American University Graduates Newsletter*, Detroit, Michigan, December 1972, p. 3.

13. 'A World Free of Violence', statement by Secretary Rogers before the UN General Assembly on 25 September 1972, *Department of State Bulletin*, LXVII, 1738 (16 October 1972), pp. 425-34.

14. Ibid.

15. UN Document A/Res. 3034 (XXVII), December 1972.

16. 'U.S. Government Approach to Terrorism: A Global Approach', address by Ambassador Lewis Hoffacker at New Orleans, La. on 28 February 1974, *Department of State Bulletin*, LXX, 1812 (18 March 1974), pp. 275-6.

17. *International Terrorism Hearings*, p. 11.

18. This agreement is viewed as the toughest move yet to combat hijackings. It calls for the discontinuation of commercial airline service to and from any country that harbours aeroplane hijackers. (*Washington Post*, 18 July 1978, p. 119.)

19. Sami Esmail is an American-born citizen of Palestinian ancestry. He was arrested in Israel in December 1978 while on his way to visit his dying father who lived on the West Bank. He was later brought to trial on charges of undergoing military training in Libya and belonging to the PFLP. He admitted visiting

Libya but denied receiving military training or being a member of the PFLP. He claimed that the confession he signed was under 'torture'. Ismail was convicted and given a fifteen-month jail sentence. His case received a great deal of publicity in the United States. See *The Washington Star*, 27 June 1978 and *New York Times*, 15 June 1978.

20. *The Washington Post*, 20 March 1978, p. 1.

UNITED STATES POLICY TOWARDS THE
PALESTINIANS AS A PEOPLE

Soon after taking office, the Carter administration plunged into Middle East diplomacy. Carter was initially optimistic.[1] In mid-February 1977, Secretary of State Vance travelled to Israel, Egypt, Lebanon, Jordan, Syria and Saudi Arabia to initiate the administration's effort. That spring, Carter met with Prime Minister Yitzhak Rabin of Israel, President Sadat of Egypt, King Hussein of Jordan and President Assad of Syria to assure them he intended to settle the conflict.[2]

The Carter administration began by promoting a comprehensive settlement. It therefore brought back into focus the issue of the Palestinians and moved further than the previous two administrations in dealing with the Palestinians and recognizing their rights. Domestic as well as international politics caused this change.

The Carter Administration and a Homeland for the Palestinians

The designation of Zbigniew Brzezinski as the Assistant to the President for National Security Affairs directed attention to an otherwise obscure Brookings Institution report on the Middle East.[3]

Brzezinski, an author of the Brookings report, concluded that any settlement had to provide for 'Palestinian self-determination' once the Palestinians had agreed to recognize Israel. Self-determination might take the form of an independent Palestinian state or of an entity voluntarily federated with Jordan.[4]

On 15 March 1977, less than two months after his inauguration, President Carter spoke out on the Palestinian issue during his town hall meeting at Clinton, Massachusetts. He said that the first prerequisite of a lasting peace was Arab recognition of Israel; the second, 'establishment of permanent borders for Israel'; and the third 'ultimate requirement for peace is to deal with the Palestinian problem'. Carter expressed understanding of Palestinian claims in the dispute with Israel and proposed:

There has to be a homeland provided for the Palestinian refugees who have suffered for many, many years. And the exact way to solve the Palestinian problem is one that first addresses itself right now to the Arab countries negotiating with Israel.[5]

A milestone had been passed in US Middle East policy. The concept of a Palestinian homeland had never been part of any official American plan since 1947 when the United States supported the UN partition plan dividing Palestine into an Arab and a Jewish state. Carter did not include in his proposal any specific provisions for Palestinian self-determination or participation in negotiations. Specifics were left to the Arab countries concerned.

Indeed, Carter had no clear idea of the shape or character of the Palestinian homeland he proposed, and consequently it meant different things to different parties. The Israeli government perceived it as a threat to its security; Palestinians saw it as an independent state where they could exercise their national rights. Carter, who viewed it as merely an idea to be worked out through negotiations by the parties involved, clarified his thoughts in a press conference on 12 May 1977.

> The exact definition of what that homeland might be, the degree of independence of the Palestinian entity, its relationship with Jordan or perhaps Syria or others, the geographical boundaries of it, all have to be worked out by the parties concerned. But for the Palestinians to have a homeland and for the refugee question to be resolved is obviously of crucial importance.[6]

Carter recognized the 'crucial importance' of resolving the Palestinian problem and realized that American peace efforts had to include efforts to accommodate the Palestinian people. His proposal for a homeland was more specific than those of his predecessors for 'justice for the refugees' or awareness of the Palestinians as a people or an entity. In an interview with *Jerusalem Post* correspondent Trude Feldman on 8 September 1977, President Carter defined homeland simply as a 'place for people to live'. It might seem that President Carter was merely trying to placate his Israeli readers by using this simple definition which bypassed the issue of establishing a Palestinian state or even describing the state's geographical boundaries. However, the implication was quite clear that the homeland would be constituted from the West Bank and Gaza. The most detailed policy statement on the homeland issue came from Vice-President Walter Mondale, speaking for the Carter administration before the World Affairs Council in San Francisco on 17 June 1977:

A further major issue is that of the future of the Palestinian people. It has been the source of continuing tragedy in the Middle East. There are two prerequisites for a lasting peace in this regard.

First, there must be a demonstrated willingness on the part of the Palestinians to live in peace alongside Israel.

Second, the Palestinians must be given a stake in peace so that they will turn away from the violence of the past, and toward a future in which they can express legitimate political aspirations peacefully.

Thus, if the Palestinians are willing to exist in peace and are prepared to demonstrate that willingness by recognizing Israel's rights to exist in peace, the President has made clear that in the context of a peace settlement, we believe the Palestinians should be given a chance to shed their status as homeless refugees and to partake fully of the benefits of peace in the Middle East, including the possibility of some arrangement for a Palestinian homeland or entity – preferably in association with Jordan.

How this would be accomplished and the exact character of such an entity is, of course, something that would have to be decided by the parties themselves in the course of negotiation. However, the President has suggested that the viability of this concept and the security of the region might be enhanced if this involved an association with Jordan, but I emphasize the specifics are for the parties themselves to decide.[7]

The Carter administration also changed US policy on the issue of Palestinian participation in peace negotiations. The State Department simply said, 'Palestinian representatives will have to be at Geneva for the Palestinian question to be resolved,'[8] without saying which Palestinians:

Along with the issues of the nature of peace negotiations, security and borders, the status of the Palestinians must be settled in a comprehensive Arab-Israeli agreement. This issue cannot be ignored if the others are to be solved.

Moreover, to be lasting, a peace agreement must be positively supported by all of the parties to the conflict, including the Palestinians.

This means that the Palestinians must be involved in the peacemaking process. Their representatives must be at Geneva for the Palestinian question to be solved.[9]

Israel immediately rejected any PLO participation in the negotiations at Geneva. Moshe Dayan said that Israel would negotiate with 'the Palestinians of the West Bank' of Jordan and the Gaza Strip, but not with the PLO and in any event not in Geneva. During meetings in Washington on 19 September 1977, between Dayan, Vance, Mondale and Carter, the Carter administration failed to win a more flexible Israeli position on the issue. Dayan said bluntly, 'We do not agree with one another on bringing Palestinians into the peace talks.' A joint statement issued at the end of the discussions confirmed the Israeli Foreign Minister's description of the talks and simply stated, 'There was an exchange of views on the question of the Palestinian representation and the question of Israeli settlements.'[10]

On 1 October, eleven days following the meeting with Dayan, the Carter administration issued a 'Joint Soviet-U.S. Statement on the Middle East'. The key section read:

> The United States and the Soviet Union believe that, within the framework of a comprehensive settlement of the Middle East problem, all specific questions of the settlement should be resolved, including such key issues as withdrawal of Israeli armed forces from territories occupied in the 1967 conflict; the resolution of the Palestinian question including insuring the legitimate rights of the Palestinian people; termination of the state of war and establishment of normal peaceful relations on the basis of mutual recognition of the principles of sovereignty, territorial integrity, and political independence.
>
> The United States and the Soviet Union believe that the only right and effective way for achieving a fundamental solution to all aspects of the Middle East problem in its entirety is negotiations within the framework of the Geneva Peace Conference, specially convened for these purposes *with participation in its work of the representatives of all the parties involved in the conflict including those of the Palestinian people*, and legal and contractual formalization of the decisions reached at the Conference.[11] [Emphasis added.]

This declaration was another milestone in the American approach to the Palestine issue. It represented a US recognition that the participation of the two superpowers was needed to solve the Middle East conflict. Kissinger had excluded the Soviet Union in his step-by-step diplomacy. The statement broke further ground by referring to the Palestinians' 'legitimate rights' and moved a step closer to accepting

PLO participation in the negotiations, accepting the reality that the PLO is recognized by over two hundred countries as the legitimate representative of the Palestinian people.

A crisis developed in American-Israeli relations. Israel objected strongly to the phrases 'legitimate rights of the Palestinian people' and 'participation of the representatives of the Palestinian people'. Israel regarded the language as an unacceptable concession to the PLO. These expressions were understood by many, in light of UN General Assembly Resolution 3236, as the right to establish an independent state in Palestine with the PLO legitimately representing the Palestinian people. Israel and the United States had both voted against that resolution, but Israel opposed the entire US-Soviet declaration as an intrusion into the negotiations by the 'pro-Arab' Soviet Union against Israel.

It took six hours of intensive negotiation in New York between Moshe Dayan and Cyrus Vance, with President Carter joining in, to solve this American-Israeli crisis. In the resulting joint working paper each side made concessions. The paper called for the Geneva conference to be opened by a plenary group consisting of Israel and a united Arab delegation. Then the conference would break down into both bilateral and multilateral working groups. The bilateral group would negotiate peace treaties between Israel and each Arab state; the multilateral groups would deal with broader issues, such as the future of the West Bank and compensation for Palestinian refugees. There was no mention of the PLO, but Dayan agreed that Israel would negotiate on some issues with more than one Arab delegation, including Palestinian representatives.[12]

Dayan held firm that no known PLO members would be accepted. He implied that as long as the Palestinian representatives did not identify themselves as PLO members, Israel would not object. Dayan promised, 'We will not check their IDs.' In return, the United States agreed that the US-Soviet declaration was 'not a prerequisite for the reconvening and conduct of the Geneva Conference'.[13] The Americans also agreed not to use military or economic sanctions to pressure Israel to make concessions. Thus, America foreswore using its main leverage − economic and military aid − to mitigate Israeli inflexibility in the peace talks, leaving only the power of persuasion. Since the Israelis were not easily persuaded, meaningful progress towards a comprehensive settlement remained remote.

The Carter administration's retreat from the joint American-Soviet statement resulted from Israeli government pressure and pressure by the pro-Israeli constituency in the United States, Jewish and non-Jewish alike. American anti-Soviet elements, particularly in Congress, objected to including the Soviet Union in Middle East peace negotiations because that might enhance the Soviet image and influence in the area. But the American retreat from the statement, instead, tarnished American image and prestige in the Arab world and in the international community.

The Carter administration's plan to reconvene the Geneva peace conference before the end of 1977 was derailed by Sadat's dramatic trip to Jerusalem in November. Subsequently, Sadat called for a meeting of all concerned parties in Cairo to prepare for the Geneva conference. Syria, Jordan and the PLO declined to attend. Egyptian, Israeli, US and UN representatives participated.[14] Another meeting of the same parties took place in Jerusalem, but Egypt soon afterwards broke off the peace talks. The Egyptian delegation was recalled from Jerusalem in protest against Israel's 'intransigence' over the issues of withdrawal from occupied Arab lands and the fate of the Palestinians.

A serious bone of contention between the Egyptian and Israeli negotiating positions was the problem of Palestinian self-determination. Egypt insisted on the Palestinian right to self-determination and to establish an independent state on the West Bank and Gaza. Israel rejected this. Menahem Begin considered the West Bank and Gaza as parts of Eretz Israel (Greater Israel). He strongly opposed any form of Palestinian self-determination in any part of Palestine, and he offered instead a plan for 'self-rule' for West Bank Palestinians. The plan envisioned that:

1. the whole area would remain under Israeli military control;
2. there would be no legal restrictions on further Jewish settlement in the area;
3. the military administration would be replaced by a cantonal or a central civilian administration;
4. after a five-year transitional period, the Palestinians would be given the choice of becoming Israeli or Jordanian citizens.[15]

The United States tried to bridge the seemingly insuperable gap between the Egyptian and Israeli proposals. President Carter summarized the American position in an interview with network reporters on 28 December 1977:

President Sadat so far is insisting that the so-called Palestinian entity be an independent nation. My own preference is that they not be an independent nation but tied in some way with the surrounding countries, making a choice, for instance, between Israel and Jordan.

But, we don't have any real choice. I have expressed an opinion, but if Israel should negotiate with the surrounding countries a different solution, we would certainly support it.

But my own personal opinion is that permanent peace can best be maintained if there is not a fairly radical, new independent nation in the heart of the Middle Eastern arena.[16]

Carter also remarked that the Begin self-rule proposals provided a 'fair basis for negotiations'. Sadat perceived this comment as tantamount to an endorsement of the Begin proposals. On 4 January 1978, Carter made a special but brief stop at Aswan, Egypt to talk with Sadat. After the ninety-minute meeting, Sadat was satisfied with clarification of the American position. Carter then restated publicly the American policy with regard to the Palestinians. The President read from a prepared statement, part of which declared, 'There must be a resolution of the Palestinian problem in all its aspects. The problem must recognize the legitimate rights of the Palestinian people and enable the Palestinians to participate in the determination of their future.'[17]

At least publicly, Sadat interpreted this as meaning self-determination. He also agreed with President Carter that a Palestinian state did not necessarily have to be part of nor a by-product of a settlement. He further accepted Carter's preference for a Palestinian entity affiliated with Jordan. Some administration officials pointed out that the Aswan statement came only a hair's breadth short of endorsement of Palestinian self-determination. The fact is that 'participation in the determination of their own future' only means that Palestinians should be included in negotiations about their future. They would have a voice, but not a free choice. They would not have self-determination. The Palestinian preference was for a free and independent Palestinian state. Such a development was unlikely to occur in the near future due to Israeli objections and American ambivalence towards a Palestinian state. In the aftermath of Sadat's November 1977 trip to Jerusalem, nothing new happened in American Palestinian policy until the signing of the Camp David accords in September 1978. Alfred Atherton, Jr, the administration's ambassador-at-large for Middle East negotiations, attempted another restatement of the policy:

While Resolution 242 calls for a just settlement of the 'refugee' problem, it does not deal in a comprehensive way with a solution to the Palestinian problem. In the decade since the passage of that

Resolution it has become inescapably clear that a solution to the Palestinian problem is essential in reaching a lasting settlement of the Middle East conflict. No party to the conflict today disputes that the Palestinians have a sense of identity which must be taken into account. President Carter has recognized this by speaking of the need for a homeland for the Palestinians. In our own view, as I said earlier, no settlement in the Middle East can endure which does not include a just solution of the Palestinian problem in all its aspects. This involves meeting the humanitarian need of the Palestinian Arabs for an identity of their own, and agreement on the future status of the West Bank and Gaza – those parts of the former Palestine mandate outside Israel's 1967 boundaries.

It also involves vital security considerations for Israel which must be taken into account, as well as interests of other Arab states, in particular Jordan and Egypt, and the interests of the Palestinian Arabs themselves, over one million of whom reside still in the West Bank and Gaza.

A way must be found for the Palestinians to participate in the determination of their own future. Any solution, if it is to be viable and lasting, must be based ultimately on the consent of the governed.[18]

The Atherton, Mondale and other main pronouncements of the Carter administration all made these points:

(1) The Palestinians had to demonstrate their willingness to live in peace with Israel by changing articles of the PLO charter related to Israel, by accepting UN Resolution 242 and by granting Israel a *de jure* recognition. Israel was, however, not asked to reciprocate by recognizing the PLO. It did not have to admit the right of the Palestinians to self-determination in a sovereign state living alongside Israel. The Palestinians, therefore, would have had to renounce for themselves and for future generations the right to return to their homeland. Elaborating on this position, PLO Chairman Yasser Arafat said that the United States was using the question of recognition to avoid the real issues. The United States had dealt with China for twenty-five years without recognizing it and had yet to recognize Cuba or East Germany. He said that recognition was the prerogative of independent and sovereign states. Once the Palestinians had their own independent state, they would decide the recognition question through democratic processes, he said.[19]

(2) The Palestinians were required to repudiate armed struggle in

exchange for a territory where they could express their legitimate political aspirations (i.e. electing local officials and electing representatives for an independent or Jordanian-affiliated parliament).

(3) The United States preferred to have a Palestinian entity connected in one form or another with Jordan, perhaps in a 'United Arab Kingdom'. Carter believed this would enhance the security of the region.[20] It implied that a totally sovereign and independent Palestinian state might present a security risk to the region, perhaps by establishing alliances or friendly relations with the Soviet Union, Libya or Iraq. Joining a West Bank state (or some form thereof) with Jordan would ensure a pro-American stance and 'moderation' towards Israel. All evidence indicated that if an independent entity or a state were established in the West Bank and Gaza neither the United States nor Israel would allow it to have an army. It would be totally demilitarized with nothing beyond a police force to maintain local order.

US policy therefore stopped well short of accepting Palestinian statehood. Carter asserted emphatically, 'I have never favored an independent Palestinian state. I still don't favor one, and I have no intention of deviating from that position.'[21] The Palestinian section of the Camp David accords negotiated in September 1978 between the United States, Egypt and Israel only reflected this anti-statehood position. (See Appendix H for text.)

The Carter Administration and Accommodation of the PLO

Initially the Carter administration continued the same approach towards the PLO as the Ford administration. The PLO was on a Justice Department list of terrorist organizations posing a political threat to the United States, and its representatives were automatically denied entry visas. In February 1977, the Justice Department denied Sabri Jiryis a visa to come to Washington DC to address a conference on peace in the Middle East sponsored by the American Friends Service Committee. In general, Carter required the PLO to recognize Israel's right to exist and accept Resolution 242 before he would deal with it. On these questions, Carter remained in the Kissinger groove.[22] Nevertheless, Carter was able to advance US policy towards future accommodation of the Palestinians in general, and the PLO in particular, in the peace negotiations.

President Carter quietly lifted the label 'terrorist' from the PLO and made it easier for its officials to visit the United States. On 17 August

1977, Carter signed legislation that eliminated the requirement that members of the PLO, as well as foreign Communist party members, obtain a special waiver from the Justice Department in order to visit the United States. The legislation was sponsored by Senator George McGovern. Only two years later, on 10 May 1979, Israel's supporters in Congress succeeded in repealing the law despite pleas by Senator McGovern and the Carter administration. PLO members could only be admitted to the United States if the Secretary of State and the Attorney-General agreed on a special waiver.[23]

The Carter administration made numerous indirect contacts with the PLO through various channels, including American citizens. Former Pennsylvania Governor William Scranton reportedly met with a high-level PLO representative in Paris in July 1977. Carter was attempting to advise the PLO that they would have to recognize Resolution 242 before he could arrange a role for them at the proposed Geneva peace talks. Recognition of Resolution 242 meant indirect recognition of Israel and its right to exist within secure and recognized boundaries. President Carter had received a message from the PLO that it was moderating its demands. Landrum Bolling, President of the Lilly Endowment, who met with Arafat frequently, carried a message to President Carter in which Arafat reportedly indicated that the PLO would accept Resolution 242 as a framework for the Geneva talks.[24] Consequently, Carter softened his position towards the PLO. Where previously the United States had said that 'unless the PLO endorses Resolution 242' it would not even consider dealing with them nor sponsoring their presence at peace talks, Carter now said that 'if' the PLO accepted Resolution 242 the United States would 'immediately' open direct talks with it.

Carter's switch to the more positive approach was calculated for its impact on Saudi Arabia, the backstage power broker in the Middle East peace efforts. Through its financial contributions, Saudi Arabia exerted significant influence over Egypt, Syria, Jordan and the PLO. Carter conveyed to the Saudis that, if they persuaded the PLO to accept Resolution 242, the United States would promptly deal directly with the PLO and bring it into peace negotiations.[25]

That signal was quickly seized upon by Saudi Arabia, which informed Secretary of State Vance on 8 August 1977 that the PLO seemed close to a change. Vance, as well as Carter, indicated that this would be sufficient to bring about a US-PLO discussion.[26]

However, on 25 August 1977, the PLO Central Council, meeting in Damascus, once more rejected Resolution 242 as inadequate because it dealt only with Palestinians as refugees. The PLO did not consider the American offer of direct talks as adequate compensation for its recognition of Resolution 242. Arafat considered it foolish to give away the PLO's trump card – recognition of Israel – in return for the privilege of direct contact with the United States. The PLO wanted a more concrete offer and assurances from the United States.

The PLO instead favoured an amendment of Resolution 242 deleting references to the refugee problem and substituting instead references to the national rights of the Palestinian people. The United States, however, rejected the idea of drafting a completely new resolution. No amending mechanism existed. The United States also anticipated that Israel would reject a new resolution. The consensus which had existed over Resolution 242 would be lost. The United States even opposed the addition to the resolution proposed by its original author, Lord Caradon, the British Ambassador to the United Nations;[27] Lord Caradon favoured addition of a section to meet the concerns of the Palestinians, one sufficient to gain PLO acceptance of the resolution.

The United States wanted to avoid the diplomatic crisis with Israel which would be inevitable upon amendment of Resolution 242 to recognize the national rights of the Palestinians. The United States also hoped that the PLO could be pressured by Arab governments to recognize Resolution 242 unchanged, though with 'reservations'. Perhaps that may explain why the Carter administration left the door open for the PLO even after its Central Council rejected Resolution 242. The joint Soviet-US statement on the Middle East already alluded to and reflected that flexible approach.

In the American-Soviet statement of 1 October 1977, the two superpowers agreed on the basis of negotiations at the Geneva peace conference, for which they were co-chairmen. Since the statement recognized the 'legitimate rights of the Palestinian people' and included their representatives in the conference, it implied the participation of the PLO, since the PLO is recognized by the Arab states and the United Nations as the legitimate representative of the Palestinian people.[28] The United States also recognized the PLO as one group representing the Palestinians, and hence the US statement intended that the PLO be included in the Geneva talks.[29] Although the Carter administration then retreated under Israeli and American domestic pressure and declared that it no longer considered the joint Soviet-US statement as the basis for reconvening the Geneva conference, the administration successfully persuaded Israel to accept the inclusion at Geneva of Palestinians who were not well-known PLO members. Israel insisted it would not accept Palestinians who admitted membership of the PLO. As a formula for Palestinian participation, the inclusion of an 'American Professor of Palestinian origin' was proposed. Arafat accepted the proposal but insisted that any Palestinian-American appointed to a united Arab delegation would have to be cleared by the PLO.[30] The formula for Palestinian participation had almost been accepted by all parties when Sadat's trip to Jerusalem completely altered the situation.

When the PLO opposed Sadat's trip to Jerusalem and joined the anti-Sadat rejectionists' conference in Tripoli, Libya, Carter's displeasure with the PLO reached its peak. His harsh criticism of the PLO reflected the long-term American ambivalence in dealing with that organization. The United States approved efforts by Israel, Jordan and Egypt to encourage the creation in the West Bank and Gaza of an alternative Palestinian leadership to the PLO. Carter denounced the PLO for its opposition to the Sadat peace initiative and its participation in the Tripoli conference:

> The PLO has been completely negative. It has not been cooperative at all in spite of my own indirect invitation to them and the direct invitation to them by Sadat . . . So, I think they have themselves removed the PLO from any immediate prospect of participation in a peace discussion . . . We want to be sure that at least moderate Palestinians are included in the discussion. And this is an attitude that is mirrored not only by myself but also by Prime Minister Begin, President Sadat and others.[31]

The PLO would be accommodated once it subscribed to a moderate position on Israel and the current peace negotiations. Carter preferred to deal with a more moderate Palestinian leadership, such as Shaikh Jabari of Hebron or Sa'id Al-Shawa of Gaza, rather than with the PLO.

Carter complained to a group of Arab-Americans at a White House meeting on 15 December 1977 of the 'countless hours' he had spent with other Arab leaders urging them to persuade the PLO to join in peace discussions. He told the group of the antagonistic response these efforts had generated among Israelis and 'Jewish Americans'.[32]

Although the Carter administration gave up its efforts to include the PLO in peace negotiations, it continued to send signals to the PLO telling of the rewards of moderation. One signal came in the statement on the PLO issued by the State Department on 29 June 1978, clarifying points of the Senate testimony of Ambassador Atherton and Deputy Assistant Secretary Harrop. The statement also condemned a bombing in Jerusalem for which Fateh claimed responsibility. The State Department condemned that organization as well as its chief, Yasser Arafat.[33] It was a rare precedent for the United States to condemn by name the head of a government or such an organization. In this case, the State Department's real message to Arafat was that it acknowledged him as in command of the PLO, as able to control its actions, and as having the power to force the organization to repudiate violence in favour of negotiating a peace settlement.

By the end of 1978, however, American policy towards the PLO had made progress on three fronts:

(1) The United States did not consider the PLO a terrorist organization, but it condemned any acts of violence carried out by elements of the PLO.

(2) The United States viewed the PLO not as the only legitimate representative of the Palestinians but rather as the largest of the groups representing them.

(3) The United States would conduct direct discussions with the PLO after it recognized Resolution 242. Subsequently, it would exert pressure upon Israel to accommodate the PLO in future peace talks.[34]

It was very unlikely that the PLO would recognize Resolution 242 or the Camp David process. However, had it given the green light to its supporters in the West Bank and Gaza to join the Palestinian autonomy negotiations, no doubt American accommodation and subsequent recognition of the PLO would have been forthcoming.

The Camp David Accords: an Evaluation

The Egyptian-Israeli agreements of Camp David generated great euphoria in the United States. In fact, the Camp David accords concerning the disposition of Israeli-occupied Sinai and the Palestinian areas of the West Bank and Gaza were not the first Arab-Israeli accords, nor were they to be the last. Previous accords included the Weizmann-Faisal agreements of 1919, the armistice agreement of 1949-50, and Israel's accord with the late King Abdullah of Jordan. These agreements became just other casualties of five Arab-Israeli wars. The Camp David accords seemed little more durable.

The Palestinians had rejected other proposals in the past, the 1947 UN partition plan of Palestine, the Dulles proposals of 1955 for refugee resettlement and integration, and the Rogers plan of 1969. All these were less detrimental to Palestinian rights than the Camp David accords. The Palestinian reaction to the Camp David agreements was thus predictable. United States officials professed disappointment at this reaction, insisting that the Camp David accords were only the first step towards a comprehensive settlement. They called the accords the 'cornerstone' of a process leading to full attainment of Palestinian rights and to peace.[35]

The Palestinians rejected the Camp David accords as threatening their rights and very survival as a people. Then what is the meaning of the accords?

Denial of Fundamental Palestinian Rights[36]

The final resolution of the Palestine problem envisaged by the accords precluded Palestinian self-determination and statehood in Palestine. It ignored the natural human right of dispersed Palestinians to return to their home and their right to choose and designate their own national representatives. Israel and the United States all along denied the Palestinian people those rights. It was Egypt's concurrence in that denial that constituted the shocking feature of the Camp David Palestine formula. Hence came the prompt negative reaction from the PLO leaders in the West Bank and Gaza, as well as from the governments of the Arab states, the nonaligned states and the socialist camp. All these parties saw the Camp David Palestine formula as violating an international consensus on the Palestine problem, repeatedly expressed in nonaligned summit conferences and at the United Nations.

Permanent Dismemberment of the Palestinian People

The Camp David framework divided the Palestinian people into separate categories with different formulas for dealing with their respective situations. It focused its attention upon the inhabitants of the West Bank and Gaza. The framework also recognized a second group of Palestinians, consisting of those who were 'displaced from the West Bank and Gaza in 1967'. It should be noted, however, that the Camp David framework does not refer at all to three other categories: Palestinians displaced or departed from the West Bank and Gaza *since* 1967; Palestinians displaced in 1948, but not registered with the UNRWA as refugees; and Palestinians in Israel.

The framers of the Camp David accords made their distinctions among various groups of Palestinians not solely for the procedural purpose of providing appropriate formulas for dealing with distinct

groups in varying situations. On the contrary, the Camp David conferees 'assigned' each of these groups a separate and distinct permanent
fate. The Camp David accords would have battered the unity of the
Palestinian people once and for all. The accords made the dismember-
ment of the Palestinian people into a permanent feature of the proposed Egyptian-Israeli-American solution of the Palestinian problem.

An Imposed Settlement

The Camp David Palestine formula has all the earmarks of the very
imposed settlement that was formerly opposed by both Israel and the
United States. The difference is that this solution is being imposed
partially by, rather than on, the Israelis. All the basic decisions on both
procedures or ultimate solutions were taken at Camp David in the
absence of Palestinian representatives and without regard for the known
wishes and widely recognized rights of the Palestinian people. As on
many occasions in the past sixty years, once again the Palestinians were
confronted with fundamental decisions about their destiny, reached
without their participation, knowledge, or consent, in the vein of the
Balfour Declaration, the League of Nations Mandate, the partition
recommendation of the United Nations General Assembly and Security
Council Resolution 242.

Procedural Substitutes for Substantive Principles

Unlike the 'Framework for the Conclusion of a Peace Treaty between
Egypt and Israel', which includes agreements on substantive, general
principles, as well as specific actions, the Camp David accords provide
only procedural formulas. Moreover, the generic procedure involved
was that of 'negotiation' which, in the absence of agreement on substantive principles, necessarily conferred upon Israel in practice a veto
power over any proposal it did not like, including proposals to consider
issues not specifically mentioned on the agenda.

Thus, the basic decisions relating to all aspects of the Palestine problem were simply deferred. Israel was assured of the ability to prevent,
when the moment of decision at last arrived, the adoption of any agreement to which it did not consent. Inasmuch as Israel was in actual
control of the situation, the failure to reach agreement as a result of an
Israeli veto was tantamount to perpetuation of the status quo.

Full Autonomy or a 'Palestinustan'?

The population of the West Bank and Gaza experienced some relaxation of direct rule by the Israeli military government and a measure of
self-rule, essentially in accordance with a proposal made by Begin on 28

December 1977. Although President Carter in his address to a joint session of Congress on 18 September 1978 described this measure of self-rule as 'self-government with full autonomy', the actual Camp David framework held that the precise 'powers and responsibilities of the self-governing authority to be exercised in the West Bank and Gaza' *had yet to be defined*, and that they would in fact be defined through negotiations among Egypt, Israel and Jordan.

The governments of each of these countries had to 'agree' on the 'powers and responsibilities' of the proposed 'self-governing' authority, giving each of those governments veto power. Accordingly, the 'self-governing' authority could not enjoy any of the attributes of 'self-government' or 'full autonomy' which the government of Israel did not consent to confer upon it. This 'full autonomy' was even less autonomous than Transkei of South Africa. It was a Palestinian Bantustan, or more precisely, a Palestinustan!

'Legitimizing' Continued Israeli Occupation

During the transitional period of five years from the time the 'self-governing' authority was to be 'established and inaugurated', the only partially withdrawn Israeli forces would continue to be stationed in the West Bank and Gaza in locations to be specified during the proposed Egyptian-Israeli-American negotiations. Having been determined in advance by agreement of the United States, Israel and Egypt at Camp David, the question of the continued presence of Israeli forces in the West Bank and Gaza throughout the five-year transitional period would not be subject to further discussion and agreement at the proposed trilateral negotiation. Acquiescence in that decision by the so-called 'self-governing' authority, which those negotiations are designed to produce, was mandatory.

The Camp David framework thus bestowed American-Egyptian 'legitimacy' upon the continued Israeli occupation of the Palestinian areas in question for years to come. The projected Egyptian-Israeli-Jordanian negotiations — stipulated to be conducted 'on the basis' of the Camp David agreement — would confer further 'legitimacy' upon that occupation through Jordanian consent if Jordan agreed to participate. And the 'self-governing' authority in the Palestinian territories would grant a spurious Palestinian 'legitimacy' to the Israeli military occupation as well.

The Camp David framework for peace therefore enabled Israeli occupation, which the entire international community had for eleven years declared illegal, to maintain itself 'legitimately' in the Palestinian territories for several more years, if not permanently.

Annexation of Jerusalem

The Camp David framework places occupied Jerusalem totally outside the scope of the powers and responsibilities of the projected 'self-governing' authority. Since the beginning of the Israeli occupation of the West Bank, Israel had formally annexed and enlarged its area by incorporating other occupied Palestinian territories. It significantly altered the city's demographic composition by displacing and deporting thousands of Palestinians and bringing in thousands of Israelis.

Retention and Enlargement of Existing Settlements

Israel and the United States came to an ill-defined agreement on the expansion of existing settlements. In regard to new settlements, nothing was concluded at Camp David. Israel made no commitments to refrain from enlarging existing settlements in the West Bank and Gaza either in the short term or during the five-year transitional period and beyond. Yet large-scale expansion of existing settlements was no less important than planting new settlements. In any event, Israel could easily establish new settlements in the guise of expanding existing ones. It resorted precisely to that strategem in early January 1978 between the end of the Begin-Sadat Ismailia summit and the convening of the military and political committees in Cairo and Jerusalem in mid-January 1978.

Even more important than the setting up of new settlements or the territorial-demographic expansion of existing ones was the question of the retention of Israeli settlements in the West Bank and Gaza. Israel made no commitments whatsoever to give up the settlements it had planted in the West Bank and Gaza since 1967. Accordingly, the difficult question of the future of Israeli settlements, unresolved even in principle at Camp David, remained open along with all other questions relating to the future of the West Bank and Gaza. Again, to defer difficult issues of such importance to future negotiations without establishing any principles to govern those negotiations was to play into the hands of the party which controlled the situation on the ground — Israel.

Meanwhile, Israeli settlements would raise a number of important problems about the powers of the 'self-governing' authority during the transitional period:

(a) Would Israeli settlers in the West Bank and Gaza take part in the elections to set up the 'self-governing' authority? The Camp David framework repeatedly referred to the 'elected representatives of the inhabitants of the West Bank and Gaza' without qualifying 'inhabitants' by nationality or citizenship.

(b) Would the 'self-governing' authority have the power to restore to the rightful owners the lands expropriated by the Israeli occupation authorities over the past eleven years and turned into Israeli settlements?

(c) Would the 'self-governing' authority exercise its powers equally over the Israeli and Palestinian inhabitants of the area it governs? Would the local police, the judiciary, and the administrative agencies of the 'self-governing' authority exercise power over the Israeli settlements? Or would Israel insist – as it initially had done with respect to its Sinai settlements – that the settlements in the West Bank and Gaza 'be linked to Israeli administration and law' and 'be defended by an Israeli force'?[37] Subsequent to the signing of the Israeli-Egyptian treaty of March 1979, Begin clarified the Israeli position by stating on several occasions that 'autonomy' would apply only to the Arab inhabitants of the West Bank and Gaza, and not to Israeli settlers, the land or its vital water resources.

The far-reaching importance of these questions for the transitional period and beyond requires no elaboration. What the *New York Times* wrote editorially on the long-range impact of Israeli settlements before Camp David applies with even greater relevance after Camp David:

> Mr. Begin asks whether he has not been generous enough in postponing Israeli claims of sovereignty in the West Bank and offering "self-rule" to the million Palestinians there and in Gaza. Why has Jordan failed to negotiate from that point? Probably because Jordan, like a growing number of prominent Israelis, understands the fine print in the offer. *While Arabs rule their own communities, Israelis financed by their Government and protected by their army would continue to buy and settle West Bank lands so that when the question of sovereignty is next examined, they will have completely altered the face of the region.* Behind a shield of security, they would have staked out claims to more territory. If it were not so, why have there been no Israeli security proposals – as for the final – that plainly renounce the ambition for territory?[38]

No Return of Displaced Persons

A final aspect of the powers and responsibilities of the proposed 'self-governing' authority was its power to decide which former inhabitants of the West Bank and Gaza could return. The General Assembly had affirmed on at least twelve occasions the right of those persons to return to their homes in Resolutions 2252 (ES-V), 2452 A (XXIII), 2535 B (XXIV), 2672 D (XXV), 2792 E (XXVI), 2963 C and D (XXVII), 3089 C (XXVIII), 3331 D (XXIX), 3419 C (XXX), 31/15 B and 32/90 E. The latest resolution passed on 13 December 1977 by a vote of 125 to 1, 'reaffirm[ed] the right of the displaced inhabitants to return to their homes and camps in the territories occupied by Israel since 1967' and 'deplore[d] the continued refusal of the Israeli authorities to take steps for the return of the displaced inhabitants'.

The agreement reached at Camp David to the effect that 'the Israeli Military Government and its civilian authorities will be withdrawn as soon as a self-governing authority has been freely elected by the inhabitants of those areas (viz., the West Bank and Gaza)' should have led inescapably to the end of Israel's authority to stop the displaced inhabitants of the West Bank and Gaza from coming back and should have given the 'self-governing' authority the right to process the return of the displaced. But the logic of Camp David decreed otherwise. The Camp David framework was based directly on paragraph 21 of Begin's original 26-point proposal of 28 December 1977:

> During the transitional period, representatives of Egypt, Israel, Jordan, and the self-governing authority will constitute a continuing committee to *decide by agreement* on the modalities of *admission* to persons displaced from the West Bank and Gaza in 1967, *together with necessary measures to prevent disruption and disorder*. (Emphasis added.)[39]

By means of this procedure, the United States and Egypt let Israel set three severe limits on the right of return:

(a) The *absolute right of return* became a *selective privilege of 'admission'*;
(b) The 'privilege' applied only to persons displaced in (but not since) 1967;
(c) Israel obtained veto power over the 'admission' of any displaced persons.

The linkage between the 'admission' of displaced persons and 'measures to prevent disruption and disorder' gave Israel the legal weapon to justify refusal to admit any Palestinians deemed politically undesirable on grounds of security.

Israel also invoked the principle of 'economic viability' to limit which and how many displaced Palestinians would be 'admitted'. At a news conference in Jerusalem on 21 September 1978, shortly after his return from Camp David, Dayan said he expected that the Palestinians would demand the right of one hundred thousand of their compatriots who fled the West Bank and Gaza Strip to return. But Israel's attitude would depend on whether this would be economically viable. 'We don't want any new Arab refugee camps', he said.[40] Israel's invoking of the principle of 'absorptive capacity' (now renamed 'economic viability') was not without historical irony. During the British Mandate, the Zionists always objected to any attempts to tie the influx of Jewish immigrants to the 'absorptive capacity' of an underdeveloped Palestine.

Beyond the Transitional Period

Deferred Agreement on All Issues

The Camp David agreement resolved none of the issues beyond the transitional period. It only delayed them. Failing to agree on principles, the Camp David conferees agreed on nothing other than negotiating procedure.

They agreed on the parties to those negotiations — Egypt, Jordan and the 'elected representatives of the inhabitants of the West Bank and Gaza'. They also agreed upon the timing (they should begin 'as soon as possible, but not later than the third year after the beginning of the transitional period' and end by the close of that period) and upon some of the issues to be negotiated. The four most important issues to be negotiated were the final status of the West Bank and Gaza, the new state's relationship with its neighbours, the location of its boundaries, and the nature of the security arrangements. Equally significant are the questions not included in the projected quadrilateral negotiations: 1) the final status of occupied Jerusalem; 2) the future of Israeli settlements; 3) withdrawal of Israeli forces; and above all, 4) sovereignty over the West Bank and Gaza.

The Position of Israel on the Outstanding Issues

Since the end of the Camp David summit, Israeli leaders have forcefully reaffirmed the position which Israel will adopt at the projected negotiations.

Occupied Jerusalem. Several statements made by Prime Minister Begin since the end of the Camp David summit were cited earlier in connection with the transitional period. Their import, however, goes beyond that period. In his address before the General Assembly on 9 October 1978, Dayan stated:

> For us, the city of Jerusalem is the one and only eternal capital of Israel. We have not, and we shall never have any other capital city, whether or not others recognize it as such . . . We have resolved never again to compromise the unity of Jerusalem, and it is our hope that other people will share our position.[41]

Appearing on CBS, Dayan denied he envisioned some Arab sovereignty over the eastern part.[42]

Israeli Settlements. Immediately after the Knesset vote approving the removal of Israeli settlements from Sinai within the framework of an Egyptian-Israeli peace treaty, the Israeli press published assurances by Begin that that decision did not establish a precedent affecting the future of Israeli settlements in the other occupied territories. 'In newspaper interviews published over the weekend', reported the Jewish Telegraphic agency *Daily News Bulletin*, Begin 'insisted that Israel would never withdraw its settlements from the West Bank and Golan Heights'.[43] And in remarks to foreign newsmen in Jerusalem on 21 September 1978, Begin stressed that 'Israel would have an open-ended right' even after a peace treaty is signed to 'settle on the West Bank'.[44] He spoke in the same vein in his address to the UN General Assembly on 9 October 1978:

> We do not regard ourselves as foreigners in those areas. The Israeli settlements in Judea, Samaria and the Gaza district are there as of right. It is inconceivable to us that Jews should be prohibited from settling and living in Judea and Samaria, which are the heart of our homeland.[45]

Withdrawal of Israeli Forces. Begin has contended that the 'security arrangements' envisaged in the Camp David framework for the transitional period 'and beyond' conferred upon Israel the 'automatic right to keep troops on the West Bank beyond the five-year interim period'.[46] He declared that Israeli troops would remain on the West Bank 'forever'.[47] While Secretary of State Vance was visiting Saudi Arabia immediately after the end of the Camp David summit, a senior official in the United States party, who asked not to be identified, told

Associated Press reporters, 'If it is necessary for Israeli security, the United States would support Israel in its determination to leave troops on the West Bank beyond the five-year period envisaged in the Camp David accords.'[48]

Sovereignty over the West Bank and Gaza. Shortly after the end of the Camp David summit, Begin told the House Foreign Affairs Committee, 'Israel had not given up its right to claim sovereignty over the West Bank. It would exercise that right if the issue came up for negotiation in the future.'[49] He assured a cheering, enthusiastic audience of more than two thousand Jewish leaders from across the United States that 'Judea, Samaria and the Gaza Strip are integral parts of the land of Israel. This is our land of right.'[50] Although Israel was willing to 'let the question of sovereignty be open', for the time being, it was ready to discuss it and reassert its claims during the negotiations on the future of those territories.[51] He repeated in *Time* magazine that Israel had 'a right and claim to sovereignty' over the West Bank and Gaza, that it had agreed at Camp David to leave that question open and that it would reassert its claim at the end of the five-year transitional period in the expectation that 'others would also come forward with a similar claim'.[52]

Harry Hurwitz, a journalist from South Africa who became Begin's public relations adviser, urged the Jewish media to 'start educating your readers to understand the right of the Jewish people to Eretz Israel'.[53] In the course of the next five years, Israel, the Jewish people and the Zionist movement would have to present a strong, substantiated claim to Judea and Samaria.[54] Asking rhetorically, 'What is Eretz Israel? Is it only the area around Tel Aviv and Netanya?', Hurwitz replied to his own question, 'I believe that when the time will come in the last years of the twentieth century, we may well have to educate the world to sustain our political association with that land.'[55] And Yehuda Blum, Israel's new permanent representative at the United Nations, said that Israel's 'concessions in Samaria and Judea' in allowing the question of sovereignty to be 'kept in abeyance', were of equal magnitude to its 'sweeping concession in the Sinai'.[56]

The Final Status of the West Bank and Gaza. On several recent occasions and particularly in his address to the Knesset during the debate on the Camp David accords, Begin repeated his famous 'three nos': no Palestinian state; no referendum on the West Bank and Gaza; and no negotiations with the Palestine Liberation Organization.[57] More importantly, however, he told the Knesset, with reference to his negotiations with Sadat and Carter at Camp David, 'I obtained an assurance that there will be no Palestinian state under any pretext whatsoever.'[58]

Neither President Carter nor President Sadat has contradicted that public assertion. Despite appearances, the Camp David framework implicitly ruled out the statehood option. It required only that the projected negotiations produce agreement on a 'peace treaty between Israel and Jordan, taking into account the agreement on the final status of the West Bank and Gaza', and that, in those negotiations, the representatives of Jordan be 'joined by the elected representatives of the inhabitants of the West Bank and Gaza'.

Disagreement Means Perpetuation of the Status Quo

It cannot be overemphasized that, by failing to agree on substantive issues and by simply deferring decisions to future negotiations, the Camp David conferees have, in effect, agreed that every party would be free to reject the proposals of any other party. Armed with such a veto power, the party in control would be able to perpetuate the *status quo*. That was precisely what Begin had in mind when he told *Time* magazine:

> [If] there is an agreement between the parties negotiating — then everybody will rejoice that there is an agreement. And if there is no agreement, the [present] arrangement . . . will continue. So in either case, nothing wrong can happen. Therefore, I am optimistic about the future.[59]

There were those who said that the West Bank and Gaza Palestinians had nothing to lose by going along with the Camp David 'autonomy' plan, and perhaps, a great deal to gain. This was not so. Faced with total Israeli opposition to a Palestinian state and an Israeli veto over the negotiations, the Palestinians could gain nothing. By electing a 'self-governing' authority to participate in negotiations which would inevitably lead to a deadlock, and thus indefinite occupation, the Palestinians would be giving up the principle of their refusal to recognize any legitimacy to Israeli occupation. If Israel continued its settlement policy during such negotiations and beyond, conceivably the Palestinians could end up losing what little they had left.

For US policy-makers, however, the Camp David accords realized three objectives:

(1) They eliminated any viable military threat to Israel, at least for the near future, thus consequently defusing the threat of total war in the Middle East.

(2) They isolated Egypt effectively from the Arab front, thus crippling joint Arab military action for the liberation of occupied Arab lands.

(3) They gained for the United States a significant strategic advantage by including Egypt in the American military camp. The United States gained an ally with sufficient military capability to oppose nationalist and radical regimes and protect US interests in the Horn of Africa. Sadat had enthusiastically volunteered Egypt for this role.

Yet despite the tangible advantages of the Camp David accord for the United States, the advantages were only temporary and in the final analysis would make the attainment of a comprehensive peace even harder, thus placing American interests in greater jeopardy. Then why did President Carter accept the Begin plan for Palestinian 'self-rule', a plan he had rejected nine months earlier? No doubt the lack of any major foreign policy accomplishments of the Carter administration, and other domestic political considerations, played a vital part in this shift.

Notes

1. Bernard Reich, 'The Continued Quest for Peace: The Carter Administration and the Arab-Israeli Conflict in 1977', (manuscript – GWU, Washington, DC), pp. 23-8.

2. Ibid.

3. PLO representative Dr. Isam Sartaw, in a telephone statement to the American Friends Service Committee Middle East Conference held in Washington, DC, 12 February 1977, quoted a statement made by Jimmy Carter to Richard Holbrooke in Louisville, Kentucky on 23 November 1975. Carter said:

> I think the community of nations has got to recognize some basic principles of a settlement on a permanent basis in the Middle East. And I think one of the integral parts of an ultimate settlement has got to be the recognition of the Palestinians as a people, as a nation, with a place to live and a right to choose their own leaders . . .
>
> But I would not as a nation recognize the PLO, or Arafat as a spokesman of the Palestinian people even though that might be an actual fact, until after Arafat agrees that Israel has a right to exist in peace as an integral part of the Middle East community.

This statement reflects Carter's lack of political understanding of foreign policy during the early phase of the presidential primary campaign. However, Carter's position on the Middle East during his campaign included, among other things, a 'homeland for the Palestinians, preferably under Jordan as a key element in settlement'.

'Candidates' Stands on Foreign Policy', *The Washington Post*, 6 October 1976, p. a-8.

4. The Brookings Institute Study-Group Report 'Toward Peace in the Middle East', (The Brookings Institute, 1975) pp. 244 and 273. Several participants of the study-group now hold top-level positions in the Carter Administration, most notably Zbigniew Brzezinski and William Quandt.

5. President Carter's response to a question on the Middle East at Clinton, Massachusetts Town Hall Meeting, 16 March 1977. *Department of State Release*, 17 March 1977, pp. 1-2.

6. Transcript of the President's News Conference on Foreign and Domestic Matters, 12 May 1977, *New York Times*, 13 May 1977, p. a-12.

7. *Department of State News Release*: Vice-President Walter Mondale's address before the World Affairs Council of North California, 'A Framework for Middle East Peace', 17 June 1977, p. 6.

8. *The Washington Post*, 20 September 1977, pp a-1 and a-6.

9. Ibid., 13 September 1977, pp. 1 and 4.

10. Ibid.; another source of controversy in American-Israeli relations has been the issue of Israeli settlements on Arab territories occupied since 1967. The United States has repeatedly protested against the building or extension of these settlements.

11. 'Joint Soviet-US Statement on the Middle East', *Public Information Series*, Bureau of Public Affairs (Department of State, Washington, DC, 1 October 1977).

12. *Newsweek*, 17 October 1977, p. 30, and the *Washington Post*, 12 October 1977, pp. a-1 and a-12. According to the *Washington Post* story based on a dispatch by the Israeli newspaper *Haaretz*, Israel had rejected two clauses that the United States wanted to include in the 'working paper'. The clauses would have called for a discussion of a Palestinian entity, such as a homeland and the participation of low-level PLO members. *Haaretz* also reported that Dayan blocked both and secured an agreement with the United States that Israel reserved the right to block any attempt to include the PLO at Geneva or to discuss a Palestinian entity.

13. *Public Information Series*, 5 October 1978, and the *Washington Post*, 10 October 1978, pp. a-1, a-10.

14. Sadat's trip to Jerusalem split the Arab world. Libya, Syria, PLO, Algeria, and South Yemen held a rejectionist conference in Tripoli to counter the Cairo meeting. Jordan, although sympathetic to Sadat, stayed away from both meetings. Israel threatened to leave the meeting in Cairo if the PLO was allowed to participate. As the PLO went instead to Tripoli, the Israeli threat was eliminated and Sadat was saved embarrassment.

15. *The Manchester Guardian Weekly*, 25 December 1977, p. 2; *Washington Post*, 16 December 1977, p. a-26.

16. 'Interview with the President by Barbara Walters (ABC), Robert McNeal (PBS), Tom Brokaw (NBC), and Bob Schieffer', Office of the White House Press Secretary, The White House, 28 December 1977, p. 5.

17. 'President Carter's Statement at Aswan', News Release, 4 January 1978 (Bureau of Public Affairs, Office of Media Services, Department of State).

18. 'The Middle East Peace Process: A Status Report', Remarks by Alfred Atherton, Jr, Ambassador-at-Large for Middle East Peace Negotiations, Los Angeles, California, 15 June 1978, (Department of State, Washington, DC).

19. 'Interview with Yasser Arafat', PLO Chairman, January 1980.

20. *Weekly Compilation of Presidential Documents*, 26 September 1977, p. 1378.

21. Ibid., vol. 13, no. 22, 21 May 1977, p. 768.

22. *Sunday Times* (London), 30 April 1971, p. 3.

23. 'Foreign Relations Authorization Act, Fiscal Year 1978', Public Law 95-104, 17 August 1977, p. 848 and *The Boston Herald American*, 24 August 1977, p. 3. *The Washington Post*, 11 May 1979.

24. *Newsweek*, 17 October 1977, p. 32.

25. Rowland Evans and Robert Novak, 'Carter's Maneuver to Bring in the PLO', *The Washington Post*, 17 August 1977, p. 17.

26. *The Washington Post*, 9 August 1977, pp. 1, 14.

27. 'PLO Put on Ice', *The Middle East*, February 1978, p. 41.

28. 'Joint Soviet-US Statement on the Middle East'. *Public Information Series* (Bureau of Public Affairs, US Department of State, Washington, DC, 7 October 1977).

29. The Arab Summit Conference at Rabat in 1974 and UN General Assembly Resolution 3236 recognized the PLO as the legitimate representative of the Palestinian people. Ambassador Alfred Atherton, speaking at Senate subcommittee hearings on 28 July 1978, stated that the PLO speaks for a substantial number of Palestinians, but the US will not deal with it so long as it does not recognize Security Council Resolution 242. See *Mideast Observer* 1 July 1978, p. 1.

30. *The Middle East*, February 1978.

31. 'Press Conference of the President of the United States', 15 December 1977 (Room 450, Old Executive Office Building, Washington, DC) p. 8.

32. 'Arab-Americans, Carter Confer; Crucial M.E. Topics Discussed'. *The Voice* of the National Association of Arab Americans, vol. 5.

33. 'Statement on the PLO' *Department of State Press Release*, 29 June 1978 and the *Washington Post*, 30 June 1978.

34. Israeli Prime Minister Menachem Begin during an interview on CBS's Face the Nation, indicated that Israel came under some pressure from the US to consider the possibility of recognizing the PLO. Begin said:

> I remember it was only some eleven, ten months ago that this suggestion was made to me by a representative of the United States – that we should take into consideration a possibility to recognize the so-called PLO. It is not now the case.

See CBS 'Face the Nation', 23 July 1978, Guest: Menachem Begin, Prime Minister of Israel.

35. Interview with Nathaniel Howell, Jr, Director, Office of Iraq, Jordan, Lebanon, and Syria Affairs. US Department of State, 1 July 1980.

36. Fayez Sayegh, ' "The Camp David accords: A Framework for Peace,' A Critical Examination,' Fay Zeady (ed.), *Camp David: A New Balfour Declaration* (AAUG, Detroit, Michigan: 1979). This section draws heavily on Dr. Sayegh's excellent discussion and analysis of the Camp David accords. This section quotes heavily from the Camp David accords, see text in appendix.

37. Quoted in ibid.

38. *New York Times*, 15 August 1978, p. 152.

39. Quoted in Sayegh, 'The Camp David accords'.

40. Ibid., p. 27.

41. UN Document, A/35/PV. 26.

42. *Jewish Week*, 15 October 1978, p. 37.

43. *Jewish Telegraphic Agency*, Daily News Bulletin, 4 October 1978, p. 1.

44. *Jewish Telegraphic Agency*, Daily News Bulletin, 22 September 1978, p. 1.

45. Ibid.

46. *Jewish Week*, 24 September 1978, p. 4.

47. Jewish Telegraphic Agency, *Daily News Bulletin*, 20 September 1978, p. 3; and *Jerusalem Post International Edition*, 26 September 1978, p. 10.

48. Associated Press Dispatch in *The Reporter Dispatch*, 23 September 1978, p. a-1 and a-14.

49. *Jerusalem Post International Edition*, 26 September 1978, p. 10.

50. Jewish Telegraphic Agency, *Daily News Bulletin*, 21 September 1978, pp. 1-2.

51. Ibid.

52. *Time*, 2 October 1978, p. 21.

53. *Jewish Week*, 1 October 1978, p. 49.

54. Ibid.

55. Ibid.

56. *Jewish Week*, 15 October 1978, p. 4.

57. Jewish Telegraphic Agency, *Daily News Bulletin*, 26 September 1978, p. 1; *Jewish Chronicle*, 29 September 1978, p. 2.

58. *Christian Science Monitor*, 26 September 1978, p. 4.

59. *Jewish Week*, 15 October 1978, p. 4.

7 WHO INFLUENCES AMERICAN-PALESTINIAN POLICY?

There is a very large body of literature that deals with the structure, staff, membership and activities of domestic interest groups in American politics. While it is not the purpose of this study to examine theoretical questions related to interest-group politics, nor to examine in extensive detail all the domestic pressure groups which are concerned with US policy toward the Palestinians, a few general observations about interest-group activities and a survey of some of the more relevant groups is essential to any discussion of the factors that have influenced the making of US policy toward Palestinians.

A very simple generalization which can be made about interest groups is that the greater their access to decision makers, the greater will be their impact on the policy process. A collaboration between interest groups on an issue where their interests are compatible is not unusual, although such co-operation is not always indicative of ideological or general compatibility of view or interests. Although even domestic policy is sometimes subject to outside pressures, it is much more the case that foreign policy issues are the battle ground of foreign and internal pressures, from all kinds of national and international actors.

Domestic Pressures

Few other areas of US foreign policy have received more attention and public concern than that of the question of the influence of domestic pressure groups on American Middle East policy. These groups fall into three general categories: the business, banking, and oil company groups; American-Arab groups; and the American Jewish lobby.

Business, Banking and Oil Interests

With their pivotal role in the power structure of the United States and their access to political decision-makers at all levels, it would be logical to assume that business, banking and oil interests would constitute an influential factor affecting US Palestinian policy, particularly considering the high stake which these business interests have in the preservation of stability and harmonious relations with the Arab world. The Arab states, with the largest proven oil reserves in the world and the highest level of oil exports, have for many years provided the oil companies with tremendous profits. Banking and other business interests have also gained enormously from Arab markets, and, in the years since the beginning of the large OPEC petrodollar surpluses, from Arab investment and bank deposits. Although these oil, banking and other business interests clearly grasp the importance of cordial relationships with Arab states, clearly they feel that maintenance of the *status quo* has served, and will continue to serve their purpose well. The Arab governments have given them no reason to believe otherwise.

These interests have expressed no more than mild dissatisfaction with some aspects of American Palestinian and Middle East policy, apparently not perceiving that their interests have been sufficiently threatened. Should they find that their interests in the Middle East were in jeopardy, they would surely bring to bear on the American policy-making process the full weight of their power.

American-Arab Groups

Unlike the pro-Israeli groups the pro-Arab groups have had only a marginal impact upon the domestic scene in the US, and even less on government decision-making on policies towards the Middle East or Palestine questions. This is mainly because the pro-Arab groups tend to play a reactive rather than a formulative or active policy-making role. They have been numerically and organizationally weak (especially if compared to the pro-Israel groups) because they are: isolated in an apathetic, perhaps even hostile domestic environment; constrained by less access to the media and thus less visible; and most importantly, denied access to policy makers which inhibits their policy preferences from being considered by core governmental decision-makers.

Three other major factors which diminish the political effectiveness of American-Arabs, even where they are located in otherwise sufficient numbers, are the facts that: (1) most of them fall into the working or lower-middle class and thus lack the financial capability and the political interest to make their views felt; (2) despite their common Arab heritage, they have a diversity of views and ideologies which hinders unified action; and (3) many American-Arabs, particularly second and later generations, are more concerned with assimilation and acceptance than with raising their children to feel the kind of link with Palestine or the Arab world that most American Jewish children are raised to feel with Israel. American-Arabs in general did not identify with their heritage until relatively recently and have tended to be politically inactive. Their relative lack of political clout is reflected in the fact that, although there has been a staff liaison person for Jewish groups on the White House staff, American-Arab groups have a hard time even being able to meet with Executive Branch officials. (Henry Kissinger refused for two years to meet with pro-Arab groups.)

There are three major American-Arab groups active on the national level, one of which, the Palestine Congress of North America, was formed only in August 1979. Both the Association of Arab American University Graduates (AAUG) and the National Association of Arab Americans (NAAA) were formed after the 1967 Middle East War. The AAUG is the more academic of the organizations, while NAAA is the only one which is a formal lobbying organization.

Ironically the role of the Arab governments in organizing and supporting the activities of American-Arabs is minimal, particularly when compared with the strong organizational and financial link between the Israeli government and Jewish groups worldwide. Whether or not American-Arabs will increase their involvement in domestic politics and make their influence felt on US Middle East policy remains to be seen.[1]

American-Jewish Lobby

American domestic politics have had a significant impact on US foreign policy towards the Palestinians since World War I. This became more intense after the formation of Israel in 1948 (see Chapter 2). The Israeli lobby or the so-called 'Jewish lobby' has challenged the decision of every American President, whenever that decision was perceived as harmful to Israeli interests, including the overtures made by the Carter administration last year towards the PLO.[2] The American Israel Public Affairs Committee (AIPAC) is the only registered group that deals exclusively with matters affecting Israeli interests. The Israeli lobby is ultimately directed by a group called the Conference of Presidents of Major American Jewish Organizations, which co-ordinates the general policy of the American Israel Public Affairs Committee. There are other Jewish groups that engage in direct contacts with public officials to affect policy matters on Israel and other matters of concern to the American Jewish community.

The extent of the impact, intrigue, resentment, admiration and publicity the AIPAC invites is unsurpassed by any other lobby in Washington. The extent of its successes and failures is directly related to the nature of the American system, its own strengths and weakness, the nature of its constituency, economic status, and the role it plays in the American polity. The amount of attention and controversy that AIPAC generates necessitates a more detailed treatment of its structure, *modus operandi*, and the extent of its influence.

The American Israel Public Affairs Committee, the officially registered domestic Jewish lobby, serves as the co-ordinator of all the Jewish lobbying efforts undertaken on Capitol Hill and as a congressional resource centre for information about the Middle East. Currently it employs four persons registered as lobbyists but not as foreign agents. It has a staff of over twenty with an annual budget (in 1978) of over $750,000 which came from over 15,000 membership contributions ranging from $25 to $5,000.[3]

AIPAC has its roots in the American Zionists Council, an umbrella organization which had been established in the 1930s to arouse support for the development of the Jewish state in Palestine. Among its other activities after the establishment of the state of Israel was an ongoing campaign among Congressmen, government officials, and various branches of the media to enlist sympathy and support for Israel's economic as well as military needs, since after 1950 the Tripartite Declaration banned the selling of arms to any state in the Middle East region. It also worked to counter activities in the US by Jewish groups opposed to Zionism such as the American Council for Judaism.

Isaiah L. Kenen, who had worked during the 1930s as a journalist in Ohio, came to Washington in 1943 as executive director of the American Zionist Conference, a group then being formed with the same goals as the Washington-based American Zionist Council.[4] The year 1948 found him in Paris as director of information for the Jewish Agency at the United Nations, and later he went on to become press officer in Ambassador Abba Eban's Israeli delegation to the UN in New York. Kenen recounts how, in 1950, when Israel was badly in need of economic assistance, President Truman informed the leading members of the American Jewish community who approached him, that he could not offer aid to Israel without balancing it with offers to the Arab states as well. He suggested, instead, that these leaders appeal to the Congress. 'Since then', Kenen explains, 'the Administration has always left it to us – virtually all important aid to Israel is initiated on the Hill.'[5] Kenen left the Israeli delegation in New York and succeeded in gathering 36 Senators and 150 House members to support a grant to Israel under the Marshall Plan, but, he said, the State Department was opposed to this. Therefore he extended his stay in Washington in order to lobby for more support in Congress. He registered with the Justice

Department as a foreign agent for the Zionist state in 1951, but later in the same year, he changed his status to domestic lobbyist for the American Zionist Council (AZC).

In 1954, the AZC closed its Washington office and the independent American Zionist Council Public Affairs Committee was established to carry on political and lobbying activities in the capital city. Mr Kenen became its executive director and has emphasized the fact that this committee from its inception was supported by taxable − not tax free − American contributions. Right away the director began a policy of meeting regularly with representatives from major American Jewish organizations in the area to discuss policy formation and support-gathering. Now presidents of most major American Jewish organizations sit on AIPAC's executive board which holds weekly meetings. The committee's chairman was Louis Lipskey in 1954 (who was president of the AZC from 1949-54), Rabbi Philip S. Bernstein from 1955-68 and Irving Kane from 1968 onwards.

Between 1954 and 1960, the year that the Jewish Agencies in New York and Jerusalem reorganized, Kenen continued assisting the AZC in his private capacity, giving speeches and arranging speakers for various conventions and reprinting them for distribution. In 1957 he founded the *Near East Report* (NER), a propagandist newsletter, which he owned and edited until recently. Regarding its bias, Kenen admitted in a letter to Senator Fulbright during the 1953 hearings that 'The views expressed in the *Near East Report* reflect judgments based on my own experience and conviction.'[6] He also explained how he withdrew from the American Zionist Council Public Affairs Committee payroll on the first day of its publication and thereafter contributed his services to that committee without payment. After 1957, the AZC paid Kenen a yearly sum of $20,000 of which $5,200 was in payment for his services while the balance covered travel, printing, office expenses, and subscriptions of the NER purchased by the council for all Congressmen as well as many government officials and newspaper editors. AZC purchases of the newsletter for this purpose were stopped in 1962 because, Kenen said, the Council was in arrears.

The effect of these payments to Kenen for his NER was that the publication was subsidized by a foreign agent, since the AZC received its money from the Jewish Agency. The newsletter did not carry a label stating this, however; the AZC was serving as a channel which insulated the publication from compliance with the FARA labelling law. Perhaps it is not irrelevant to note here that after the 1953 hearing, attempts were made to make the FARA more effective, eliminating possible evasions of the law such as this, but that by 1975 only four groups of organizations had been investigated under the revised regulations. One of these four was the Arab League Information Centers.[7]

Now, AIPAC, since 1975 under the executive director Morris J. Amitay (who is also a contributing editor of NER), provides funds for about four thousand subscriptions of the newsletter to the professionals mentioned above as well as to some embassies and UN delegations.

While AIPAC has grown in number and strength in the past thirty years (it now maintains a branch office in New York), it is not merely the existence of this official Washington committee which assures the success of the Jewish lobby. It depends to a great extent on the support it receives from an extensive network of interconnecting organizations and individuals who work in the interest of Israel and Jewish concerns not only within Washington but throughout the country.

This network may be broadly divided into four categories which are only formally independent of AIPAC: (1) Congressmen, Jewish or non-Jewish who have a personal commitment to the Jewish cause; (2) Congressional staff members; (3) other Jewish lobbyists, organizations, the Israeli Embassy, and influential or strategically placed Jewish individuals in the Administration; and (4) Jewish constituents in the Congressmen's home states.

Among those Senators and Representatives who have been outspoken in their support for Israel in the past are Senator Henry M. Jackson (D-Wash.), Senator Jacob K. Javits (R-N.Y.), Senator Abraham Ribicoff (D-Conn.), Senator Stuart Symington (D-Mo.), Senator Richard Stone (D-Fla.), Senator Hugh Scott (R-Pa.), Senator Herman E. Talmadge (D-Ga.), and Representatives Charles A. Vanik and Jonathan Bingham. The strongly anti-Soviet Senator Jackson was once tagged as the 'most influential spokesman for Israel',[8] and indeed his record is impressive. Although not Jewish himself, he sees parallels between his Norwegian and the Jewish background and is likewise impressed by the strong family tradition among the Jews. To cite one example of his activities; it was under his direction in 1970, that the Senate Armed Services Committee and afterwards the Senate approved by 87 votes to 7 a $500 million appropriation for Israeli arms. After the appropriation had been signed into law, Jackson used his influence to get the Defense Department to allow Israel to repay the money on much easier credit terms than usually applied.[9] Most recently the Senator has gained recognition for his sponsorship of the Jackson-Vanik Amendment to the Trade Reform Act. Senator Symington has also been outspoken in urging arms supplies to the state of Israel and

Senator Javits will drop everything in times of perceived crisis by Israel in order to meet with embassy and administration officials. One remark by Kenen in 1972 is very revealing concerning the initiating role that these Congressmen play in shaping American policy to Israel. 'I also have to spend time trying to hold back Congressmen to prevent them from doing things that would exacerbate relations [between the US and the Arab countries]. Many times, people in the Senate want to go too far.'[10]

If not more important than the Congressmen themselves are their aides, because they have more time to devote to the details of developing contacts and support and a fine understanding of the issues involved. Mr Amitay has explained that there are a lot of people around who are willing to look at matters purely in terms of their Jewishness.

> These are all guys who are in a position to make the decisions in these areas for these Senators . . . You don't need that many to get something done in the Senate . . . if they're willing to become involved, you can get an awful lot done just at the staff level . . . the Senators have a million things to do and they'll take the recommendation of the administrative assistants most time.[11]

A list of the more active past and present aides includes Richard Perle on Senator Jackson's staff, Winslow Wheeler or Albert Lakeland on Senator Javits's staff, Jay Berman on Birch Bayh's, Dan Spiegel on Humphrey's, Mark Talisman on Vanik's and Jerome Levison and Jack Blum on Church's.

One illustrative incident underscores the role a staff member can sometimes play. It concerns Stephen Bryen, at one time a professional staff member on the Senate Foreign Relations Subcommittee on Near Eastern and South Asian Affairs, who reportedly met with four Israelis from the embassy in a coffee shop in Washington and according to Michael Saba, former executive director of the National Association of Arab Americans, who happened to be sitting nearby, handed over Pentagon documents on Saudi military installations to the Israelis.[12] The matter was debated but remained unsettled.

The close links AIPAC maintains with other Jewish organizations also lightens the lobby's task considerably. David Brody of the B'nai B'rith Jewish Defense League worked together at one time with Kenen and now works closely with Amitay, although attempts are made to avoid appearing as a team. Close ties exist as well with the Israeli embassy, although likewise and for obvious reasons the embassy tries to keep its distance from AIPAC in public. The embassy has in the past co-operated in financing junkets to Israel for various Congressmen, and members from the embassy meet from time to time not only with AIPAC officials but with the most involved Congressmen. Officials from the Israeli Government will often testify before Congressional Committees as well as members of other Jewish organizations. In fact, AIPAC maintains a list of persons who remain 'on call' to appear for testimony upon short notice whenever necessary.

Another familiar individual to Congressmen is Hyman Bookbinder of the American Jewish Committee who guards in practice a small distance from AIPAC with whose policies he does not always agree. Indeed, although the lobby's greatest strength is the wide support which it enjoys from the vast number of American Jewish organizations, at the same time this is also the source of its greatest weakness, since each organization maintains its own individual point of view, causing some serious divisions. The most divisive issues currently seem to be the question of Israeli settlements on the West Bank, its policy of retaliatory bombings, and the problem of Palestinian refugees. Divisions among the different groups have become more apparent recently since many disapprove of Amitay's heavy-handed and often offensive tactics which have been counterproductive to a certain extent, irritating and alienating some Congressmen. Senator Ribicoff, a strong supporter of Israel, remarked that members of the lobby act as 'self-appointed spokesmen who try to give the impression they speak for the Jews . . . But there is no monolithic view'.[13] A further indication of this is Breira, a new organization which appeared in 1971 and gives voice to the more moderate points of view, stressing the need to discuss withdrawal of post-1967 settlements. Its president Bob Loeb once said of Amitay, 'The most military anti-Israeli Arabs should give him a medal.'[14]

On the other hand, most Jewish groups are able to work together on the crucial policies. The visible forms of this co-operation are AIPAC's executive and national boards, on which, as mentioned earlier, sit the presidents of most of the American Jewish organizations as well as a 32-member group called the Conference of Presidents of Major American Jewish Organizations. By definition this conference overlaps AIPAC's executive committee and thus works closely with it, participating in annual policy conferences, for example, and activating their members at AIPAC's request.

The main purposes of the Conference of Presidents of Major American Jewish Organizations (CPMAJO), however, are to lobby the White

House and the State Department, two areas which AIPAC has been unable to penetrate directly, and to serve as a liaison between the executive branch and the American Jewish community. For example, when President Ford wanted assurance that the lobby would help in the passage of his Sinai accord through Congress, he arranged a meeting with the conference. Rabbi Alex M. Schindler, the CPMAJO president in 1978, has said that the conference was founded at the suggestion of the State Department. According to him, Secretary of State Dulles suggested to Dr Nahum Goldman, then president of the World Jewish Congress, that all of the Jewish presidents get together and send one representative to see him, rather than tying him up with separate interviews with each one. The conference was thus informally established in March 1955 with Goldman as president and began meeting off and on to discuss issues of concern and reach a consensus. After 1960, this *ad hoc* character changed and the conference was organized on a permanent basis, formalizing procedures, employing a professional staff and adopting a regular budget. In 1966, an official resolution was passed designating the conference as the central representative body of the major American Jewish organizations. Yet Schindler also commented about the differing viewpoints among members. Like Ribicoff and Bookbinder he emphasized that a consensus may be reached but that a truly unified viewpoint is never achieved.

In the past, the White House has employed an official liaison to the Jewish community, although Nixon did not maintain this post and Carter's Mark Spiegel resigned. Usually, however, there are influential members within the administration who perform that service unofficially, Max Fisher and Rabbi Israel Miller in the Nixon administration, for example.

It is generally agreed that the most effective way of influencing policy is through personal contact. A good example of this is the influence of Eddie Jacobson on President Truman's staff. One recent influential personality who lobbied on various levels in his private capacity is Myer Feldman. In 1972 he outlined some of his activities:

1. Conferring on a regular basis with members of the Israeli government on issues of concern to them in the US.
2. Getting pro-Israeli ideas across to influential newspaper columnists.
3. Advising Democratic candidates for office on Middle East issues.
4. Intervening with 'people in Congress, when I am asked to, sometimes by people in Israel, more often by leaders of the American Jewish community'.[15]

In the 1960s, AIPAC began a regular policy of bringing constituents to Washington to appeal to wavering law-makers. The voice of the Congressman's Jewish constituents has a great impact on him because Jews are politically active in disproportion to their actual number; they supply 60 per cent of Democratic and 40 per cent of Republican campaign contributions, and produce an estimated turn-out of 90 per cent in most national elections. Thus in some districts, in close races, their collective vote can make or break a candidate.

In fact, three main factors seem to influence a Congressman's decision about a particular issue, with constituents' desires perhaps the most powerful. The other two areas would be what have been identified as operational factors within the Congressional system, and the individual perspective factor.[16] AIPAC operates by reaching into each one of these areas which act on the Congressman's final decision. It reaches out into the community to keep its members well informed and vocal. While the NER remains officially independent from AIPAC, it serves as the committee's mouthpiece with its circulation of 30,000 throughout the country. It is a tool particularly useful in informing constituents of how their Congressmen vote on all issues which affect Israel or world Jewry. It offers its own rewards and punishments; a particular Senator will be lauded for any positive statement or action undertaken, while anyone daring to speak out against the lobby's stance will be severely reprimanded. When Senator Abourezk spoke out on the Senate floor in 1974 for the rights of Arab refugees in the Middle East, the NER printed an angry article on his 'fantasies' and followed up this action by sending out letters containing the article to supporters of Abourezk's campaign in his home state. Abourezk also spoke out about the lobby's activity in motivating Jewish constituents in Arkansas to support Dale Bumber who unseated Senator Fulbright, at one time the lobby's most outspoken enemy. Likewise Jews supported Wayne Morse in Senator Hatfield's 1974 re-election campaign in Oregon, angered by Hatfield's independent thinking on Middle East matters. In 1976, NER had a 'campaign column' where it reprinted statements made by presidential hopefuls about the Middle East as well as their past records. In their guide, 'Effective Community Action', which was prepared for the 1978 policy conference, AIPAC advises,

> AIPAC will be happy to supply constituents with the public record on new votes — but you can help us by clipping news items about your legislator's activities and positions in local newspapers or media which we do not have access to and sending them to us.

Besides election votes, the lobby has well-organized methods of making sure its constituents' voices are heard by the Congressman in his Washington office. Letters and phone calls are helpful, but are most effective, one lobbyist cautions his supporters, when 'coordinated with the goals of the strategists in Congress and among the pressure groups'.[17] Kenen's own words best outline how he gets a campaign started.

> When something comes up, I send out a letter to about 700 people. They go to the national and local level leaders of the American Jewish community as well as to the local boys here in Washington. I may call them to my office — just to alert them to what is going on and urge them to do what they can. The (Senators) haven't signed. Please do what you can.[18]

An interesting insight into the methods used to flood senators' offices with hundreds, sometimes thousands of pieces of mail within a short period of time is given by AIPAC's 'Effective Community Action' guide. It details how to establish mailgram banks which 'permits one individual to trigger a number of mailgrams or telegrams to a Congressman in the name of different constituents'. With regard to telephone bombardment, some Congressmen have reported receiving calls throughout the night until agreeing to join up with the lobby's cause. Remarks Amitay,

> With a Senator from the far west, we won't bother on something like the Jackson Amendment. But if we get a Senator from an industrial state, a state with any sizable Jewish population and he doesn't come out, we don't let him get away with it. That's when we call for outside help.[19]

Concerning the operational factor in decision-making, AIPAC not only distributes free copies of NER among Congressmen, but maintains a research library on the Middle East to which Congressmen as well as journalists and members of the State Department turn for assistance. Its collection includes a set of bound volumes containing 'every single statement or document on a Middle Eastern topic that has appeared in the *Congressional Record* during the past 26 years'.[20] Noted for its efficiency, the lobby can, within four hours, have on the desk of every Senator and Congressman 'a carefully researched, well-documented statement of its views'.[21] AIPAC's lobbyists also testify at Committee hearings or arrange for others to testify. Winning the approval of a committee can be a key to winning Congress, since many will often vote according to the committee's recommendation. Trips to Israel for Congressmen are financed by AIPAC as are regular luncheon briefings for aides and a Capitol Hill banquet on Israel's national day every year. In addition, AIPAC lobbies other lobbies on the hill, notably the Americans for Democratic Action, and the AFL-CIO. Amitay often works by making and unmaking alliances on different bills, 'in return for which he obtains his debtors' support for the defence of Israel's interest'.[22]

Although traditionally most Jews have tended to be registered Democrats, AIPAC appeals to both parties, accepting support from whoever will not refuse to offer it. AIPAC's lobbyists now include one Republican as well as one gentile 'for credibility's sake'.[23]

Outside the CPMAJO, AIPAC's only way to pressure the White House is to generate pressure among the Congressmen to pressure the Executive. Congressional petitions and letters to the President have a history which begins long before the establishment of AIPAC; in 1936 President F.D. Roosevelt received a petition from 51 Senators, 194 Congressmen, and 30 state Governors in an effort to persuade him to request Britain not to alter the Palestine Mandate without US approval. More recently, AIPAC inspired two Senate letters to President Ford, one in December 1974, the other four months later in April, and a House letter to President Carter in October 1977.

When, in 1973, the $2.2 billion aid package to Israel was passed in the Senate, 66 votes to 9, Kenen wasn't even in Washington. The lobby played less of a role in securing this aid for the Zionist state than did the sympathy of the Congressmen themselves. Yet, while some Members of Congress may be predisposed to giving generous aid to the state, they may need some prodding to support more ambiguous measures such as the Jackson-Vanik amendment to the Trade Reform Act and the letters to the President, as well as the blocking of arms sales to moderate Arab nations. In these cases the lobby managed to muster considerable support, but not quite enough.

Kenen and AIPAC took the lead in 1972-3 in making Soviet Jewish emigration a major issue on Capitol Hill, which led to Senator Jackson's amendment to the Trade Reform Act, denying most favoured nation status to 'non-market countries' that restricted free emigration or US investment in those countries or imposed 'more than nominal exit visas or . . . other fees'.[24] Representative Vanik introduced a similar bill in the House. Although the amendment eventually passed by a 2:1 margin, it proved counterproductive in more than one way. Not only did the Soviets reject the trade act, but they further restricted emigration. Furthermore, AIPAC's lobbying tactics irritated several Congressmen. When AIPAC threatened reluctant Senators with sending their constituents hostile election-year mail campaigns directed against them,[25] Ohio Republican Senator William Saxbe lifted his name from among the signatures of the amendment, and Wisconsin Democratic Senator Gaylord Nelson refused to cosponsor it. Yet other Senators succumbed to the pressure. When Senator Javits wavered in his support for the amendment, he was warned that the Jewish constituents of New York would be forced to support his opponent in the Senate race, former US Attorney General Ramsey Clark.[26] Democrat Lloyd Bentsen of Texas was also not initially in favour of the amendment, but supported it 'after AIPAC generated pressure from Texas rabbis and a Jewish staff assistant on the Special Committee on Aging'.[27] Bookbinder recounts how Kenen called him, asking if he knew anyone who might get Senator Herman Talmadge of Georgia to be a cosponsor. Bookbinder said that the American Jewish Committee chapter chairman in Atlanta was Talmadge's law partner and gave him a call. A few days later, Talmadge indeed signed his name on the list of sponsors.[28]

The December 1974 letter to President Ford, written by Dan Spiegel of Senator Humphrey's staff and signed by 71 Senators, denounced the UN decision to invite Yasser Arafat to the General Assembly and to admit the Palestine Liberation Organization to observer status. The April 1975 letter, which 76 Senators signed, was drafted by Amitay, and cosponsors included Henry Jackson, Jacob Javits, Abraham Ribicoff, Richard Stone, Lloyd Bentsen, Walter Mondale, and Herman Talmadge. The letter expressed discontent with President Ford's 're-assessment' of Middle East policy at that time. Chuck Percy from Chicago refused to sign the letter and wrote his own letter explaining his viewpoint to the President. In order to reduce the effect of this letter, Amitay slipped the 76-Senator letter to the *Washington Post* the day before it reached President Ford.[29] Following up this action, Amitay decided to 'make an example of Percy', according to one aide, so that 'no one else would dare to do what Percy did'.[30] Percy's office was flooded with over 20,000 pieces of critical mail before the lobby campaign was over. Remarked Joseph Alsop:

> As a flagrant foreign interference, it further shocked a good many of Israel's staunchest American friends, myself included, and it left a bad taste on Capitol Hill, because of the armtwisting . . . foolishly employed to get the maximum number of Senatorial signatures.[31]

The incident over the 1975 arms sales to Jordan further illustrates some of the mechanics, strategies and weaknesses of the AIPAC lobby. In July 1975, staff members of Senator Clifford Case and Jonathan Bingham passed on to Amitay a Pentagon letter to members of the Senate Foreign Relations and House International Committees, which formally announced the contract of sale for three Hawk anti-aircraft missile batteries to Jordan (to be expanded over a period of four years to a total of 14). Under law, the members of Congress had 20 days to disapprove of the sale. After meeting with Israeli defence attachés, Amitay produced a two-page statement saying that such weapons could be used to 'shield an advancing Jordanian force from air attack'.[32] Amitay sent his statement to all the members of Congress as well as to 397 city and regional Jewish organizations. As phone calls and letters began pouring in, the Americans for Democratic Action, other Jewish organizations, and AIPAC divided up the lobbying duties. Amitay sent out a second memo on 18 July and testified before the Senate Foreign Relations Committee on 21 July. Representative Bingham introduced a bill in the House to block the sale, which acquired almost one hundred cosponsors and was voted out, after an AIPAC-inspired phone blitz. Senator Case introduced a similar bill in the Senate. However, the administration, anxious to remain on good terms with King Hussein, proposed that a stipulation be added onto the sale contract, so that the batteries would be made immobile. Since it was turning out that there was little reason to oppose the sales, both Senator Case and Representative Bingham withdrew their bills. After King Hussein pointedly checked out a Soviet offer for some lower-priced Soviet missiles, the US sales went through.

Again, in 1976, another conflict arose over President Ford's agreement to sell six C-130 troop transport planes to Egypt. Although the lobby campaigned against it, the sale was eventually approved.

There is much to remark in these examples, for AIPAC's task may be getting rougher rather than easier, despite the increased amount of aid recently promised to Israel under the peace treaty. Problems to be overcome include healing the personality conflicts which have been developing since Amitay's arrival as AIPAC's director, as well as bridging the gaps between Washington (AIPAC) and the American Jewish community and the Israeli government.

During the past few years, the Israeli lobby has achieved most of its legislative objectives, including a law that restricts Soviet-American trade — US trade relations being conditional on free emigration for Soviet Jews. Other legislative feats achieved by this lobby were: the letter to President Ford from 76 Senators calling for strong financial aid for Israel at a time when that administration's support for Israel seemed to be eroding; a resolution requesting the examination of US membership in the UN if it expelled Israel; halting American aid to UNESCO because of its anti-Israel actions; legally limiting American business's compliance with the Arab boycott of Israel; the modification or cutting-off of proposed military aid to certain Arab states. Of course, it is impossible to assess proportionately to what extent legislators were motivated by lobbying efforts or by their own personal support of Israel.

The Israeli lobby has lost some key battles, especially since the Carter administration took office. Most significant was perhaps its first major defeat in Congress in the Summer of 1979 over the sale of arms to Egypt and Saudi Arabia. The fact remains that the lobby has demonstrated its enormous power in the US, power far beyond that which one might expect from a Jewish community of about six million people or three per cent of the total American population.

What accounts for this political clout? American Jews participate in the political process to a much greater extent than other minorities. They vote more regularly, they are more active in political campaigns, and they contribute generously to their favourite candidates. Indeed, campaign contributions by American Jews are far more important than their actual voting power (see Table 7.1). Stephen Isaacs, in his *Jews and American Politics*, estimated that Jews have provided about 60 per cent of all campaign funds for Democratic candidates in past elections, and over 40 per cent of Republican campaign funds.[33] *The Congressional Quarterly* said in 1974: 'More than half of over $10,000 contributions to Democratic candidates' came from Jewish contributors. President Carter discovered the extent of American Jewish contributions to the Democratic Party funds when he addressed a fund-raising dinner in Los Angeles, following the US-Soviet joint statement of October 1977. Many of the Jewish contributors were angered by the inclusion in the statement of 'the legitimate rights of the Palestinian people', which many of them regarded as a euphemism for 'the destruction of Israel'. They refused to attend the dinner in protest at Carter's policy, which resulted in half of the $1,000-a-plate tickets not being sold.[34]

Because of the educational, economic, and cultural tradition of the Jewish community in the US, it is rather well represented within the upper-middle strata of the political institutions. Such access to power, which has been denied to many minorities, most obviously influences the decision-making process. In certain instances, policies could be

Table 7.1: The Demographic Distribution of the American Jewish Population

State	Total population	Estimated Jewish population	Estimated Jewish %	Estimated Arab population	Estimated Arab %
Alabama	3,691,000	9,465	0.25	16,200	0.44
Alaska	413,000	190	0.005		
Arizona	2,305,000	20,485	0.89	15,800	3.82
Arkansas	2,152,000	3,065	0.14		
California	2,887,000	693,085	3.16	258,000	1.18
Colorado	2,625,000	25,140	0.95	17,400	0.66
Connecticut	3,107,000	103,730	3.34	30,000	0.97
Delaware	582,000	8,540	1.47		
DC	685,000	15,000	2.19		
Florida	8,466,000	189,280	2.24	42,000	0.50
Georgia	5,041,000	26,310	0.52	25,000	0.50
Hawaii	891,000	1,000	0.11		
Idaho	856,000	500	0.06		
Illinois	11,228,000	283,180	2.52	116,000	1.03
Indiana	5,350,000	24,385	0.46	35,000	0.65
Iowa	2,888,000	7,500	0.26		
Kansas	2,320,000	3,575	0.15	8,500	0.37
Kentucky	3,468,000	11,200	0.32	10,200	0.30
Louisiana	3,930,000	15,630	0.40		
Maine	1,084,000	8,185	0.81		
Maryland	4,137,000	177,115	4.28	39,400	0.95
Massachusetts	5,777,000	229,635	3.97	62,000	1.07
Michigan	9,418,000	97,995	1.04	95,000	1.01
Minnesota	3,980,000	33,565	0.84	26,000	0.65
Mississippi	2,386,000	4,075	0.17		
Missouri	4,822,000	80,685	1.67	33,000	0.68
Montana	766,000	615	0.08		
Nebraska	1,555,000	8,100	0.52		
Nevada	637,000	2,380	0.37		
New Hampshire	850,000	4,260	0.50		
New Jersey	7,338,000	387,220	5.28	44,000	0.60
New Mexico	1,196,000	3,645	0.30		
New York	17,923,000	2,521,755	14.06	195,000	1.09
North Carolina	5,515,000	9,450	0.17	56,000	1.01
Ohio	10,696,000	160,715	1.50		
Oklahoma	2,817,000	6,480	0.23	14,000	0.50
Oregon	2,385,000	9,045	0.38	1,500	0.48
Pennsylvania	11,796,000	443,595	3.76	115,000	0.9
Rhode Island	937,000	23,000	2.45	8,500	0.91
South Carolina	2,878,000	7,285	0.25	9,000	0.38
South Dakota	688,000	520	0.08		
Tennessee	4,292,000	16,710	0.39	16,400	0.38
Texas	12,806,000	65,520	0.51		
Utah	1,270,000	1,650	0.60	9,000	0.71
Vermont	482,000	2,330	0.48		
Virginia	5,095,000	37,350	0.73	51,000	1.00
Washington	3,681,000	15,485	0.42		
West Virginia	1,853,000	4,760	0.26	15,800	0.85
Wisconsin	4,610,000	32,295	0.70	49,500	1.07
Wyoming	406,000	710	0.18		

Source: *Statistical Abstract of the United States*, 100th Edition (US Department of Commerce, Bureau of Census), pp. 14 and 54. Irving J. Sloan (ed.), *The Jews in America* (Dobbs Ferry, NY: Ocean Publications, 1971), pp. 14-21.

shaped by such influences (though this is not to infer that the Jewish community is monolithic even on such issues as the direction and future of Israel). Jews, very understandably, believe they must involve themselves politically to obviate repercussions of a regenerated anti-Semitism, if that should ever prevail in the US as it once did in Europe. While Jewish contributions are given to promote many interests, they are not given to a candidate who opposes Israel, regardless of the remainder of his platform.

The pro-Israel strength in Congress is so extensive that various administrations have utilized it to assist in promoting legislation on other issues. Aid for the *junta* which controlled Greece was argued on the grounds that the US needed support facilities in Greece for the security of Israel. To ensure Congressional approval, aid ear-marked for Cambodia was attached to foreign assistance legislation for Israel.[35] Political candidates usually make an ostentatious contest over who would be a better friend of Israel, and if elected they try to surpass their opponents in the extent of support they have demonstrated for Israel. The 1972 Nixon-McGovern presidential race and the 1976 Ford-Carter contests manifest these points.[36]

Other Factors

Israel's support in the US is not limited to the Jewish community, rather it extends to a significant proportion of the articulate public. Ever since Jews began immigrating to the US at the end of the last century, they have been in the forefront of American liberal and labour movements and have forged strong ties.

It is not only American Jews who pressure the government to support Israel's interests. George Meany and Lane Kirkland, the AFL-CIO leaders, black leaders, Vernon Jordan of the National Urban League, Benjamin Hooks of the NAACP, UN Ambassador Andrew Young, the National Council of Churches and organized Catholic and Protestant groups have long supported Israeli interests.

It is quite clear that domestic support of Israel goes well beyond the boundaries of Israeli and American-Jewish lobbying groups. There is a strong sentiment in American moderate and liberal circles (and often among conservatives as well) that Israel is a nation 'in the image' of the US: 'democratic', 'progressive', and western in outlook. Certain American fundamentalist groups even regard the establishment of Israel as the fulfillment of biblical prophecy. In addition, Israel is perceived by many American supporters as an essential, strategic ally in an unstable region, the 'bulwark against communism and radical nationalism' in the Middle East.[38]

Beyond the identifiable and distinct sources of Israel's backers, there is the entire domestic political environment that surrounds the government's policy-making system. The ability of pro-Israel groups to marshall and maintain the support of the mass media, public opinion and a broad cross-section of American associations (such as the afore-mentioned organized interest groups) have enabled them to disseminate their views far beyond their own organizational structures. These groups, and Israel, are conscious of such power and never hesitate to use it. Neither is the opposition allowed to forget its control. Israeli Ambassador Dinitz threatened Kissinger with unleashing its wrath during the 1973 October War when American arms were delayed in resupplying Israel.[39] Another case in point was that of Senator Charles Percy (R-Ill.) who, after his return from visiting the Middle East in 1975, publicly called upon Israel to negotiate with the PLO and further warned that the Israelis could no longer count on automatic majorities in the Congress. In response to his statements, Percy received a massive amount of mail denouncing his position. This forced him to cancel previous engagements so that he could go back to Illinois to mollify angry Jewish constituents and fund-raisers. One of Percy's aides who is Jewish and supportive of the Senator's resistance to the Israeli lobby, commented: 'There were some meetings in Chicago when I wondered if we'd get out unharmed.'[40]

William Quandt, in *Decade of Decisions*, pointed out that pro-Israeli groups are often most influential when they do nothing at all to influence policy. Merely their existence is sufficient to constrain the actions of policy-makers. What Carl J. Friedrich, in *Man and His Government*, defines as the 'law of anticipated reaction' is applicable to this situation. Various courses of action are frequently rejected because of expected negative reaction from pro-Israeli groups and their supporters in Congress.[41] This is perhaps the plausible explanation for President Carter's halt in his efforts to accommodate the PLO in 1979. Furthermore, the White House, concerned about reaction to the administration's Middle East policy, recently began to publish a weekly summary of the Jewish press. This publication exists for internal use only, and is similar to the President's daily news summary of domestic and foreign events. The Jewish news round-up is drawn from all US Jewish publications as well as *The Jerusalem Post*.[42] This is a recognition by the White House of the domestic strength of pro-Israeli groups. It is an indication of the part these groups play in determining US-Palestinian policy. If American interests remain relatively constant (and the global situation is not

completely transformed), this influence will certainly continue to domi-
nate as long as a significant countervailing pressure remains absent.

Foreign Pressures

In addition to the pressures brought to bear by domestic groups, the
United States – or indeed any other nation – responds to the actions
and demands of other actors in the international system. This response
may take the form of acquiescence to, or refusal of, a demand or
request, or simply a negative reaction to others' actions or policy. There
are a number of foreign factors which have been brought to bear on US
Palestinian policy, including pressures from the governments of Israel,
the Arab States and other nations as well as from the Palestinians themselves.

The Israeli Government

Israel as a state, and independent of its lobby, has a certain, though
measurable, amount of influence on US policy towards the Palestinians. This influence is born out of the 'special relationship' that
characterizes the nature of relations between the two states.[43]

Although it has been the United States which has played the bene-
factor role in supplying Israel with billions of dollars worth of economic and military assistance (in addition to allowing the tax-deductible
status of private contributions to Israel) over the past years, interest-
ingly it is rather Israel that has more influence over American policy
toward the Palestinians than the reverse. This dearth of American
influence and the complementary, disproportionate Israeli influence
on the American policy process *vis-à-vis* the Palestinians is not only
due to the significance of domestic pressure in favour of Israel, but
also to the prevalent, if illusory, conception – particularly among
conservatives and fundamentalist Christian groups – that Israel is the
bastion of pro-American anti-communism in the Middle East. An
increasing number of Americans reject this conception of Israel's role
in the Middle East and actually see Israel as the irritant which forced
many of the Arab states to turn away from the United States and towards the only other superpower capable of supplying them with the
money and materials for their defence.

Another public misconception which may underlie Israel's ability
both to resist any American pressure and to bring pressure upon the
United States is the contention that only a strong and perfectly secure

Israel can reasonably be expected to make any concessions on the Palestinian issue. Yet Israel has decisively won four wars, has obtained virtually all the sophisticated weaponry it has requested from the United States, possesses undoubted military superiority, was able to hold by military occupation an area which increased its size by 250 per cent, and has neutralized Egypt, its most powerful enemy. But measured by its willingness to make genuine concessions on the Palestinian question, Israel is less secure than ever.

As early as 1949, in a note to Israeli Prime Minister Ben Gurion, President Truman expressed his disappointment at Israel's failure to make any of the desired concessions on the Palestinian territory and its refugees. Truman thought Israel should allow, at the very least, the return of 200,000 refugees. He termed Israel's attitude as dangerous to peace, and implied a threat that the US would reconsider its attitude towards Israel (see Chapter 3). Israel rejected the American appeal and argued against the return of the refugees. Subsequently, the United States retreated from that position. Furthermore, following the second Palestinian exodus of 1967, the US made a strong appeal to Israel for the return of the refugees to the West Bank and Gaza. Israel permitted the return of only slightly less than ten per cent of those who had fled from the West Bank and Gaza (see also Chapter 3). A more recent example of Israeli influence on US policy positions is the veto power given to Israel by Kissinger over PLO participation in the peace talks, and his commitment that the US would not negotiate with the PLO unless it recognized Israel's right to exist. This is not to suggest that the United States has never successfully exerted pressure on Israel, although, as former Under-Secretary of State George Ball has noted, the last time such a thing occurred was when Eisenhower compelled the Israelis to withdraw from Sinai after the Suez War in 1956. Observation of American diplomatic behaviour over the past thirty years suggests that the United States will avoid exerting pressure on Israel whenever possible.[44]

Not only does Israel enjoy the position of being able successfully to influence the United States in the area of Middle East policy, it also guards jealously its traditional position as the only major nation involved in the Arab-Israeli conflict to have such influence. When, after the October War of 1973, the United States began to develop cordial relations with Sadat of Egypt, the Israelis became concerned. In response to this concern, American officials took great pains to reassure the Israelis that this special relationship would not be adversely affected by the increasing rapport with Egypt or any other friendly Arab country.

Assistant Secretary of State Harold Saunders, during an appearance before the House Subcommittee on Europe and the Middle East on 12 June 1978, emphasized that the United States was definitely not reducing its support for Israel in favour of the Arab nations. Saunders explained that:

> close relations with one party do not mean diminished relations with others. None of our friends, nor we, will gain from a diminished U.S. relationship with any of the key states there. To the contrary, a closer relationship with each party enhances our ability to pursue objectives common to all.[45]

Arab Governments

The Arab governments which have the most direct impact on US Middle East policy are Saudi Arabia, Egypt, Syria and Jordan. Other than Saudi Arabia — which is becoming a major financial power with the means to affect the American economy, and which exerts leverage on most of the Arab countries involved in the Middle Eastern conflict through extensive financial support — these countries have been military participants in the thirty year-old conflict with Israel.

The Saudis have increasingly played a larger role in peace negotiations, and have proved to be a moderating force upon the Arab governments and the major Palestinian groups. Indeed, since 1973 the Saudi capital has become a frequent stop for American Secretaries of State on trips to the area to resume negotiations. King Faisal and his successors have consistently urged the American administrations to accommodate the Palestinians and recognize their right to self-determination. Following the 1973 October War, King Faisal, meeting with Secretary of State Kissinger, asked that the Palestinians be allowed to return to their homeland in exchange for lifting the oil embargo; Kissinger had asked the King to lift the embargo, and Faisal responded, 'I should like to rescind it immediately. I, too, am in a difficult position. It would be easier if the United States would announce that Israel must withdraw and permit the Palestinians to return to their homes.'[46] Kissinger complained that this would cause a strong reaction and asked Faisal to reflect. King Khaled and Crown Prince Fahd, the current policy-makers of Saudi Arabia, seem to be slightly more malleable and co-operative with the United States than their predecessors. It is possible that King Khaled and Crown Prince Fahd are reluctant to apply strong pressure to the United States because they fear that the United States has sufficient power in Saudi Arabia to promote a rival group in the royal family or in the army, and thus undermine the present regime.

It is clear that, taken together, the Arab oil-producing nations could exert enormous influence on the process by which American policy toward the Middle East is made. Saudi Arabia and other Arab oil producers have repeatedly demanded that the Palestinians be granted the right of self-determination and that the Israelis return the occupied lands, particularly Jerusalem. So far their potential power to affect US policy and their apparent willingness to do so have not been combined into an effective tool of influence other than the 1973 oil embargo. Officials of these nations seem to feel that the most productive approach is through persuasion rather than strong-arm tactics. Saudi Arabia in particular follows the approach of making clear that they have the power to affect the American economy, and using that potential weapon to influence the United States. This Saudi tactic has been neutralized by America's continual capacity to persuade the Saudis that it is doing the best it can and that no greater efforts are possible under the current circumstances. 'Current circumstances' seem to be a never-ending cycle of American Presidential elections, Congressional elections, and Israeli Knesset elections.

If the Arab oil-producing states were seriously interested in influencing American policy, they could apply a gradual progression of sanctions starting with the withholding of bank deposits and Treasury note purchases with surplus petrodollars, proceeding to the reduction of trade by degrees to only the most essential products, and actual withdrawal of existing bank deposits and Treasury notes, and finally coming to successive ten per cent drops in oil exports to the United States. There can be little doubt about the potency of such steps given that: the estimated petrodollar surplus for 1980 of the OPEC nations is $115 billion, two-thirds of which is Arab nations' surpluses;[47] the total Arab import of US products for 1979 was $11.05 billion (particularly significant considering that the overall US trade deficit for 1979 was $37.29 billion); it is estimated that Arab investment, deposits and Treasury notes in the United States amount to $130 billion; and the US economy is increasingly dependent upon oil imports from the Arab nations.[48] However, the United States seems to proceed on the assumption that such steps will never be taken because these states need the United States more than it needs them.

Syria, and up to 1979 Egypt, have always insisted on American recognition of the Palestinian right to self-determination and have urged US negotiations with the PLO. They stressed that the Palestine problem must be recognized as the crux of the entire Arab-Israeli conflict. During and after the negotiations for disengagement both Egypt and Syria impressed upon the US the importance, for the peace process and for the region, of American recognition of the Palestinians as an independent entity and the necessity of involving the PLO in that process.[49] Syrian President Assad gained Kissinger's acquiescence for the participation of the PLO in a debate on the Palestinian question in the UN Security Council in January 1976. Further Arab pressures on the US surely affected the Saunders document, which defined the Palestinian dimension as the heart of the Arab-Israeli conflict (see Chapter 5). After 1977 Sadat began to change his position on the Palestinian issue and in 1979 he took upon both himself and his Camp David partners the responsibility of deciding the Palestinians' fate for them and reneged upon his support for the establishment of an independent Palestinian state.

Jordanian pressure on the United States was unsurpassed by other Arab states: King Hussein tried to gain US backing for his proposed 'United Arab Kingdom' plan. This plan envisioned that upon the West Bank being returned to Jordan by Israel, a referendum would be held to offer the Palestinians federation with Jordan. Hussein also hoped to prevent the US from recognizing the PLO as the legitimate representative of the Palestinian people or from recognizing a Palestinian government in exile.[50] The King is a longtime friend of the American government, and it is clear that it prefers to deal with him than with the PLO. Although the US did not endorse the 'United Arab Kingdom' plan, the Carter administration made public its preference for some kind of a Palestinian entity to be affiliated with Jordan.

International Factors

The Palestinians have not only managed to survive two wars in Jordan and Lebanon within a six-year period, but have also succeeded in gaining official recognition and prominence in the international community. At a myriad of international conferences (such as the Islamic Summit Conference in Algiers in 1973, among others), resolutions were passed that reaffirmed the right of the Palestinians to self-determination. Also the PLO has gained full membership in the League of Arab States, the Afro-Asian Conference, the Non-Aligned Conference, UNESCO, the International Labor Organization, observer status at the United Nations, and in the Organization of African Unity.

The question of Palestinian political and human rights is frequently discussed at international summit meetings. Hope for resolution of the problem is often expressed by joint communiqués emanating from these meetings, including the Ford-Brezhnev summit at Vladivostock in 1974, and the Carter-Tito, Carter-Ceausescu summits in 1978 in Washington. The United States found itself in the lone company of such countries as Israel, Haiti and Bolivia in the United Nations voting on Middle East questions. With 89 nations voting in favour of and only one against UN General Assembly Resolution 3237, recognizing the PLO as the sole legitimate representative of the Palestinians, and with PLO diplomatic missions in over 65 countries, the United States has felt increasingly at odds with the international community concerning legitimate Palestinian rights. At a time when it is in a state of tension with the Soviet Union, the American government has found it politically necessary to mellow its pro-Israel stance.

United States Palestinian policy has also caused some degree of American isolation from its European and Far Eastern friends, whose stake in the security and stability of the Middle East is even greater than that of the United States. The Europeans are ambivalent about the Camp David process, and the June 1980 joint statement on Palestinian rights by the members of the European community was a means of voicing their interest in a more equitable and practical approach to the Arab-Israeli conflict. Most European nations have gone much further than the United States in supporting the inalienable rights of the Palestinian people and in establishing cordial official relations with the PLO, while the United States supports only certain Palestinian rights and has no official relationship with the PLO. These policy differences with its closest friends and allies are likely to be even more influential on American policy than is the general international isolation which has resulted from US Middle East policy.

The Palestinians

The United States has been intertwined with the Palestinian problem from the very early months of the tragedy of 1948. It has observed their growth and advancement into a more united people, despite their dispersion. Palestinians constitute the most educated and highly-trained people in the Arab world. However, the US did not have to deal directly with solving their problem of having been forcibly removed from the land. Instead, it dealt only with the Arab governments, who had appointed themselves as trustees for Palestinian interests in the conflict. After the 1967 war, the Palestinians threw off that mantle of trusteeship and emerged as an independent force with which the US had to reckon. This phenomenon had an impact on regional and international circumstances. The following factors could be cited as being partially responsible for the changes in American attitudes and policies towards the Palestinians.

(1) Despite tremendous attempts to liquidate them, in Jordan and in Lebanon, the Palestinian people have shown determination and a great capacity to survive. The United States has been impressed with the varied political, social, economic, and educational institutions they have created and maintained for their people which exhibit this same will of survival.

(2) Both Palestinians inside the 'Green line' and in the diaspora have overwhelmingly supported the PLO. Its position as legitimate spokesman of the Palestinian people is well recognized and relatively unchallenged internationally.

(3) Palestinian violence, which was used primarily to draw attention to their problem and to achieve recognition of their rights, consequently infers that continued non-recognition remains a major source of violence. This portends further upheaval and instability with grave consequences for the entire region. Not only does the United States fear the destabilizing effects of direct Palestinian violence in and out of the region, but also the potential impact of actions by the thousands of Palestinians — many of them highly placed — living in the Arab states of the Gulf in the event of greater menace to the Palestinian liberation movement, or even just continued failure to resolve the issue. There are indications that, in response to this potential threat to vital American interests in the Gulf, the Pentagon has undertaken studies to determine the nature and extent of relations between Palestinians working in the Gulf area and the PLO.

(4) Most importantly, the main leadership of the PLO has shifted its position. It has reduced its demands for a Palestinian state in all of Palestine to that of accepting, in all probability, a state only in the West Bank and Gaza. It has given *de facto* recognition to UN Security Council Resolution 242 by agreeing to go to Geneva, if invited, since Resolution 242 is the basis for negotiations at the Geneva Conference; *de facto* recognition of Resolution 242 means also *de facto* recognition of the State of Israel. The December 1977 PLO statement from Tripoli rejecting Resolution 242 and Geneva can only be seen as a political attempt to improve relations among the rejectionists in the Arab world, particularly in light of President Sadat's visit to Jerusalem and his defection from the Arab front. Subsequent PLO statements from Beirut and specifically from Yasser Arafat have indicated that the PLO would

accept a sovereign Palestinian state in Gaza and the West Bank, which would not threaten Israel's security.[51] The Carter administration termed Arafat's statement helpful but not sufficient to establish direct talks with the PLO.

The role of pressure groups — both foreign and domestic — on the formulation of American policy towards the Middle East and the Palestinians is obviously significant, but generally the policy-makers' perceptions of vital national interest supercede all other factors. Whenever any administration perceives that a particular decision is critical from the point of view of military or economic security, all efforts by other governments or pressure groups are neutralized. Major examples include Roosevelt's successful efforts to get Congress to shelve the 1944 pro-Zionist resolution, Eisenhower's adamant insistence on Israeli withdrawal from the Sinai and Gaza in 1956-7, and decisions by several administrations to sell weapons to friendly Arab states such as Jordan, Saudi Arabia and Egypt.

Notes

1. The oil companies do not exert any significant pressure or have any significant effect on US Middle-East policymaking. See Robert Trice, *Congress and the Arab-Israeli Conflict*, and Quandt, *Decade of Decisions*.

2. The purpose of this section is not to examine the Israeli interest groups in the United States, but rather to point out their significance and impact on foreign policy decision-making with regard to the Palestinians. For a comprehensive discussion of the Israeli lobby see Reich, *Quest for Peace*, pp. 349-464, and Russell W. Howe and Sarah H. Trott, *The Power Peddlers* (Garden City, New York: Doubleday & Co., Inc., 1977), pp. 271-361.

3. Lynn Elmehdaoui and Nancy Jo Nelson, *Perspectives on the Israeli Lobby* (unpublished paper, Georgetown University, Washington, DC, 1979). The contributions of Miss Elmehdaoui and Miss Nelson were vital to this section.

4. *National Journal*, 8 January 1972, p. 63.

5. Howe and Trott, *Power Peddlers*, p. 288.

6. US Congress, Senate Committee on Foreign Relations. *Activities of Non-diplomatic Representatives of Foreign Principals in the United States*. 88th Cong., 1st sess., 1 August 1963, Part 12 (Washington: US Government Printing Office, 1963), p. 1780.

7. Howe and Trott, *Power Peddlers*, p. 26.

8. *National Journal*, 1972, p. 64.

9. Ibid., p. 65.

10. Ibid., p. 62.

11. Stephen Isaacs, 'Jewish Lobby, Part of American Texture', *Washington Post*, 23 November 1974.

12. William J. Lanouette, *National Journal*, 13 May 1978, p. 755.

13. Ibid., p. 752.

14. Howe and Trott, *Power Peddlers*, p. 349.

15. *National Journal*, 1972, p. 71.

16. David Garnham, 'Factors Influencing Congressional Support for Israel During the 93rd Congress'.

17. Lanouette, *National Journal*, p. 755.

18. Ibid., p. 63.

19. Isaacs, 'Jewish Lobby'.

20. Sanford J. Ungar, 'Washington: Jewish and Arab Lobbyists', *Harpers*, April 1978, p. 10.

21. Ibid., p. 10.

22. Eric Rouleau, 'Carter and the Jewish Lobby', *Manchester Guardian Weekly*, July 1977.

23. Ungar, 'Washington: Jewish and Arab Lobbyists', p. 10.

24. Howe and Trott, *Power Peddlers*, p. 228.

25. Ibid., p. 233.

26. Ibid.

27. Ibid.

28. Ibid., p. 316.

29. Ibid., p. 273.

30. Ibid., p. 276.

31. Garnham, 'Factors Influencing Congressional Support for Israel', p. 25.

32. Howe and Trott, *Power Peddlers*, p. 295.

33. For a detailed discussion of the significance of American Jews and their impact on the American political process, see Stephen D. Isaacs, *Jews and American Politics*, (Garden City, New York: Doubleday & Co., 1974).

34. *The Washington Post*, 6 October 1977, p. 8.

35. Reich, *Quest for Peace*, p. 431.

36. Ibid., pp. 431-3.

37. The American Jewish community is obviously heterogeneous. It is composed of a large number of groups ranging from right wing Zionists whose support is unwavering, to the anti-Zionist group, Jewish Alternative to Zionism, headed by Rabbi Elmer Berger, who supports the political, national, and human rights of the Palestinians and the PLO, though with some reservations. A large number of the Jewish community sympathize with the Palestinian plight, though it would be safe to say that a majority is opposed to the PLO. For further discussions on this subject see Reich, *Quest for Peace* and Howe and Trott, *Power Peddlers*.

38. See Reich, *Quest for Peace*, pp. 365-9 for further elaboration on American support for Israel.

39. Kalb and Kalb, *Kissinger*, pp. 537-8.

40. Howe and Trott, *Power Peddlers*, p. 273.

41. Quandt, *Decade of Decisions*, Chapter I, and Carl J. Friedrich, *Man and His Government*, (New York: McGraw and Hill, 1963), Chapter II.

42. *The Middle East Observer*, 1 January 1978, p. 2.

43. For a discussion of the American-Israeli relationship see Reich, *Quest for Peace*.

44. For a detailed discussion of American-Israeli relations see ibid., and Association of Arab-American University Graduates, *The United States, Israel and the Arab States*, Information Series, no. 3 (Chicago, Illinois: AAUG, December 1970), and Quandt, *Decade of Decisions*.

45. 'Annual Review of U.S. Policy in the Middle East', statement by Assistant Secretary Harold H. Saunders before the House Subcommittee on Europe and the Middle East, 12 June 1978, Department of State, Washington, DC, 12 June 1978, p. 13.

46. Sheehan, *Foreign Policy*, p. 20.

47. CBS News Reports, 12 June 1980.

48. *Highlights of U.S. Export and Import Trade*, US Department of Commerce, Bureau of Census Report FT990/December 1979, (US Government Printing Office, Washington, DC) pp. 11, 39-40, and 88-9.

49. Sadat broke relations with the PLO after they denounced his trip to Jerusalem. He invited some West Bank and Gaza leaders to Cairo to co-ordinate peace negotiating efforts. This was understood to be an attempt on Sadat's part to find an alternative Palestinian leadership to the PLO. Additionally, he has retreated from his interpretation of Palestinian self-determination — from that of their right to form an independent state to the position that this does not have to include an independent state.

49. Although King Hussein accepted publicly the Rabat Summit decision about the PLO representing the Palestinians, he does not recognize it as the Palestinian representative of the Palestinians living in areas under his control.

51. *New York Times*, 2 May 1978, p. 1. There are those, including many Israelis, who assert that the PLO's acceptance of a Palestinian state in the West Bank and Gaza is not a modification in its position and merely represents the first stage of strategy which still aims at the ultimate recovery of all of mandated Palestine. Israel rejects the establishment of a Palestinian state in the West Bank and Gaza even if the PLO Charter were to be amended. The PLO has refused to amend that part of its charter, Article 6, which calls for the destruction of Israel as a Jewish state, reasoning that to do so under outside pressure would constitute an unacceptable interference in their internal affairs. However, Palestine National Council decisions of the last few years, accepting a Palestinian state in any part of Palestine, are considered by many Palestinians as the equivalent of an amendment to the PLO charter.

It is interesting to note that, while the US had earlier demanded an amendment to the Palestinian National Charter as a prerequisite for direct talks with the PLO, now it appears that amendment of the charter is no longer a precondition of such contact. Carter had indicated that PLO recognition of UN Security Council Resolution 242 would suffice. See *The Voice*, vol. 5, p. 1.

8 CONCLUSION

American involvement in the question of Palestine dates back to the early part of this century. In the pre-1948 period the American part in the Palestinian-Zionist-British conflict was minimal. Although American policy supported Zionist aspirations, the United States did not become actively involved in the affairs of Palestine until the end of World War II. Such policy as there was took cognizance of Palestine as a territory. As for the Palestinians themselves, they were treated as a non-people.

From 1948 to 1980 American policy toward the Palestinians passed through three distinct phases that in retrospect seem little more than tactical shifts to accommodate changing circumstances. The first phase, between 1948 and 1967, was a policy of pacification. Humanitarian concerns were combined with a fear that the refugee problems would unleash political and economic chaos in the region. The United States faithfully continued its financial support of UNRWA and developed detailed economic proposals for refugee resettlement outside the home-land – proposals for the most part technically sound but politically unrealistic.

During the second phase of American policy towards the Palestinians, lasting from 1967 to 1976, the emphasis shifted to confrontation. The United States condemned as terrorism the guerrilla actions taken against targets inside and outside Israel, and developed anti-terrorist tactics. Nevertheless, towards the end of the period, the United States began to recognize a Palestinian national entity 'with legitimate rights and aspirations'.

During the third phase of policy, 1976-80, the American stance shifted further towards a grudging accommodation of the Palestinians, as it became clear that peace could not last without their participation. The United States thus acknowledged the legitimate rights of the Palestinian people, including the right to a homeland. It still refused, however, to recognize their right to self-determination. The US made a brief but unsuccessful attempt to deal directly with the PLO and to include the Palestinians in peace talks. It failed to engage the Palestinians in the autonomy talks precisely because the Camp David accords narrowly defined autonomy to exclude true self-determination. Instead it devised a formula that Palestinians perceived as a lethal threat to their rights and survival as a people.

Just as American conceptions of an acceptable solution to the Middle East problem changed from 1948 to 1980, so did those of the Palestinians. In 1947 the United States voted for UN General Assembly Resolution 181 providing for an independent Palestinian state alongside Israel. Understandably the Palestinians unequivocally rejected this resolution (see Figures 1.1-1.4). Only in 1978 did PLO Chairman Yasser Arafat express Palestinian acceptance of a settlement based on UN resolutions, including Resolution 181. Meanwhile, the United States recanted its support of Resolution 181 and other UN resolutions providing for Palestinian refugee repatriation. Instead the United States wanted to resettle Palestinians outside their homeland. These changes in American policy only fed Palestinian suspicions.

While specific US policy toward the Palestinians shifted uncertainly toward accommodation, quite another trend was evident in overall US policy towards the Middle East. During the 1948-67 period the United States concentrated on solving what it regarded as primarily a refugee problem. By solving the refugee problem, it could encourage a settlement between Israel and the Arab states. Policy towards the Palestinians, albeit only as refugees, took centre stage. After this approach failed, the United States tried the reverse strategy. It sought to settle differences between the various states first, and hoped that the Palestinian problem would work itself out later. The American reasoning here rested on the assumption that the Palestinians would obligingly go along with whatever the Arab states might work out for them. This approach assigned the Palestinians a less central role in US policy-making than before, even though the Palestinian problem remained at the hub of the Middle East conflict.

American spokesmen made much of these tactical shifts in US policy, ascribing to each a strong symbolic importance. Words became grave portents of policy. Between 1917 and 1978, US references to the Palestinians evolved from the 'non-Jewish population of Palestine', 'Arab refugees', and 'Arab terrorists' to 'Palestinian terrorists', 'Palestinians', a 'Palestinian entity', and finally the 'Palestinian people'. The object of US policy actions evolved from 'Palestine, a mandated territory', 'repatriation and compensation or resettlement and integration', 'justice for the refugees', and 'anti-terrorism' to 'Palestinian interests', 'legitimate Palestinian interests', and finally 'legitimate rights and a homeland for the Palestinian people and participation in the determination of their own future'. The US government studiously avoided giving these terms a precise operational definition. Indeed, part of their usefulness was their ambiguity, by which they could suggest changes in policy orientation without specific policy content. The tactic was effective in persuading Arab governments and public opinion of motion and flexibility in US policy.

While tactics shifted, certain themes remained constant. The United States persistently sought to contain the Arab-Israeli conflict, to pacify the recalcitrant Palestinian liberation movement, and to provide full support to Israel. Above all, the American perception of its interests in the Middle East remained remarkably constant, even as alliances, partnerships and adversaries changed.

As America's new imperial role and vital interests grew, so did its involvement in the Middle East and Palestinian affairs. American decision-makers tailored their Palestinian policy — central to much of Middle East policy — to protect and promote their perceived interests. The United States penetrated, shaped and controlled the political and economic structures of a dozen nominally independent Arab states. The tools were numerous and sophisticated, ranging from military aid, training and equipment for loyal regimes to foreign aid for ports and communications and the cultivation of elite classes growing rich from dealings with American corporations. At times the chosen instrument was a CIA network or outright bribery of officials. At other times 'free world' cultural and ideological propaganda and the effervescent wonders of Coca-Cola sufficed. Finally, direct US intervention was used to keep friendly regimes in power, in Iran in 1953, in Lebanon in 1958, and in Jordan in 1970.

Cultural and strategic interests only reinforced the huge US economic stake in the Middle East, particularly in oil, consumer goods, markets and access to surplus petrodollars. The American position came under increasing attack. Soviet influence rose and fell, marking a nadir in 1979 as Sadat became a fully-fledged American ally. Soviet policy generally supported radical regimes, provided them with external economic and military aid and supported national liberation movements.

The increasing aspirations of Arab countries to control their own resources and to choose their own friends posed a further threat to US domination of the region. The influence of the Arab liberation movements, in which Palestinian liberation forces were extremely active, rose steadily. Responding to both the Soviet and Arab revolutionary threat, the United States froze the Russians out of the negotiations, consolidated conservative Arab regimes, and sent yet more aid to Israel.

Particularly in the Arab world, commentators ascribed perfervid US support of Israel to the activities of the US Jewish community. Important as that domestic constituency was, other factors also bound Israel and the United States together. Both had common enemies in the Soviet Union and the Arab liberation movement. Both had a stake in the *status quo* and access to oil and markets. The United States helped build Israel's military machine into a regional surrogate. Israel assumed the role of junior partner to the United States, acting both as conquering power and regional gendarme on the side of counter-revolutionary forces, as its role in Lebanon illustrated. Conflicts of interest nevertheless persisted between Israel's ceaseless quest to expand its settlements and the quiet preference of the US State Department and corporations to maintain the *status quo*. US arms made Israel far less vulnerable to attack and also intransigent and overweening, creating numerous embarrassments in US relations with the Arab states. 'In Israel we have created ourselves a monster', said NATO chief Alexander Haig despairingly.[1]

US and Arab government interests both conflicted and converged. Points of essential agreement were oil supply, financial markets and weapon supply. Divergences arose over Israel — its occupation of Arab lands and its uprooting of the Palestinian people. Washington hoped for order and security in the Middle East and supplied arms to both the Arabs and Israel, a policy that also kept weapons research contracts coming, arms factories rolling and profits flowing. Petrodollars paid for Arab weapons, US taxpayers' dollars for Israeli weapons.

US policy also created points of conflict with Western Europe and Japan, which are more dependent on Middle East oil, trade and investment. The Europeans and Japanese went much further than the United States in recognizing the PLO and the Palestinian right to self-determination.

The American public, too, has shown signs of restiveness regarding US policy in the Middle East and its obvious double standards. The United States cut off arms to Turkey after it used them illegally in Cyprus, but looked the other way as Israeli pilots flew US-provided aircraft to bomb villages in southern Lebanon and as Israel resold US warplanes on the international weapons market in flagrant violation of US military assistance law. US willingness to talk and negotiate with such disparate groups as the Zimbabwe liberation organizations, the National Liberation Front of South Vietnam, and even the ex-terrorist Menachem Begin of Israel also stood ill beside the refusal to talk officially with the PLO. To gain the privilege of talking with the United States, the PLO had to give up in advance its most crucial negotiating position — recognition of Israel's right to exist. Far from being required to make a reciprocal recognition in advance of negotiations, Israel was not even required to recognize the Palestinians' right to choose their own representatives to the negotiations (for Israel had already refused to deal with any Palestinian representative who is a member of the PLO). Even worse, Israel denied that the Palestinians have a right to self-determination which could legitimaty culminate in the establishment of a sovereign Palestinian state. Israel continued to explicitly deny that such a state has the right to exist.

Another contradiction in American policy was highlighted by its firm and repeated denunciation of Soviet forces in Afghanistan. Although the Israeli army had occupied the Golan Heights, the West Bank and Gaza for thirteen years, and had repeatedly violated both human rights and international law in their occupation policies, there was never a direct criticism of the occupation itself, much less any suggestion of a boycott.

Israel was cited for systematic violation of human rights in the occupied lands by a myriad of organizations, including the United Nations Commission on Human Rights, the London *Sunday Times*, the Swiss League of Human Rights and Amnesty International. Yet despite the Carter administration's attempt to project strong support for human rights internationally, the United States refused even to acknowledge that Israel had systematically violated the human rights of the Palestinians, much less criticise or withhold aid. Blatant Israeli violations of international law — the illegal expropriation of over 30 per cent of the land of the West Bank and Gaza since 1967, and the continuous creation of illegal civilian settlements in these areas — were greeted by the United States with nothing more than verbal criticism.

A final example of the double standard of American policy applied to the Palestinians and to Israel dates back to the 1950s when the United States began to call for the Arab countries in which Palestinian refugees were located to resettle them and offer them citizenship. American policy-makers were convinced of the reasonableness of this demand, and it was difficult to understand why, if such a demand could be made of the Arabs up to 1967, it could not be made of the Israelis since 1967, particularly when one considers that the Israeli government actually controlled the lands and homes from which these refugees were originally driven. Indeed, after 1967 Arab governments were still being asked to resettle Palestinian refugees although no similar demands were made of Israel.

US policy presented a façade of moralism and humanitarianism for public consumption, but after thirty years the façade was wearing thin. The US administration rationalized their policies as best they could to bring about a comprehensive peace. They saw ultimate peace producing

Arab recognition of Israel, containment of Arab progressive movements, an end to Soviet influence in the Middle East, the growth of trade and financial relationships with the Arabs and a pledge by the Arab states to keep down oil prices. As for Israel, it would give back some occupied Arab lands and accept a 'Palestinian autonomy'. Israel would then benefit immensely. It would get open borders, an end of the Arab economic boycott, an end to international isolation, and the establishment of economic relations with the Arab states which would probably lead to joint economic ventures and inflows of Arab surplus petrodollars. Israel would probably also retain or even enhance its military power and expand its role as a regional policeman against any revolutionary movement. Such were the hopes in Washington. But the conflict between the Arabs and Israel was too sharp to allow such wholesale Arab-Israeli co-operation to occur without Israel abandoning its Zionist policies and claim to all of Palestine. American policies would have to change as well. In 1980 these scenarios seemed most likely:

A change in Jordan which would bring about a return of Palestinian commando bases and the escalation of guerrilla warfare from Jordan as well as southern Lebanon. Prolonged incursions would bleed Israel sufficiently to make it resort to desperate action such as the use of tactical nuclear weapons, or invasion and occupation of Jordan and south Lebanon and perhaps parts of Syria as well, if Syria became involved. Invasion and further occupation of Arab lands would inevitably bring in the Soviet Union to check Israeli expansion and assist the Arabs in regaining their lands. A confrontation between the United States and the Soviet Union would become a real possibility. The greater the threat of Israeli tactical nuclear weapons, the more the Arabs would be forced to acquire them as deterrents. The whole region would step to the brink of a holocaust.

Another scenario has some Arab regimes — with US and Israeli blessings — attempting physically to liquidate the PLO in Lebanon, forcing the whole movement underground to initiate a guerrilla campaign against American and Israeli companies, personnel and installations, as well as the Arab regimes allied with the United States. With the whole region in turmoil, oil supply and economic activities would be jeopardized, threatening an explosion of unpredictable magnitude.

Another real possibility is that continued occupation of Syrian and Palestinian lands, with the elimination of Egypt from the Arab front, would lead to Syrian preparations for military action. Syria would need Soviet backing for any military move, at least air cover. Such a situation could cause Israel to strike pre-emptively. With Soviet involvement, a cease-fire might not materialize before liberation of at least a portion of the Arab lands. The United States would come in to defend Israel and its conquests and lead once more to superpower confrontation with possible disastrous consequences.

American policies are largely responsible for the precipitation of any of these disasters. American decisions related to the Palestinian question have sought an illusory 'quick fix' treatment to generate domestic political support for foreign policy 'successes' while temporarily defusing a dangerous situation. While such approaches can sometimes prevent war, they do not produce peace. Indeed, indefinitely postponing a genuine resolution can even increase the power of the eventual explosion.

The Camp David agreements are a setback to a genuine resolution of the Palestinian question. Despite Carter's more humane perception of the Palestinian people and their right to a homeland, Palestinians justifiably view the Camp David accords as a path to disaster. 'Participation in the determination of their own future' as codified in the Camp David agreements differs drastically from the inalienable right to self-determination. Even going beyond numerous other objections, the core of Palestinian rejection of the Camp David approach lies in the fact that, if an agreement satisfactory to Israel is reached, it can exercise a permanent veto of Palestinian rights and indefinitely perpetuate occupation.

Moreover, Palestinians perceive 'full autonomy', envisioned by the Begin government as no more than a cosmetic legalization of military occupation, as a 'neo-mandate', in which Palestinians would exercise no more rights than under the present military occupation by Israel, and indeed, fewer rights than under the British Mandate, which at least was subject to annual international review. Israeli insistence that 'full autonomy' would not include control over legislation, land, water or other less critical areas of administration, in addition to the continual Israeli land expropriation and settlement policies, amply demonstrate that Palestinian fears are well grounded.

It should be kept in mind that the Camp David agreement addresses only one-third of the Palestinian people. It contains no provisions for the rights of the Palestinians in the *Ghurbah* (diaspora), although it appears to assume that the majority of them will be somehow settled outside Palestine. Such a proposal will have no chance of being accepted by the Palestinians, as their attachment to the land of Palestine is far too intense. Palestinian culture is deeply rooted in the land, and since it is difficult to separate a people from their culture, it follows that the tie between the Palestinians and their land is an enduring bond.

Any viable settlement must, therefore, include the Palestinian right to return to their homeland, to determine their destiny and to establish their own independent state. No settlement that ignores these rights can be either morally acceptable or politically practicable. Nor can such an agreement bring about the peace that is so deeply desired by the Palestinians, and, indeed, by all the peoples of the Middle East.

American policy-makers appear to have paid little attention to the damaging effects on the United States itself of its unsuccessful policy toward the Palestinian question. America's unwillingness to force Israel to listen to reason under any conditions led to an erosion of American credibility internationally and strains on the American economy. In 1979, when the American economy was already on the downswing, Israel received $4.8 billion in foreign aid, more than half of the entire US foreign aid programme. Thus the approximately 130 million American taxpayers provided Israel with an average of $37 apiece, more than the individual US taxpayer average for mass transit, urban renewal, higher education or alternative energy research, and only slightly less than each taxpayer provided for social services, including both welfare and aid to the elderly.[2]

Continued pursuit of the current US Palestinian policy was costly and threatened disaster not only to American interests in the Middle East but to its European allies as well. The fact that the American approach had relatively contained the conflict during the previous thirty years had little relevance for the future. For the objective conditions have changed. The US interventions in Lebanon and the Dominican Republic, the 1970 contingency plans for intervention in Jordan and the more recent Soviet intervention in Afghanistan were glaring reminders of superpower willingness to take more risks to defend their 'vital' interests. More alarming yet was the proliferation of nuclear weapons into the hands of regional powers such as Israel and South Africa who were more likely to use them if they felt their power genuinely threatened, thereby dragging their senior partners to the brink of nuclear holocaust.

The importance of the Palestine issue was greater than the fate of the four million Palestinians alone. It was the conscience of the Arab world and a pulsating vein of the Islamic world; it was perhaps the only issue where Arab nationalism and Islamic revivalism were joined. The United States could no longer afford to adopt 'interim' or 'transitional' solutions to this explosive situation. After thirty years, opiates could no longer substitute for the radical surgery needed to treat a malignant tumour. The explosion could come at any time. The experience of the wars of 1956, 1967 and 1973, all illustrated that changes come very rapidly without much warning, threatening a chain reaction.

In 1981, therefore, the Palestinian question remains a powder keg set to explode at any moment. After thirty years, the time has come for America to recognize the natural right of the Palestinians to self-determination and an independent homeland.

Notes

1. Barry Rubin, 'Anatomy of an Imperial Strategy', *Journal of Palestine Studies*, vol. II, no. 3, (Spring 1973), Fu'ad Moghrabi, 'American Foreign Policy Decision Making Process', *Shu'un Filastinia*, (July 1979), Edward Said, *The Palestine Question and the American Context*, 1, Institute For Palestine Studies, 1979. These articles were instrumental in developing some of the ideas in this chapter.

2. *U.S. FY 1979 Budget* and National Association of Arab Americans, 'Summary of Statement on US Taxes and Israel', (Washington, DC 1980), pp. 1, 9.

APPENDICES

Appendix A

THE PALESTINIAN NATIONAL CHARTER

DECISIONS OF THE NATIONAL CONGRESS OF THE PALESTINE
LIBERATION ORGANIZATION HELD IN CAIRO FROM 1-17 JULY
1968.

Article 1: Palestine is the homeland of the Arab Palestinian people;
it is an indivisible part of the Arab homeland, and the Palestinian
people are an integral part of the Arab nation.

Article 2: Palestine, with the boundaries it had during the British
Mandate, is an indivisible territorial unit.

Article 3: The Palestinian Arab people possess the legal right to their
homeland and have the right to determine their destiny after achieving
the liberation of their country in accordance with their wishes and
entirely of their own accord and will.

Article 4: The Palestinian identity is a genuine, essential and in-
herent characteristic; it is transmitted from parents to children. The
Zionist occupation and the dispersal of the Palestinian Arab people,
through the disasters which befell them, do not make them lose their
Palestinian identity and their membership of the Palestinian community, nor do they negate them.

Article 5: The Palestinians are those Arab nationals who, until
1947, normally resided in Palestine regardless of whether they were
evicted from it or have stayed there. Anyone born, after that date, of a
Palestinian father — whether inside Palestine or outside it — is also a
Palestinian.

Article 6: The Jews who had normally resided in Palestine until the
beginning of the Zionist invasion will be considered Palestinians.

Article 7: That there is a Palestinian community and that it has
material, spiritual and historical connection with Palestine are indisput-
able facts. It is a national duty to bring up individual Palestinians in an

Arab revolutionary manner. All means of information and education must be adopted in order to acquaint the Palestinian with his country in the most profound manner, both spiritual and material, that is possible. He must be prepared for the armed struggle and ready to sacrifice his wealth and his life in order to win back his homeland and bring about its liberation.

Article 8: The phase in their history, through which the Palestinian people are now living, is that of national struggle for the liberation of Palestine. Thus the conflicts among the Palestinian national forces are secondary, and should be ended for the sake of the basic conflict that exists between the forces of Zionism and of imperialism on the one hand, and the Palestinian Arab people on the other. On this basis the Palestinian masses, regardless of whether they are residing in the national homeland or in the diaspora, constitute – both their organizations and the individuals – one national front working for the retrieval of Palestine and its liberation through armed struggle.

Article 9: Armed struggle is the only way to liberate Palestine. Thus it is the overall strategy, not merely a tactical phase. The Palestinian Arab people assert their absolute determination and firm resolution to continue their armed struggle and to work for an armed popular revolution for the liberation of their country and their return to it. They also assert their right to normal life in Palestine and to exercise their right to self-determination and sovereignty over it.

Article 10: Commando action constitutes the nucleus of the Palestinian popular liberation war. This requires its escalation, comprehensiveness and the mobilization of all the Palestinian popular and educational efforts and their organization and involvement in the armed Palestinian revolution. It also requires the achieving of unity for the national struggle among the different groupings of the Palestinian people, and between the Palestinian people and the Arab masses so as to secure the continuation of the revolution, its escalation and victory.

Article 11: The Palestinians will have three mottoes: national unity, national mobilization and liberation.

Article 12: The Palestinian people believe in Arab unity. In order to contribute their share towards the attainment of that objective, however, they must, at the present stage of their struggle, safeguard their Palestinian identity and develop their consciousness of that identity, and oppose any plan that may dissolve or impair it.

Article 13: Arab unity and the liberation of Palestine are two complementary objectives, the attainment of either of which facilitates the attainment of the other. Thus, Arab unity leads to the liberation of

Palestine; the liberation of Palestine leads to Arab unity; and work towards the realization of one objective proceeds side by side with work towards the realization of the other.

Article 14: The destiny of the Arab nation, and indeed Arab existence itself, depends upon the destiny of the Palestine cause. From this interdependence springs the Arab nation's pursuit of, and striving for, the liberation of Palestine.

The people of Palestine play the role of the vanguard in the realization of this sacred national goal.

Article 15: The liberation of Palestine, from an Arab viewpoint, is a national duty and it attempts to repel the Zionist and imperialist aggression against the Arab homeland, and aims at the elimination of Zionism in Palestine. Absolute responsibility for this falls upon the Arab nation — peoples and governments — with the Arab people of Palestine in the vanguard. Accordingly the Arab nation must mobilize all its military, human, moral and spiritual capabilities to participate actively with the Palestinian people in the liberation of Palestine. It must, particularly in the phase of the armed Palestinian revolution, offer and furnish the Palestinian people with all possible help, and material and human support, and make available to them the means and opportunities that will enable them to continue to carry out their leading role in the armed revolution, until they liberate their homeland.

Article 16: The liberation of Palestine, from a spiritual point of view, will provide the Holy Land with an atmosphere of safety and tranquillity, which is turn will safeguard the country's religious sanctuaries and guarantee freedom of worship and of visit to all, without discrimination of race, colour, language, or religion. Accordingly, the people of Palestine look to all spiritual forces in the world for support.

Article 17: The liberation of Palestine, from a human point of view, will restore to the Palestinian individual his dignity, pride and freedom. Accordingly the Palestinian Arab people look forward to the support of all those who believe in the dignity of man and his freedom in the world.

Article 18: The liberation of Palestine, from an international point of view, is a defensive action necessitated by the demands of self-defence. Accordingly, the Palestinian people, desirous as they are of the friendship of all people, look to freedom-loving, justice-loving and peace-loving states for support in order to restore their legitimate rights in Palestine, to re-establish peace and security in the country, and to enable its people to exercise national sovereignty and freedom.

Article 19: The partition of Palestine in 1947 and the establishment of the state of Israel are entirely illegal, regardless of the passage of time, because they were contrary to the will of the Palestinian people and to their natural right in their homeland, and inconsistent with the principles embodied in the Charter of the United Nations, particularly the right to self-determination.

Article 20: The Balfour Declaration, the Mandate for Palestine and everything that has been based upon them, are deemed null and void. Claims of historical or religious ties of Jews with Palestine are incompatible with the facts of history and the true conception of what constitutes statehood. Judaism, being a religion, is not an independent nationality. Nor do Jews constitute a single nation with an identity of its own; they are citizens of the states to which they belong.

Article 21: The Arab Palestinian people, expressing themselves by the armed Palestinian revolution, reject all solutions which are substitutes for the total liberation of Palestine and reject all proposals aiming at the liquidation of the Palestinian problem, or its internationalization.

Article 22: Zionism is a political movement organically associated with international imperialism and antagonistic to all action for liberation and to progressive movements in the world. It is racist and fanatic in its nature, aggressive, expansionist and colonial in its aims, and fascist in its methods. Israel is the instrument of the Zionist movement, and a geographical base for world imperialism placed strategically in the midst of the Arab homeland to combat the hopes of the Arab nation for liberation, unity and progress. Israel is a constant source of threat *vis-à-vis* peace in the Middle East and the whole world. Since the liberation of Palestine will destroy the Zionist and imperialist presence and will contribute to the establishment of peace in the Middle East, the Palestinian people look for the support of all the progressive and peaceful forces and urge them all, irrespective of their affiliations and beliefs, to offer the Palestinian people all aid and support in their just struggle for the liberation of their homeland.

Article 23: The demands of security and peace, as well as the demands of right and justice, require all states to consider Zionism an illegitimate movement, to outlaw its existence, and to ban its operations, in order that friendly relations among peoples may be preserved, and the loyalty of citizens to their respective homelands safeguarded.

Article 24: The Palestinian people believe in the principles of justice, freedom, sovereignty, self-determination, human dignity, and in the right of all peoples to exercise them.

Article 25: For the realization of the goals of this Charter and its principles, the Palestine Liberation Organization will perform its role in the liberation of Palestine in accordance with the Constitution of this Organization.

Article 26: The Palestine Liberation Organization, representative of the Palestinian revolutionary forces, is responsible for the Palestinian Arab people's movement in its struggle — to retrieve its homeland, liberate and return to it and exercise the right to self-determination in it — in all military, political and financial fields and also for whatever may be required by the Palestine case on the inter-Arab and international levels.

Article 27: The Palestine Liberation Organization shall co-operate with all Arab states, each according to its potentialities; and will adopt a neutral policy among them in the light of the requirements of the war of liberation; and on this basis it shall not interfere in the internal affairs of any Arab state.

Article 28: The Palestinian Arab people assert the genuineness and independence of their national revolution and reject all forms of intervention, trusteeship and subordination.

Article 29: The Palestinian people possess the fundamental and genuine legal right to liberate and retrieve their homeland. The Palestinian people determine their attitude towards all states and forces on the basis of the stands they adopt *vis-à-vis* the Palestinian case and the extent of the support they offer to the Palestinian revolution to fulfill the aims of the Palestinian people.

Article 30: Fighters and carriers of arms in the war of liberation are the nucleus of the popular army which will be the protective force for the gains of the Palestinian Arab people.

Article 31: The Organization shall have a flag, an oath of allegiance and an anthem. All this shall be decided upon in accordance with a special regulation.

Article 32: Regulations, which shall be known as the Constitution of the Palestine Liberation Organization, shall be annexed to this Charter. It shall lay down the manner in which the Organization, and its organs and institutions, shall be constituted; the respective competence of each; and the requirements of its obligations under the Charter.

Article 33: This Charter shall not be amended save by [vote of] a majority of two-thirds of the total membership of the National Congress of the Palestine Liberation Organization [taken] at a special session convened for that purpose.

Appendix B

Security Council Resolution No. 242 (1967) of 22 November 1967,
STATING THE PRINCIPLES OF A JUST AND LASTING PEACE IN
THE MIDDLE EAST

The Security Council,

Expressing its continuing concern with the grave situation in the Middle East,

Emphasizing the inadmissibility of the acquisition of territory by war and the need to work for a just and lasting peace in which every State in the area can live in security,

Emphasizing further that all Member States in their acceptance of the Charter of the United Nations have undertaken a commitment to act in accordance with Article 2 of the Charter,

1. *Affirms* that the fulfilment of Charter principles requires the establishment of a just and lasting peace in the Middle East which should include the application of both the following principles:

(i) Withdrawal of Israel armed forces from territories occupied* in the recent conflict;

(ii) Termination of all claims or states of belligerency and respect for and acknowledgement of the sovereignty, territorial integrity and political independence of every State in the area and their right to live in peace within secure and recognized boundaries free from threats or acts of force;

2. *Affirms further* the necessity

(a) For guaranteeing freedom of navigation through international waterways in the area;

(b) For achieving a just settlement of the refugee problem;

(c) For guaranteeing the territorial inviolability and political independence of every State in the area, through measures including the establishment of demilitarized zones;

3. *Requests* the Secretary-General to designate a Special Representative to proceed to the Middle East to establish and maintain contacts with the States concerned in order to promote agreement and assist efforts to achieve a peaceful and accepted settlement in accordance with the provisions and principles in this resolution;

4. *Requests* The Secretary-General to report to the Security Council on the progress of the efforts of the Special Representative as soon as possible.

Appendix C

Security Council Resolution No. 338 (1973) of 22 October 1973,
CALLING FOR A CEASE-FIRE AND FOR THE IMPLEMENTATION
OF RESOLUTION 242 IN ALL OF ITS PARTS

The Security Council,

1. *Calls upon* all parties to the present fighting to cease all firing and terminate all military activity immediately, no later than 12 hours after the moment of the adoption of this decision, in the positions they now occupy;

2. *Calls upon* the parties concerned to start immediately after the cease-fire the implementation of Security Council resolution 242 (1967) in all of its parts;

3. *Decides* that, immediately and concurrently with the cease-fire, negotiations start between the parties concerned under appropriate auspices aimed at establishing a just and durable peace in the Middle East.

Appendix D

General Assembly Resolution No. 181 (II) of 29 November 1947,
RECOMMENDING A PARTITION PLAN FOR PALESTINE

The General Assembly,

Having met in special session at the request of the mandatory Power to constitute and instruct a Special Committee to prepare for the consideration of the question of the future Government of Palestine at the second regular session;

Having constituted a Special Committee and instructed it to investigate all questions and issues relevant to the problem of Palestine, and to prepare proposals for the solution of the problem, and

Having received and examined the report of the Special Committee (document A/364)[1] including a number of unanimous recommendations and a plan of partition with economic union approved by the majority of the Special Committee,

Considers that the present situation in Palestine is one which is likely to impair the general welfare and friendly relations among nations;

Takes note of the declaration by the mandatory Power that it plans to complete its evacuation of Palestine by 1 August 1948;

Recommends to the United Kingdom, as the mandatory Power for Palestine, and to all other Members of the United Nations the adoption and implementation, with regard to the future Government of Palestine, of the Plan of Partition with Economic Union set out below;

Requests that:

(a) The Security Council take the necessary measures as provided for in the plan for its implementation;

(b) The Security Council consider, if circumstances during the transitional period require such consideration, whether the situation in Palestine constitutes a threat to the peace. If it decides that such a threat exists, and in order to maintain international peace and security, the Security Council should supplement the authorization of the General Assembly by taking measures, under Articles 39 and 41 of the Charter, to empower the United Nations Commission, as provided in this resolution, to exercise in Palestine the functions which are assigned to it by this resolution;

(c) The Security Council determine as a threat to the peace, breach of the peace or act of aggression, in accordance with Article 39 of the Charter, any attempt to alter by force the settlement envisaged by this resolution;

(d) The Trusteeship Council be informed of the responsibilities envisaged for it in this plan;

Calls upon the inhabitants of Palestine to take such steps as may be necessary on their part to put this plan into effect;

Appeals to all Governments and all peoples to refrain from taking any action which might hamper or delay the carrying out of these recommendations, and

Authorizes the Secretary-General to reimburse travel and subsistence expenses of the members of the Commission referred to in Part I, Section B, Paragraph I below, on such basis and in such form as he may determine most appropriate in the circumstances, and to provide the Commission with the necessary staff to assist in carrying out the functions assigned to the Commission by the General Assembly.

Appendix E

General Assembly Resolution No. 194 (III) of 11 December 1948,
ESTABLISHING A UN CONCILIATION COMMISSION, RESOLVING
THAT JERUSALEM SHOULD BE PLACED UNDER A PERMANENT
INTERNATIONAL REGIME, AND RESOLVING THAT THE
REFUGEES SHOULD BE PERMITTED TO RETURN TO THEIR
HOMES

The General Assembly,

Having considered further the situation in Palestine,

1. *Expresses* its deep appreciation of the progress achieved through the good offices of the late United Nations Mediator in promoting a peaceful adjustment of the future situation of Palestine, for which cause he sacrificed his life; and

Extends its thanks to the Acting Mediator and his staff for their continued efforts and devotion to duty in Palestine;

2. *Establishes* a Conciliation Commission consisting of three States Members of the United Nations which shall have the following functions:

(a) To assume, in so far as it considers necessary in existing circumstances, the functions given to the United Nations Mediator on Palestine by resolution 186 (S-2) of the General Assembly of 14 May 1948;

(b) To carry out the specific function and directives given to it by the present resolution and such additional functions and directives as may be given to it by the General Assembly or by the Security Council;

(c) To undertake, upon the request of the Security Council, any of the functions now assigned to the United Nations Mediator on Palestine or to the United Nations Truce Commission by resolutions of the Security Council; upon such request to the Conciliation Commission by the Security Council with respect to all the remaining functions of the United Nations Mediator on Palestine under Security Council resolutions, the office of the Mediator shall be terminated;

3. *Decides* that a Committee of the Assembly, consisting of China, France, the Union of Soviet Socialist Republics, the United Kingdom and the United States of America, shall present, before the end of the first part of the present session of the General Assembly, for the approval of the Assembly, a proposal concerning the names of the three States which will constitute the Conciliation Commission;

4. *Requests* the Commission to begin its functions at once, with a

view to the establishment of contact between the parties themselves and the Commission at the earliest possible date;

5. *Calls upon* the Governments and authorities concerned to extend the scope of negotiations provided for in the Security Council's resolution of 16 November 1948[15] and to seek agreement by negotiations conducted either with the Conciliation Commission or directly, with a view to the final settlement of all questions outstanding between them;

6. *Instructs* the Conciliation Commission to take steps to assist the Governments and authorities concerned to achieve a final settlement of all questions outstanding between them;

7. *Resolves* that the Holy Places – including Nazareth – religious buildings and sites in Palestine should be protected and free access to them assured, in accordance with existing rights and historical practice; that arrangements to this end should be under effective United Nations supervision; that the United Nations Conciliation Commission, in presenting to the fourth regular session of the General Assembly its detailed proposals for a permanent international regime for the territory of Jerusalem, should include recommendations concerning the Holy Places in that territory; that with regard to the Holy Places in the rest of Palestine the Commission should call upon the political authorities of the area concerned to give appropriate formal guarantees as to the protection of the Holy Places and access to them; and that these undertakings should be presented to the General Assembly for approval;

8. *Resolves* that, in view of its association with three world religions, the Jerusalem area, including the present municipality of Jerusalem plus the surrounding villages and towns, the most eastern of which shall be Abu Dis; the most southern, Bethlehem; the most western, Ein Karim (including also the built-up area of Motsa); and the most northern Shu'fat, should be accorded special and separate treatment from the rest of Palestine and should be placed under effective United Nations control;

Requests the Security Council to take further steps to ensure the demilitarization of Jerusalem at the earliest possible date;

Instructs the Commission to present to the fourth regular session of the General Assembly detailed proposals for a permanent international regime for the Jerusalem area which will provide for the maximum local autonomy for distinctive groups consistent with the special international status of the Jerusalem area:

The Conciliation Commission is authorized to appoint a United Nations representative, who shall co-operate with the local authorities with respect to the interim administration of the Jerusalem area;

9. *Resolves* that, pending agreement on more detailed arrangements among the Governments and authorities concerned, the freest possible access to Jerusalem by road, rail or air should be accorded to all inhabitants of Palestine;

Instructs the Conciliation Commission to report immediately to the Security Council, for appropriate action by that organ, any attempt by any party to impede such access;

10. *Instructs* the Conciliation Commission to seek arrangements among the Governments and authorities concerned which will facilitate the economic development of the area, including arrangements for access to ports and airfields and the use of transportation and communication facilities;

11. *Resolves* that the refugees wishing to return to their homes and live at peace with their neighbours should be permitted to do so at the earliest practicable date, and that compensation should be paid for the property of those choosing not to return and for loss of or damage to property which, under principles of international law or in equity, should be made good by the Governments or authorities responsible;

Instructs the Conciliation Commission to facilitate the repatriation, resettlement and economic and social rehabilitation of the refugees and the payment of compensation, and to maintain close relations with the Director of the United Nations Relief for Palestine Refugees and, through him, with the appropriate organs and agencies of the United Nations;

12. *Authorizes* the Conciliation Commission to appoint such subsidiary bodies and to employ such technical experts, acting under its authority, as it may find necessary for the effective discharge of its functions and responsibilities under the present resolutions;

The Conciliation Commission will have its official headquarters at Jerusalem. The authorities responsible for maintaining order in Jerusalem will be responsible for taking all measures necessary to ensure the security of the Commission. The Secretary-General will provide a limited number of guards for the protection of the staff and premises of the Commission;

13. *Instructs* the Conciliation Commission to render progress reports periodically to the Secretary-General for transmission to the Security Council and to the Members of the United Nations.

14. *Calls upon* all Governments and authorities concerned to cooperate with the Conciliation Commission and to take all possible steps to assist in the implementation of the present resolution;

15. *Requests* the Secretary-General to provide the necessary staff

and facilities and to make appropriate arrangements to provide the necessary funds required in carrying out the terms of the present resolution.

Appendix F

General Assembly Resolution No. 3236 (XXIX) of 22 November 1974,
RECOGNIZING THE RIGHTS OF THE PALESTINIAN PEOPLE

The General Assembly,

Having considered the question of Palestine,

Having heard the statement of the Palestine Liberation Organization, the representative of the Palestinian people.

Having also heard other statements made during the debate,

Deeply concerned that no just solution to the problem of Palestine has yet been achieved and recognizing that the problem of Palestine continues to endanger international peace and security,

Recognizing that the Palestinian people is entitled to self-determination in accordance with the Charter of the United Nations,

Expressing its grave concern that the Palestinian people has been prevented from enjoying its inalienable rights, in particular its right to self-determination,

Guided by the purposes and principles of the Charter,

Recalling its relevant resolutions which affirm the right of the Palestinian people to self-determination,

1. *Reaffirms* the inalienable rights of the Palestinian people in Palestine, including:

(a) The right to self-determination without external interference;

(b) The right to national independence and sovereignty;

(2) *Reaffirms also* the inalienable right of the Palestinians to return to their homes and property from which they have been displaced and uprooted, and calls for their return;

3. *Emphasizes* that full respect for and the realization of these inalienable rights of the Palestinian people are indispensable for the solution of the question of Palestine;

4. *Recognizes* that the Palestinian people is a principal party in the establishment of a just and durable peace in the Middle East;

5. *Further recognizes* the right of the Palestinian people to regain its

rights by all means in accordance with the purposes and principles of the Charter of the United Nations;

6. *Appeals* to all States and international organizations to extend their support to the Palestinian people in its struggle to restore its rights, in accordance with the Charter;

7. *Requests* the Secretary-General to establish contact with the Palestine Liberation Organization on all matters concerning the question of Palestine;

8. *Requests* the Secretary-General to report to the General Assembly at its thirtieth session on the implementation of the present resolution;

9. *Decides* to include the item entitled "Question of Palestine" in the provisional agenda of its thirtieth session.

Appendix G

General Assembly Resolution No. 3237 (XXIX) of 22 November 1974,
GRANTING OBSERVER STATUS TO THE PALESTINE LIBERATION ORGANIZATION

The General Assembly,

Having considered the question of Palestine,

Taking into consideration the universality of the United Nations prescribed in the Charter,

Recalling its resolution 3102 (XXVIII) of 12 December 1973,

Taking into account Economic and Social Council resolutions 1835 (LVI) of 14 May 1974 and 1840 (LVI) of 15 May 1974,

Noting that the Diplomatic Conference on the Reaffirmation and Development of International Humanitarian Law Applicable in Armed Conflicts, the World Population Conference and the World Food Conference have in effect invited the Palestine Liberation Organization to participate in their respective deliberations,

Noting also that the Third United Nations Conference on the Law of the Sea has invited the Palestine Liberation Organization to participate in its deliberations as an observer,

1. *Invites* the Palestine Liberation Organization to participate in the sessions and the work of the General Assembly in the capacity of observer,

2. *Invites* the Palestine Liberation Organization to participate in the

sessions and the work of all international conferences convened under the auspices of the General Assembly in the capacity of observer.

3. *Considers* that the Palestine Liberation Organization is entitled to participate as an observer in the sessions and the work of all international conferences convened under the auspices of other organs of the United Nations;

4. *Requests* the Secretary-General to take the necessary steps for the implementation of the present resolution.

Appendix H

TEXT OF AGREEMENTS SIGNED 17 SEPTEMBER 1978 AT CAMP DAVID

A FRAMEWORK OF PEACE IN THE MIDDLE EAST AGREED AT CAMP DAVID

Muhammad Anwar al-Sadat, President of the Arab Republic of Egypt, and Menachem Begin, Prime Minister of Israel, met with Jimmy Carter, President of the United States of America, at Camp David from 5 September to 17 September 1978, and have agreed on the following framework for peace in the Middle East. They invite other parties to the Arab-Israeli conflict to adhere to it.

PREAMBLE

The search for peace in the Middle East must be guided by the following:

— The agreed basis for a peaceful settlement of the conflict between Israel and its neighbours is United Nations Security Council Resolution 242, in all its parts.

— After four wars during thirty years, despite intensive human efforts, the Middle East, which is the cradle of civilization and the birthplace of three great religions, does not yet enjoy the blessings of peace. The people of the Middle East yearn for peace so that the vast human and natural resources of the region can be turned to the pursuits of peace and so that this area can become a model for coexistence and cooperation among nations.

—The historic initiative of President Sadat in visiting Jerusalem and the reception accorded to him by the Parliament, government and people of Israel, and the reciprocal visit of Prime Minister Begin to Ismailia, the peace proposals made by both leaders, as well as the warm reception of these missions by the peoples of both countries, have created an unprecedented opportunity for peace which must not be lost if this generation and future generations are to be spared the tragedies of war.

—The provisions of the Charter of the United Nations and the other accepted norms of international law and legitimacy now provide accepted standards for the conduct of relations among all states.

—To achieve a relationship of peace, in the spirit of Article 2 of the United Nations Charter, future negotiations between Israel and any neighbour prepared to negotiate peace and security with it, are necessary for the purpose of carrying out all the provisions and principles of Resolutions 242 and 338.

—Peace requires respect for the sovereignty, territorial integrity and political independence of every state in the area and their right to live in peace within secure and recognized boundaries free from threats or acts of force. Progress toward that goal can accelerate movement toward a new era of reconciliation in the Middle East marked by cooperation in promoting economic development, in maintaining stability, and in assuring security.

—Security is enhanced by a relationship of peace and by cooperation between nations which enjoy normal relations. In addition, under the terms of peace treaties, the parties can, on the basis of reciprocity, agree to special security arrangements such as demilitarized zones, limited armaments areas, early warning stations, the presence of international forces, liaison, agreed measures for monitoring, and other arrangements that they agree are useful.

FRAMEWORK

Taking these factors into account, the parties are determined to reach a just, comprehensive, and durable settlement of the Middle East conflict through the conclusion of peace treaties based on Security Council Resolutions 242 and 338 in all their parts. Their purpose is to achieve peace and good neighbourly relations. They recognize that, for peace to endure, it must involve all those who have been most deeply affected by the conflict. They therefore agree that this framework as appropriate is intended by them to constitute a basis for peace not only between Egypt and Israel, but also between Israel and each of its other neighbours which is prepared to negotiate peace with Israel on this basis. With that objective in mind, they have agreed to proceed as follows:

A. *West Bank and Gaza*

1. Egypt, Israel, Jordan and the representatives of the Palestinian people should participate in negotiations on the resolution of the Palestinian problem in all its aspects. To achieve that objective, negotiations relating to the West Bank and Gaza should proceed in three stages:

(a) Egypt and Israel agree that, in order to ensure a peaceful and orderly transfer of authority, and taking into account the security concerns of all the parties, there should be transitional arrangements for the West Bank and Gaza for a period not exceeding five years. In order to provide full autonomy to the inhabitants, under these arrangements the Israeli military government and its civilian administration will be withdrawn as soon as a self-governing authority has been freely elected by the inhabitants of these areas to replace the existing military government. To negotiate the details of a transitional arrangement, the Government of Jordan will be invited to join the negotiations on the basis of this framework. These new arrangements should give due consideration both to the principle of self-government by the inhabitants of these territories and to the legitimate security concerns of the parties involved.

(b) Egypt, Israel, and Jordan will agree on the modalities for establishing the elected self-governing authority in the West Bank and Gaza. The delegations of Egypt and Jordan may include Palestinians from the West Bank and Gaza or other Palestinians as mutually agreed. The parties will negotiate an agreement which will define the powers and responsibilities of the self-governing authority to be exercised in the West Bank and Gaza. A withdrawal of Israeli armed forces will take place and there will be a redeployment of the remaining Israeli forces into specified security locations. The agreement will also include arrangements for assuring internal and external security and public order. A strong local police force will be established, which may include Jordanian citizens. In addition, Israeli and Jordanian forces will participate in joint patrols and in the manning of control posts to assure the security of the borders.

(c) When the self-governing authority (administrative council) in the West Bank and Gaza is established and inaugurated, the transitional period of five years will begin. As soon as possible, but not later than the third year after the beginning of the transitional period, negotiations will take place to determine the final status of the West Bank and Gaza and its relationship with its neighbours, and to conclude a peace treaty between Israel and Jordan by the end of the transitional period. These negotiations will be conducted among Egypt, Israel, Jordan, and the elected representatives of the inhabitants of the West Bank and Gaza. Two separate but related committees will be convened, one committee, consisting of representatives of the four parties which will negotiate and agree on the final status of the West Bank and Gaza, and its relationship with its neighbours, and the second committee, consisting of representatives of Israel and representatives of Jordan to be joined by the elected representatives of the inhabitants of the West Bank and Gaza, to negotiate the peace treaty between Israel and Jordan, taking into account the agreement reached on the final status of the West Bank and Gaza. The negotiations shall be based on all the provisions and principles of UN Security Council Resolution 242. The negotiations will resolve, among other matters, the location of the boundaries and the nature of the security arrangements. The solution from the negotiations must also recognize the legitimate rights of the Palestinian people and their just requirements. In this way, the Palestinians will participate in the determination of their own future through:

1) The negotiations among Egypt, Israel, Jordan and the representatives of the inhabitants of the West Bank and Gaza to agree on the final status of the West Bank and Gaza and other outstanding issues by the end of the transitional period.

2) Submitting their agreement to a vote by the elected representatives of the inhabitants of the West Bank and Gaza.

3) Providing for the elected representatives of the inhabitants of the West Bank and Gaza to decide how they shall govern themselves consistent with the provisions of their agreement.

4) Participating as stated above in the work of the committee negotiating the peace treaty between Israel and Jordan.

2. All necessary measures will be taken and provisions made to assure the security of Israel and its neighbours during the transitional period and beyond. To assist in providing such security, a strong local police force will be constituted by the self-governing authority. It will be composed of inhabitants of the West Bank and Gaza. The police will maintain continuing liaison on internal security matters with the designated Israeli, Jordanian, and Egyptian officers.

3. During the transitional period, representatives of Egypt, Israel, Jordan, and the self-governing authority will constitute a continuing committee to decide by agreement on the modalities of admission of

persons displaced from the West Bank and Gaza in 1967, together with necessary measures to prevent disruption and disorder. Other matters of common concern may also be dealt with by this committee.

4. Egypt and Israel will work with each other and with other interested parties to establish agreed procedures for a prompt, just and permanent implementation of the resolution of the refugee problem.

B. *Egypt-Israel*

1. Egypt and Israel undertake not to resort to the threat or the use of force to settle disputes. Any disputes shall be settled by peaceful means in accordance with the provisions of Article 33 of the Charter of the United Nations.

2. In order to achieve peace between them, the parties agree to negotiate in good faith with a goal of concluding within three years.

C. *Associated Principles*

1. Egypt and Israel state that the principles and provisions described below should apply to peace treaties between Israel and each of its neighbours — Egypt, Jordan, Syria and Lebanon.

2. Signatories shall establish among themselves relationships normal to states at peace with one another. To this end, they should undertake to abide by all the provisions of the Charter of the United Nations. Steps to be taken in this respect include:

(a) full recognition;

(b) abolishing economic boycotts;

(c) guaranteeing that under their jurisdiction the citizens of the other parties shall enjoy the protection of the due process of law.

3. Signatories should explore possibilities for economic development in the context of final peace treaties, with the objective of contributing to the atmosphere of peace, cooperation and friendship which is their common goal.

4. Claims Commissions may be established for the mutual settlement of all financial claims.

5. The United States shall be invited to participate in the talks on matters related to the modalities of the implementation of the agreements and working out the timetable for the carrying out of the obligations of the parties.

6. The United Nations Security Council shall be requested to endorse the peace treaties and ensure that their provisions shall not be violated. The permanent members of the Security Council shall be requested to underwrite the peace treaties and ensure respect for their

provisions. They shall also be requested to conform their policies and actions with the undertakings contained in this Framework.

For the Government
of the Arab
Republic of Egypt:

For the Government
of Israel:

A. SADAT

M. BEGIN

Witnessed by:

JIMMY CARTER

Jimmy Carter, President
of the United States of America

APPENDIX I

Distribution by place of registration of total registered Palestinian refugee population and of camp population

	Total registered population	Number of camps		Number of persons officially registered in established camps[a]	Number of persons actually living in camps[b]	
		Established	Emergency		Established	Emergency[c]
East Jordan	663 773	4	6	74 212	90 321	126 407
West Bank	302 620	20	–	75 956	77 999	–
Gaza Strip	346 007	8	–	196 203	198 826	–
Lebanon	201 171	13	–	90 904	94 980	–
Syrian Arab Republic	192 915	6	4	31 047	36 551	19 774
Total	1 706 486	51	10	468 322	498 677	146 181

[a] Persons officially registered in these camps are refugees registered with UNRWA who are shown in UNRWA records as living in camps, irrespective of their category of registration (RSN), although some may have moved to villages, towns or cities in other parts of the country and their removal has yet to be reported to the Agency. The figures do not include refugees in camps who are not given shelter by UNRWA but benefit from sanitation services.

[b] Of the 498,677 persons actually living in these camps, 488,652 are UNRWA-registered refugees and their unregistered dependants. The balance of 10,025 are not UNRWA-registered refugees and are thus not eligible for UNRWA assistance.

[c] Persons actually living in these camps comprise 108,839 UNRWA-registered refugees and 37,342 other persons displaced as a result of the June 1967 hostilities or subsequent fighting in the Jordan valley in early 1968.

Detailed statement of income to UNRWA[a] (1 May 1950-31 December 1977) (in United States dollars)

Contributor	For the period 1 May 1950 to 31 December 1972	1973	1974	For the year 1975	1976	1977[b]	Total
			I. Contributions by Governments				
Abu Dhabi	190 927	—	—	—	—	—	190 927
Argentina	127 000	—	—	—	—	5 000	148 000
Australia	4 777 916	240 213	321 020	340 784	368 612	414 870	6 464 415
Austria	166 859	35 000	50 000	70 000	70 000	107 000	498 859
Bahrain	43 867	10 000	—	20 000	15 000	15 000	103 867
Belgium	1 538 590	261 766	674 335	770 810	996 255	757 388	4 999 144
Benin	250	—	—	—	—	403	653
Bolivia	5 000	—	—	—	—	—	5 000
Brazil	25 000	—	10 009	10 000	10 000	—	55 009
Burma	9 546	—	—	—	—	—	9 546
Canada	28 473 546	2 050 000	2 094 275	3 120 602	3 646 406	3 783 750	43 168 579
Central African Empire	2 198	—	—	—	—	—	2 198
Chile	5 000	—	2 000	2 000	2 000	2 000	13 000
China	153 279[d]	—	—	—	—	—	153 279
Congo	—	—	—	4 717	—	—	4 717
Cuba	5 000	—	—	—	—	—	5 000
Cyprus	4 994	713	697	502	750	482	8 138
Democratic Kampuchea	7 141	—	—	—	—	—	7 141
Democratic Yemen	750	—	—	—	—	—	750
Denmark	5 028 439	889 792	1 108 893	1 186 195	1 567 255	1 554 368	11 334 942
Dominican Republic	6 000	—	—	—	—	—	6 000

(Appendix J cont'd)

I. Contributions by Governments

Contributor	For the period 1 May 1950 to 31 December 1972	1973	1974	For the year 1975	1976	1977[b]	Total
Dubai	40 000	–	–	–	–	–	40 000
Egypt	5 475 976	–	7 680	7 680	–	7 680	5 499 016
El Salvador	500	–	–	–	–	–	500
Ethiopia	35 500	–	–	–	–	–	35 500
European Economic Community	2 649 191	6 891 245	24 041 348	13 771 493	14 320 477	16 905 363	78 579 117
Finland	680 500	210 000	258 340	293 107	298 265	250 000	1 990 212
France	19 612 186	1 269 365	1 343 345	1 295 312	1 568 322	1 324 315	26 412 845
Gambia	30						30
Gaza authorities	1 671 751	77 925	78 105	89 367	74 532	76 317	2 067 997
Germany, Federal Republic of	19 677 824	4 967 589	2 963 424	3 303 930	3 311 649	3 257 288	37 481 704
Ghana	46 500	4 000	4 000	5 220	5 220	5 220	70 160
Greece	483 517	184 100	17 000	17 000	25 940	22 796	750 353
Guinea				1 000			1 000
Haiti	6 000	1 000					7 000
Holy See	89 965	2 500	3 000	5 000	2 500	2 500	105 465
Honduras	2 500						2 500
Iceland	42 439	12 000	12 500	12 500	13 000	14 000	106 439
India	427 435	14 903	15 493	12 579	12 579	12 579	495 568
Indonesia	250 268	5 500	6 000	6 000	6 000	6 000	279 768
Iran	138 047	18 000	18 000	18 000	30 000	30 000	252 047
Iraq	731 006		240 256		121 600	122 000	1 214 862
Ireland	463 876	80 000	100 000	80 800	89 040	98 040	911 716
Israel	3 986 415	403 422	1 263 176	776 730	896 080	1 118 900	8 444 723

(Appendix J cont'd)

I. Contributions by Governments (Continued)

Contributor	For the period 1 May 1950 to 31 December 1972	1973	1974	For the year 1975	1976	1977[b]	Total
Italy	2 487 837	160 321	152 697	148 039	200 000	200 000	3 348 894
Jamaica	7 370	3 000	3 000	6 000	–	3 000	25 370
Japan	2 084 218	350 000	5 750 000	5 000 000	5 500 000	5 500 000	24 184 218
Jordan	2 860 848	289 083	251 709	263 634	252 037	239 625	4 156 936
Kuwait	2 942 860	220 000	400 000	400 000	1 600 000	600 000	6 162 860
Laos	4 687	–	–	–	–	–	4 687
Lebanon	999 019	64 797	70 450	128 389	106 504	96 720	1 465 879
Liberia	56 500	5 000	5 000	5 000	–	5 000	76 500
Libyan Arab Jamahiriya	1 414 000	600 000	600 000	602 100	600 000	1 000 000	4 816 100
Luxembourg	69 560	4 560	5 900	144 258	53 736	9 450	286 904
Madagascar	586	586	612	–	–	–	1 784
Malawi	280	–	–	–	–	–	280
Malaysia	51 785	1 500	1 500	1 500	1 500	1 500	59 285
Malta	5 000	–	–	–	–	–	5 000
Mauritania	–	–	–	–	1 000	1 000	2 000
Mauritius	–	–	989	943	2 000	2 000	5 932
Mexico	135 691	7 500	–	–	–	–	143 191
Monaco	7 625	215	1 667	241	211	201	10 160
Morocco	414 182	57 000	51 236	57 000	45 000	50 667	675 085
Netherlands	1 933 736	135 135	564 574	1 561 728	1 836 835	1 799 640	7 831 648
New Zealand	2 720 045	81 844	143 692	143 885	123 839	125 000	3 338 305
Niger	4 920	–	–	–	–	–	4 920
Nigeria	51 200	6 080	–	6 080	–	–	63 360
Norway	2 765 760	845 488	1 401 664	1 843 341	1 980 202	2 450 000	11 286 455
Oman	20 000	25 000	25 000	25 000	25 000	25 000	145 000
Pakistan	719 618	20 805	21 804	20 797	20 909	21 000	824 933
Panama	500	–	–	–	–	–	500
Philippines	23 750	1 250	1 250	1 500	1 750	3 000	32 500
Qatar	180 728	–	60 000	1 060 000	500 000	60 000	1 860 728

(Appendix J cont'd)

Contributor	For the period 1 May 1950 to 31 December 1972	1973	1974	For the year 1975	1976	1977[b]	Total
				I. Contributions by Governments (Continued)			
Republic of Korea	21 500	7 000	10 000	–	10 000	5 000	53 500
Rhodesia and Nyasaland	39 200	–	–	–	–	–	39 200
Romania	5 555	–	–	–	–	–	5 555
San Marino	–	–	–	–	–	6 000	11 750
Saudi Arabia	4 346 081	397 000	947 000	11 200 000	11 200 000	1 200 000	29 290 081
Senegal	3 988	–	–	–	–	–	3 988
Sierra Leone	6 656	10 400	9 680	9 680	–	–	37 926
Singapore	6 500	1 500	1 500	1 500	1 500	1 500	12 500
Socialist Republic of Vietnam	36 000	3 000	3 000	–	–	–	42 000
Spain	3 152 416	827 586	1 000 000	1 000 000	1 000 000	1 000 000	7 980 002
Sri Lanka	13 800	1 000	1 000	1 000	1 000	1 000	18 800
Sudan	163 104	5 761	6 027	–	6 027	6 027	186 946
Swaziland	–	660	–	–	–	–	660
Sweden	18 733 396	3 718 600	4 193 336	5 561 966	6 071 978	8 009 153	46 288 429
Switzerland	4 925 125	1 232 726	1 545 394	1 180 854	1 548 223	1 477 229	11 909 551
Syrian Arab Republic	1 982 041	102 192	101 981	106 666	102 363	106 042	2 501 285
Thailand	19 175	10 619	–	–	43 720	27 600	101 114
Togo	1 000	–	–	–	–	–	1 000
Trinidad and Tobago	7 130	1 810	2 899	3 000	3 000	2 487	20 326
Tunisia	51 000	6 000	7 000	7 000	8 000	8 000	87 000
Turkey	150 759	20 000	20 000	20 000	20 000	35 000	265 759
United Arab Emirates	200 000	220 000	250 000	2 275 000	270 000	300 000	3 515 000
United Kingdom of Great Britain and Northern Ireland	123 614 254	4 960 000	4 760 000	6 808 585	6 929 337	6 020 000	153 092 176
				42 054 924	44 700 000[e]	48 700 000	712 664 592
				1 887			1 887
	5 000	–	–	–	–	–	5 000

(Appendix J cont'd)

Contributor	For the period 1 May 1950 to 31 December 1972	1973	1974	For the year 1975	1976	1977[b]	Total
I. Contributions by Governments (Continued)							
United Republic of Cameroon	5 000		–	–	408	400	5 808
United States of America	525 724 592	23 200 000	28 285 076	42 054 924	44 700 000[e]	48 700 000	712 664 592
Upper Volta	–	–	–	1 887	–	–	1 887
Uruguay	5 000	–	–	–	–	–	5 000
Venezuela	–	–	–	–	5 000	–	5 000
Yugoslavia	673 700	35 000	25 000	25 000	25 000	25 000	808 700
Zaire	20 000	–	–	–	–	1 500	21 500
Sundry Governments through World Refugee Year Stamp Plan	238 211	–	–	–	–	–	238 211
	803 189 666	55 269 051	85 320 533	106 902 825	112 261 271	109 018 000	1 271 961 346
II. Contributions by United Nations agencies							
United Nations	–	–	–	2 813 150	3 759 513	4 058 387	10 631 050
United Nations Children's Fund (UNICEF)	10 000	10 000	10 000	–	–	–	30 000
United Nations Educational, Scientific and Cultural Organization (UNESCO)	5 077 298	771 511	959 521	1 159 942	1 095 075	1 182 900	10 246 247
United Nations Truce Supervision Organization in Palestine (UNTSO)	–	–	100	–	–	–	100
World Food Programme (WFP)	1 259 290[f]	–	–	–	–	391 576[f]	1 650 866
World Health Organization (WHO)	1 228 053	141 624	155 220	182 401	219 503	231 920	2 158 721
	7 574 641	923 135	1 124 841	4 155 493	5 074 091	5 864 783	24 716 984
III. Contributions from non-governmental sources							
	15 241 330	1 200 806	1 244 623	1 498 079	1 449 141	1 500 000	22 133 979

(Appendix J cont'd)

Contributor	For the period 1 May 1950 to 31 December 1972	For the year 1973	1974	1975	1976	1977[b]	Total
IV. Miscellaneous income and exchange adjustments	13 357 129	1 225 161	1 527 352	1 021 829	1 934 166	1 200 000	20 265 637
Total income	939 362 766	58 618 153	89 217 349	113 578 226	120 718 669[c]	117 582 783	1 339 077 946

[a.] The figures in this table generally show for each year government and United Nations agency contributions applicable to that year regardless of when they were received. Certain of these contributions, however, may be shown in a year later than that to which they relate because of late notification (if a minor amount).

[b.] Estimated figures.

[c.] Now part of the United Arab Emirates.

[d.] Received up to 24 October 1971. By resolution 2758 (XXVI) of 25 October 1971, the General Assembly, *inter alia*, decided 'to restore all its rights to the People's Republic of China and to recognize the representatives of its Government as the only legitimate representatives of China to the United Nations, and to expel forthwith the representatives of Chiang Kai-shek from the place which they unlawfully occupy at the United Nations and in all the organizations related to it'.

[e.] Includes $6,000,000 pledged for 1976 not reflected in the Agency's audited accounts for that year due to late notification.

[f.] Special contributions to the Government of Jordan (in 1971) and the Syrian Arab Republic (in 1977) for the benefit of the Palestine refugees for which UNRWA acted as executing agent. As these contributions were used for purposes budgeted for by UNRWA, they have been included in the Agency's income and expenditure accounts.

APPENDIX K

Total registered Palestinian refugee population according to category of registration[a]

Year ended	Members of families registered for rations 'R' category[b]			4 Other members of T families eligible for services only	'S' category[c] 5 Registered for all services but no rations	'N' category[d] 6 Registered for limited services only and no rations	7 Grand total
	1 Eligible for all services including full-rations[e]	2 Eligible for all services including half-rations[e]	3 Infants and children registered for services only				
1950	(N.A.)	(N.A.)	(N.A.)	—	—		960 021[f]
1951	826 459	51 034	2 174	—	—	24 455	904 122[f]
1952	805 593	58 733	18 347	—	—	32 738	915 411[f]
1953	772 166	64 817	34 765	—	—	45 013	916 761
1954	820 486	17 340	49 232	—	—	54 793	941 851
1955	828 531	17 228	60 227	—	—	63 403	969 389
1956	830 266	16 987	75 026	—	—	74 059	996 338
1957	830 611	16 733	86 212	18 203	4 462	62 980	1 019 201
1958	836 781	16 577	110 600	19 776	5 901	63 713	1 053 348
1959	843 739	16 350	130 092	21 548	6 977	68 922	1 087 628
1960	849 634	16 202	150 170	22 639	8 792	73 452	1 120 889
1961	854 268	15 998	169 730	23 947	9 515	77 566	1 151 024
1962	862 083	15 805	176 772	20 004	9 027	91 069	1 174 760
1963	866 369	15 705	197 914	21 195	10 420	98 567	1 210 170
1964	863 284	15 617	226 494	23 369	13 168	104 653	1 246 585
1965	859 048	15 546	251 131	29 387	18 589	107 122	1 280 823
1966	845 730	15 392	284 025	39 485	24 367	108 750	1 317 749
1967	845 790	15 328	312 649	39 997	25 331	106 991	1 346 086
1968	824 366	14 704	316 166	60 219	26 900	121 939	1 364 294
1969	806 366	13 602	326 185	73 738	27 315	148 004	1 395 074
1970	804 576	13 466	342 009	77 735	27 238	160 059	1 425 219
1971	821 338	9 688	352 143	91 442	26 683	166 867	1 468 161
1972	821 749	9 521	375 224	90 007	25 686	184 453	1 506 640
1973	820 279	9 418	394 449	90 072	25 077	201 399	1 540 694
1974	820 748	9 320	420 267	98 827	26 329	208 155	1 583 646
1975	818 844	9 061	459 197	96 416	27 851	221 338	1 632 707
1976	819 115	8 999	484 673	93 944	28 243	233 231	1 668 205
1977	821 785	9 022	510 706[g]	89 571	29 124	246 278	1 706 486

a. These statistics are based on UNRWA's registration records, which do not necessarily reflect the actual refugee population owing to factors such as unreported deaths and births, false or duplicate registrations or absences from the area of UNRWA operations.

b. The 'R' category (columns 1 to 4) comprises registered families with some or all members eligible for all Agency assistance including basic rations.

c. The 'S' category (column 5) comprises refugees whose income is above that of 'R' category refugees, but below that of 'N' category refugees, and who are eligible for general education and health services and some other UNRWA assistance, but not for basic rations. However, in Gaza, for technical reasons, there is no 'S' category and 'N' category refugees enjoy 'S' category eligibility.

d. 'N' category (column 6) comprises the following, subject to what is said about Gaza refugees in foot-note *c* above:

   (i) Refugees who are members of families whose absence from the area or the level of whose reported income disqualifies all family members for basic rations, general education and health services; or
   (ii) Refugees who have themselves received or whose families have received assistance enabling them to become self-supporting.

e. Before 1954, half rations were issued to bedouins and infants as well as to frontier villagers in Jordan. Since then, bedouins have been regarded as eligible to receive full rations and infants have also been eligible for full rations after their first anniversary if the ration ceiling permits. Half rations are issued only to frontier villagers on the West Bank (9,022). Frontier villagers displaced to east Jordan as a result of the hostilities of June 1967 (3,342) are issued with full rations under the normal programme and are therefore included in the figure of full ration recipients (column 1). Also included in column 1 are Gaza Poor (919) and Jerusalem Poor (1,347).

f. This grand total included refugees receiving relief in Israel who were UNRWA's responsibility through 30 June 1952.

g. The total of 510,706 comprises:

   (i) 14,702 infants under the age of one year who are eligible for services but not for rations;
   (ii) 457,768 children registered for services (CRS) aged one year and over (some of whom are now adults) who are not receiving rations because of ration ceilings; and
   (iii) 38,236 displaced children registered for services (CRS) who receive rations donated by the Government of Jordan on an emergency and temporary basis.

BIBLIOGRAPHY

Primary Sources

Acheson, Dean. *Present at the Creation* (New York: W.W. Norton and Company, 1969)

'A Lasting Peace in the Middle East: An American View', address by Secretary Rogers on 9 December 1969, *Department of State Bulletin*, LXII, 1953 (5 January 1970), 7-11

'A Survey of the Arab Refugee Situation', *Department of State Bulletin*, XXX, 760 (18 January 1954), 95-102

Battle, Lucius D. 'Objectives and Directives of U.S. Policy in the Near East', address, *Department of State Bulletin*, LIV, (3 June 1968), 710-14

'Behind the News in the Near East', speech by David D. Newson on 28 April 1959, *Department of State Bulletin*, XLI, 1056, (21 September 1969)

'Bolstering the Near East and Africa as a Barrier to Aggression', statement by Assistant Secretary of State George McGhee on 20 July 1951, *Department of State Bulletin*, XXV (6 August 1951), 213-19

Byroade, Henry A. 'Facing Realities in the Arab-Israeli Dispute', *Department of State Bulletin*, XXX (10 May 1954)

'Conclusions from Progress Reports of the UN Mediator on Palestine', excerpts from UN Document A/648, 16 September 1948, *Department of State Bulletin* XIX (3 October 1948), 436-40

'Continuation of Assistance to Arab Refugees', statement by James P. Richards in the *ad hoc* Political Committee on 4 November 1953, *Department of State Bulletin*, XXIX (30 November 1953), 759-61

Crum, Bartley C. *Behind the Silken Curtain* (New York: Simon and Schuster, 1947)

Department of State Bulletin, LX, 1550 (10 March 1969), 197-8

Department of State Bulletin, LXII, 1594 (12 January 1970), 50-1

'Discussion of the Palestine Situation in Committee I', statement by Philip C. Jessup, US Delegate to the General Assembly, on 20 November 1948, *Department of State Bulletin*, XIX, 490 (21 November 1948), 657-9

Eisenhower, Dwight D. 'U.S. Press. Program for the Near East, an address before the U.N.' *General Assembly*, 13 August 1958

'Encouraging the Rule of Reason in Eastern Europe and the Middle East', address by President Johnson on 10 September 1968, *Department of State Bulletin*, LIX, 1528 (7 October 1968), 345-9

Fulbright, William J. 'Old Myths and New Realities, II: the Middle East', *116 Congressional Record* S14022, S14028, S14029, S14036 (24 August 1970)

Great Britain, Palestine Land Transfer Regulations, Cmd. 6180, (London: His Majesty's Stationery Office, 1940), pp. 7-8

H. Cong. Res. 52, 67th Congress, 2nd Session, printed in *The New York Times*, 5 April 1922, p. 3

Howard, Harry N. 'The Development of United States Policy in the Near East, South Asia and Africa, 1951-1952', *Department of State Bulletin*, XXVII, 702 (8 December 1952), 891-8

Hull, Cordell. *The Memoirs of Cordell Hull* (New York: The Macmillan Company, 1948)

Hurewitz, Jacob C. 'Diplomacy in the Near and Middle East', Vols. I and II, D. Van Nostrand (ed.), *A Collection of Basic Documents on the Middle East* (Princeton NJ: Princeton University Press, 1953)

Johnston, Eric. 'Mission to the Middle East', *Department of State Bulletin*, XXX (20 February 1954), 282-4

Josiah W. Bailey replies to Committee for Abrogation of British White Paper Relating to Jewish Immigration into Palestine (Flint, Michigan)

Khadduri, Walid (ed.), *International Documents on Palestine 1969* (Beirut, Lebanon: Institute for Palestine Studies, 1972)

—— *International Documents on Palestine 1970* (Beirut, Lebanon: Institute for Palestine Studies, 1973)

Ludlow, James N. 'The Arab Refugees: A Decade of Dilemma for the United Nations', *Department of State Bulletin*, XXXIV, 1812 (17 November 1958), 755-81

McDonald, James G. *My Mission in Israel* (New York: Simon and Schuster, 1951)

'Members of House of Representatives to Secretary Dulles', letter dated 3 February 1956, *Department of State Bulletin*, XXXIV (20 February 1956), 287

'The Middle East', speech by John Foster Dulles on 26 August 1955, *Department of State Bulletin*, XXXIII, 845 (5 September 1955), 378, 380

Millis, Walter (ed.), *The Forrestal Diaries* (New York: The Viking Press, 1951)

National Archives, Washington, DC, State Department File 867.01

'Need for Progress in Dealing with Palestine Refugee Problem', statement by Francis O. Wilcox on 16 November 1960, *Department of State Bulletin*, XLIX, 1123 (2 January 1961), 28-31

Nielson, Jorgen S. *International Documents on Palestine 1972* (Beirut, Lebanon: The Institute for Palestine Studies, 1975)

—— *International Documents on Palestine 1973* (Beirut, Lebanon: The Institute for Palestine Studies, 1975)

—— *International Documents on Palestine 1974* (Beirut, Lebanon: The Institute for Palestine Studies, 1977)

'No Compromise on Essential Freedoms', address by Secretary of State Marshall on 23 September 1948, *Department of State Bulletin*, XIX, 483 (3 October 1948), 432-5

'Objectives and Directives of U.S. Policy in the Near East', speech by Lucius D. Battle on 16 May 1968, *Department of State Bulletin*, LVIII, 1510 (3 June 1968), 677-9

'Press Release', *Department of State Bulletin*, XIX, 483 (3 October 1948), 436

'Press Release', statement by President Eisenhower on 16 October 1953, *Department of State Bulletin*, XXIX (26 October 1953), 553

'Principles of Peace in the Middle East', statement by President Johnson on 19 June 1967, *Department of State Bulletin*, LVII, 1463 (10 July 1967), 31-4

'Question of Financing Aid to Palestine Refugees', statement by Genoa S. Washington in November 1957, *Department of State Bulletin*, XXXVIII, 967 (6 January 1958), 36

'Secretary Rogers's News Conference of June 25', *Department of State Bulletin*, LXIII, 1620 (13 July 1970), 25-33

'Secretary Rogers and Secretary Laird Interviewed on Issues and Answers', *Department of State Bulletin*, LXIII, 1936 (2 November 1970), 542-53

'Secretary Rusk's News Conference of 8 September', *Department of State Bulletin*, LVII, 1474 (25 September 1967), 383-90

'Security Council Affairs Principles for Peace in the Middle East', statement by Arthur Goldberg on 15 November 1967, *Department of State Bulletin*, LVII, 1486 (18 December 1967), 834-44

Statistical Abstract of the United States, 1944-1945 (Washington: US Department of Commerce, 1945), p. 34

The Statutes-at-large of the United States of America, Vol. LXII, Part 1 (Washington, DC: US Government Printing Office, 1923), p. 1012

'Stimson's Letter to Bloom', *Supplemental Statements to Hearings on H. Res. 418 and H. Res. 419, etc.* (Washington: US Government Printing Office, 1944), p. 2

Tomeh, George J. *United Nations Resolutions on Palestine and the Arab-Israeli Conflict, 1947-1974* (Beirut, Lebanon: The Institute for Palestine Studies, 1975)

Truman, Harry S. *Memoirs* Vol. I. *Years of Decision* (Garden City, NY: Doubleday and Company, 1955)

—— *Memoirs* Vol. II. *Years of Trial and Hope* (Garden City, NY: Doubleday and Company, 1955)

'U.N. Adopts Resolutions on Aid to Refugees and Status of Jerusalem', statements by Ambassador Goldberg on 3 July 1967, *Department of State Bulletin*, LVII, 1465 (24 July 1967), 108-13

'U.N. Calls for Increased Efforts to Meet Needs of Palestine Refugees in the Near East', statements by Joseph Johnson in the Special Political Committee on 25 November 1969, *Department of State Bulletin*, LXII, 1594 (12 January 1970), 46-51

United Nations Conciliation Commission for Palestine, *Final Report of the United Nations Economic Survey Mission for the Middle East*. UN Doc. A/AC. 25/6 (Lake Success: United Nations, 1949)

'United Nations Extends UNRWA to June 30, 1972', statement by Senator John S. Cooper on 6 December 1968, *Department of State Bulletin*, LX, 1542 (13 January 1969), 39-42

UN, General Assembly, 18th Session, 1 July 1962-30 June 1963, *Report of the Commissioner-General of the United Nations Relief and Works Agency for Palestine Refugees in the Near East*. Supplement No. 13 (A/5513)

UN, General Assembly, 19th Session, 1 July 1963-30 June 1964, *Report of the Commissioner-General of the United Nations Relief and Works Agency for Palestine Refugees in the Near East*. Supplement No. 13 (A/5813)

UN, General Assembly, 20th Session, 1 July 1964-30 June 1965, *Report of the Commissioner-General of the United Nations Relief and Works Agency for Palestine Refugees in the Near East*, Supplement No. 13 (A/6013)

UN, General Assembly, 22nd Session, 1 July 1966-30 June 1967, *Report of the Commissioner-General of the United Nations Relief and Works Agency for Palestine Refugees in the Near East*. Supplement No. 13 (A/6713)

UN, General Assembly, 24th Session, 1 July 1968-30 June 1969, *Report of the Commissioner-General of the United Nations Relief and Works Agency for Palestine Refugees in the Near East*. Supplement No. 14 (A/7614)

UN, General Assembly, 25th Session, 1 July 1969-30 June 1970, *Report of the Commissioner-General of the United Nations Relief and Works Agency for Palestine Refugees in the Near East*. Supplement No. 13 (A/8013)

UN, General Assembly, 26th Session, 1 July 1970-30 June 1971, *Report of the Commissioner-General of the United Nations Relief and Works Agency for*

Palestine Refugees in the Near East. Supplement No. 13 (A/8413)

UN, General Assembly, 27th Session, 1 July 1971-30 June 1972, *Report of the Commissioner-General of the United Nations Relief and Works Agency for Palestine Refugees in the Near East*. Supplement No. 13 (A/8713)

UN, General Assembly, 30th Session, 1 July 1974-30 June 1975, *Report of the Commissioner-General of the United Nations Relief and Works Agency for Palestine Refugees in the Near East*. Supplement No. 13 (A/10013)

UN, General Assembly, 15th Session, *Addendum to the Report of the United Nations High Commissioner for Refugees*. Supplement No. 11A (A/4378/Rev. 1/Add. 1)

UN, General Assembly, 15th Session, *Report of the United Nations High Commissioner for Refugees*. Supplement No. 13 (A/4378/Rev. 1)

UN, General Assembly, *First Interim Report of the United Nations Economic Survey Mission for the Middle East*. 4th Session, UN, Doc. A/1106, 17 November 1949

UN, General Assembly, *Official Records*, Second Special Session. Vols. I and II, 16 April-14 May 1948

UN, General Assembly, *Official Records*, Second Special Session. Supplement No. 1, Report of Palestine Commission to the General Assembly, 1948

UN, Relief and Works Agency for Palestine Refugees. *Twice in a Life Time*. New York, NY: November 1968

UN, Relief and Works Agency for Palestine Refugees. *Sequel*. New York, NY: November 1968

UN, Secretary-General, 14th Session, *Proposals for the Continuation of United Nations Assistance to Palestine Refugees*. Supplement No. 13A (4121)

'UN Security Council Continues Debate on Near East', *Department of State Bulletin*, LVII, 1462 (3 July 1967), 9

'UN Votes to Continue Assistance to Palestine Refugees', statement by Virgil Hancher, US Representative to the General Assembly, on 20 November 1959, *Department of State Bulletin*, XLII, 1071 (4 January 1960), 31-4

'The United States and Israeli-Arab Dispute', speech by Joseph Sisco on 11 April 1969, *Department of State Bulletin*, LX, 1558 (5 May 1969), 391-4

US Congress. House. Committee on Foreign Affairs. *The Arab Refugees and Other Problems in the Near East*. 83rd Congress, 2nd Session, 24 February 1954. (Washington: Government Printing Office, 1954)

US Congress. House. Committee on Foreign Affairs. *Arab Refugees from Palestine. Report of a Special Study Mission to the Near East*. 88th Congress, 1st Session, 4 April 1963. (Washington: Government Printing Office, 1963)

US Congress. House. Committee on Foreign Affairs. *Foreign Economic Assistance*. Report, 81st Congress, 2nd Session, 22 March 1950. (Washington: Government Printing Office, 1950)

US Congress. House. Committee on Foreign Affairs. *The Impact of the October Middle East War. Hearings Before the Subcommittee on the Near East and South Asia of the Committee on Foreign Affairs*. 93rd Congress, 1st Session, 3, 23, 24 October and 29 November 1973. (Washington: Government Printing Office, 1973)

US Congress. House. Committee on Foreign Affairs. *International Terrorism. Hearings Before the Subcommittee on the Near East and South Asia of the Committee on Foreign Affairs*. 93rd Congress, 2nd Session, 11, 18, 19, 24

June 1974. (Washington: Government Printing Office, 1974)

US Congress. House. Committee on Foreign Affairs. *The Middle East, 1974: New Hopes, New Challenges. Hearings Before the Subcommittee on the Near East and South Asia of the Committee on Foreign Affairs.* 93rd Congress, 2nd Session, 9 April, 7, 14, 23 May and 27 June 1974. (Washington: Government Printing Office, 1974)

US Congress. House. Committee on Foreign Affairs. *Palestine Refugees.* Hearings, 81st Congress, 2nd Session, 16-17 February 1950. (Washington: Government Printing Office, 1950)

US Congress. House. Committee on Foreign Affairs. *Problems of Protecting Civilians Under International Law in the Middle East Conflict. Hearing Before the Subcommittee on International Organizations and Movements of the Committee on Foreign Affairs.* 93rd Congress, 2nd Session, 4 April 1974. (Washington: Government Printing Office, 1974)

US Congress. House. Committee on Foreign Affairs. *Report of the Special Study Mission to the Middle East, South and Southeast Asia, and the Western Pacific.* 84th Congress, 2nd Session, 10 May 1956. (Washington: Government Printing Office, 1956)

US Congress. House. Committee on Foreign Affairs. *Report of the Special Study Mission to the Near East and Africa.* 85th Congress, 2nd Session, 29 May 1958. (Washington: Government Printing Office, 1958)

US Congress. House. Committee on Foreign Affairs. *Report of the Survey Mission to the Far East, South Asia and the Middle East.* 84th Congress, 1st Session, 24 March 1955. (Washington: Government Printing Office, 1955)

US Congress. House. Committee on Foreign Affairs, Subcommittee on the Near East. *The Near East Conflict.* Hearings, 91st Congress, 2nd Session, 21-23, 28-30 July 1970. (Washington: Government Printing Office, 1970)

US Congress. Senate. Committee on Appropriations. *Foreign Aid Appropriations for 1951.* Hearings, 81st Congress, 2nd Session, 13 June 1950. (Washington: Government Printing Office, 1950)

US Congress. Senate. Committee on Foreign Relations. *A Decade of American Policy. Basic Documents 1941-1949.* 81st Congress, 1st Session, 1950. (Washington: Government Printing Office, 1950)

US Congress. Senate. Committee on Foreign Relations. *Early Warning System in Sinai. Hearings Before the Committee on Foreign Relations.* 94th Congress, 1st Session, 6-7 October 1975. (Washington: Government Printing Office, 1975)

US Congress. Senate. Committee on Foreign Relations. *The Far East and the Middle East. Report of Senator John Sparktan.* 86th Congress, 2nd Session, 30 November 1960. (Washington: Government Printing Office, 1960)

US Congress. Senate. Committee on Foreign Relations. *The Middle East and Southern Europe. Report of Senator Hubert H. Humphrey on a Study Mission.* 85th Congress. 1st Session, July 1957. (Washington: Government Printing Office, 1957)

US Congress. Senate. Committee on Foreign Relations. *United States Foreign Policy, Middle East.* Staff Study, 86th Congress, 2nd Session, 9 June 1960. (Washington: Government Printing Office, 1960)

US Congress. Senate. Committee on Foreign Relations. *War or Peace in the Middle East.* Report, 90th Congress, 1st Session, 10 April 1967. (Washington:

Government Printing Office, 1967)

US Congress. Senate. Committee on Foreign Relations, Subcommittee on the Near East and Africa. *Palestine Refugee Problem. Report on the Problem of Arab Refugees from Palestine.* 83rd Congress, 1st Session, 24 July 1953. (Washington: Government Printing Office, 1953)

US Congress. Senate. Committee on Foreign Relations, Subcommittee on the Near East and Africa. *Palestine Refugee Program.* Hearings, 83rd Congress, 1st Session, 20-21, 25 May 1953. (Washington: Government Printing Office, 1953)

US Congress. House. Committee on International Relations. *The Palestinian Issue in Middle East Peace Efforts. Hearings Before the Special Subcommittee on Investigations of the Committee on International Relations.* 94th Congress, 1st Session, 30 September, 1, 8 October and 12 November 1975. (Washington: Government Printing Office, 1976)

US Congress. Senate. Committee on the Judiciary. *The Colonization of the West Bank Territories by Israel. Hearing Before the Subcommittee on Immigration and Naturalization of the Committee on the Judiciary.* 95th Congress, 1st Session, 17 and 18 October 1977. (Washington: Government Printing Office, 1978)

US Congress. Senate. Committee on the Judiciary. *U.S. Apparatus of Assistance to Refugees Throughout the World. Hearings Before the Subcommittee to Investigate Problems Connected with Refugees and Escapees of the Committee on the Judiciary.* 89th Congress, 2nd Session, 14, 19, 20, 21, 26, 27, 28 July, 2, 3, 4 August 1966. (Washington: Government Printing Office, 1966)

US Congress. *Congressional Record*, Vol. LXII, 67th Congress, 2nd Session, 1922

US Congress. *Congressional Record*, Vol. XC, 78th Congress, 2nd Session, 1944

US Congress. *Congressional Record*, Vol. XCI, 79th Congress, 1st Session, 1945

US Congress. *Congressional Record*, Vol. XCIII, 80th Congress, 1st Session, 1947

US Congress. *Congressional Record*, Vol. XCIV, 80th Congress, 2nd Session, 1948

US Congress. *Congressional Record*, Vol. XCV, 81st Congress, 1st Session, 1949

US Congress. *Congressional Record*, Vol. XCVII, 82nd Congress, 1st Session, 1951

US Congress. *Congressional Record*, Vol. CI, 84th Congress, 1st Session, 1955

US Congress. *Congressional Record*, Vol. CII, 84th Congress, 2nd Session, 1956

US Congress. *Congressional Record*, Vol. CIII, 85th Congress, 1st Session, 1957

US Congress. *Congressional Record*, Vol. CIV, 85th Congress, 2nd Session, 1958

US Congress. *Congressional Record*, Vol. CVI, 86th Congress, 2nd Session, 1960

US Congress. *Congressional Record*, Vol. CVII, 86th Congress, 1st Session, 1961

US Congress. *Congressional Record*, Vol. CIX, 87th Congress, 1st Session, 1963

US Congress. *Congressional Record*, Vol. CX, 87th Congress, 2nd Session, 1964

US Congress. *Congressional Record*, Vol. CXI, 88th Congress, 1st Session, 1965

US Congress. *Congressional Record*, Vol. CXII, 88th Congress, 2nd Session, 1966

US Congress. *Congressional Record*, Vol. CXIII, 89th Congress, 1st Session, 1967

US Congress. *Congressional Record*, Vol. CXIV, 89th Congress, 2nd Session, 1968

US Congress. *Congressional Record*, Vol. CXV, 90th Congress, 1st Session, 1969

US Congress. *Congressional Record*, Vol. CXVI, 91st Congress, 2nd Session, 1970

US Congress. *Congressional Record*, Vol. CXVII, 92nd Congress, 1st Session, 1971

US Department of State. Division of Publications, Office of Public Affairs. *The*

Palestine Refugee Program. Publication 3757, Near and Middle East Series 3. (Washington: n.n. 1950)

US Department of State, *Foreign Relations of the United States. The Conference at Malta and Yalta, 1945*. (Washington: Government Printing Office, 1955)

'U.S. Extends Mandate of Relief Agency for Palestine Refugees', statement by James J. Wadsworth in the *ad hoc* Political Committee on 19 November 1954, *Department of State Bulletin*, XXXII, 810 (3 January 1955), 24-8

'U.S. Foreign Policy for the 1970's Building for Peace', report to the Congress by President Nixon on 25 February 1971, *Department of State Bulletin*, LXIV, 1656 (22 March 1971), 341-432

'U.S. Foreign Policy in the Middle East', speech by Henry A. Byroade before the Chicago Council on Foreign Relations on 5 December 1952, *Department of State Bulletin*, XXVII, 703 (15 December 1952), 931-5

'U.S. Foreign Policy: Some Major Issues', statements by Secretary Rogers before the Senate Foreign Relations Committee on 27 March 1969, *Department of State Bulletin*, LX, 1555 (14 April 1969), 305-312

'U.S. Gives Views in U.N. General Assembly Debate on the Situation in the Middle East', statements by Ambassador Yost on 4 November 1970, *Department of State Bulletin*, LXIII, 1639 (23 November 1970), 656-63

U.S. President, *Seventh Report to Congress on Lend Lease Operations*, December, 1942. Washington: 1942

'U.S. Reaffirms Concern for Near East Refugees', *Department of State Bulletin*, LIX, 1539 (23 December 1968), 662

'U.S. Support Continuation of Aid to Near East Refugees', statement by Ambassador Wiggins on 18 November 1968, *Department of State Bulletin*, LLX, 1539 (23 December 1968), 677-79

'U.S. Urges Support for New Plan of Assistance to Palestine Refugees', statement by Philip C. Jessup in the *ad hoc* Political Committee on 17 January 1952, *Department of State Bulletin*, XXVI (11 February 1952), 224-27

'U.S. Views on Aid to Palestine Refugees', statement by George Harrison on 10 November 1959, *Department of State Bulletin*, XL, 1022 (26 January 1959), 137-42

U.S. *Weekly Compilation of Presidential Documents*, Vol. 13, No. 22. 21 May 1978. pp. 768-9

Welles, Sumner. *We Need Not Fail* (Boston: Houghton Mifflin Company, 1948)

Zahlan, Anne R. *International Documents on Palestine 1971* (Beirut, Lebanon: The Institute for Palestine Studies)

Interviews

Farouq Qaddumi, Head, PLO Political Department

Dr Nathaniel Howell, Jr, Director, Office of Iraq, Jordan, Lebanon, and Syria Affairs

Yasser Arafat, PLO Chairman

Safiq El-Hout, PLO Envoy

US Ambassador Talcott Seeley, Envoy to Syria

Secondary Sources

Books and Pamphlets

Abboushi, W.F. *Political Systems of the Middle East in the Twentieth Century* (New York: Dodd, Meade and Company, 1970)

Abu-Lughod, Ibrahim (ed.), *The Arab-Israeli Confrontation of June, 1967: An Arab Perspective* (Evanston: Northwestern University Press, 1970)

—— (ed.), *The Transformation of Palestine: Essays on the Origin and Development of the Arab-Israeli Conflict* (Evanston: Northwestern University Press, 1971)

Adams, Michael. *Chaos or Rebirth: The Arab Outlook* (London: The British Broadcasting Corporation, 1968)

Agwani, Mohammed Shabi. *The United States and the Arab World, 1945-62* with an introduction by A.R. Havrani (Aligarh: Institute of Islamic Studies, Muslim University, 1955)

Alroy, Gil Carl. *Behind the Middle East Conflict: The Real Impasse Between Arabs and Jews* (New York: Putnam, 1975)

—— *The Kissinger Experience* (New York: Horizon Press, 1975)

American Friends of a Jewish Palestine *Construction and ByLaws of the American Friends of a Jewish Palestine, Inc.* (New York: n.d.)

American Interests in the Middle East, 1969 (Middle East Institute)

American Zionist Council. *Israel and the Arab States, the Issues in Dispute: Israel's Frontiers and the Arab Refugees* (New York: American Zionist Council, 1951)

American Zionist Emergency Council. *The American Zionist Emergency Council, A Report of Activities, 1940-1946* (New York: 1946)

Antonius, George. *The Arab Awakening: The Story of the Arab National Movement* (New York: Putnam, 1965)

Badeau, John S. *The American Approach to the Arab World* (New York: Harper and Row, 1968)

Baker, Roscoe. *The American Legion and American Foreign Policy* (New York: Bookman Associates, 1954)

Al-Bazzaz, Abdul Rahman. *On Arab Nationalism* (London: Embassy of the Republic of Iraq, 1965)

Beal, John Robinson. *John Foster Dulles* (New York: Harper and Brothers, 1957)

Beling, Willard A. (ed.), *The Middle East, Quest for an American Policy* (New York: 1973)

Ben-Gurion, David. *Israel: Years of Challenge* (New York: Holt, Rinehart and Winston, 1963)

Berger, Earl. *The Government and the Sword* (London: Routledge and Kegan Paul, Ltd, 1965)

Bernadotte, Folke. *To Jerusalem* (London: Hodder and Stoughton, 1951)

Berque, Jacques. *The Arabs* (New York: Frederick S. Praeger, 1964)

Binder, Leonard. *The Ideological Revolution in the Middle East* (New York: John Wiley and Sons, Inc., 1964)

Bull, Vivian A. *The West Bank. Is It Viable?* (London, Toronto: Lexington Books, Lexington, Mass: D.C. Health and Company, 1975)

Burdett, Winston. *Encounter with the Middle East* (New York: Atheneum, 1969)

Campbell, John C. *Defense of the Middle East* (New York: Harper and Brothers, 1958)

—— *Defense of the Middle East, Problems of American Policy* (Rev. New York: Published for the Council on Foreign Relations by Harper, 1960)

Carmichael, Joel. *The Shaping of the Arabs* (New York: The Macmillan Company, 1967)

Carvely, Andrew. *US-UAR Diplomatic Relations and Zionist Pressure* (Alhambra, California: Books International of D-H T.E. International, 1969)

Cattan, Henry, *Palestine, the Arabs, and Israel* (London: Longmans, 1969)

Childs, James Rives. *Foreign Service Farewell: My Years in the Near East* (Charlottesville: The University of Virginia Press, 1969)

Churba, Joseph. *Perceiving Options in the Middle East Morewell Air Force Base* (Alabama University: Documentary Research Division, Aerospace Studies Institute, Air 1970)

—— *The Politics of Defeat* (New York and London: Cyrco Press Inc. Publishers, 1977)

Cohen, Israel. *The Zionist Movement* (New York: Zionist Organization of America, 1946)

Crossman, Richard. *Palestine Mission* (New York: Harper and Brothers, 1947)

Daher, Adel. *Current Trends in Arab Intellectual Thought* (Santa Monica: The Rand Corporation, 1969)

Daniels, Jonathan. *The Man of Independence* (New York and Philadelphia: J.B. Lippincott Co., 1950)

Davis, John H. *The Evasive Peace* (London: John Murray, 1968)

de Azcarate, Pablo. *Mission in Palestine 1948-1952* (Washington: The Middle East Institute for Palestine Studies, 1968)

De Novo, John A. *American Interests and Policies in the Middle East* (Minneapolis: University of Minnesota, 1963)

Dickinson, William, Jr, (ed.), *Editorial Research Reports* Vol. II. [n.p.], 1970

Dodd, Peter and Halim, Barakat. *River Without Bridges* (Beirut: Institute for Palestine Studies, 1968)

Donovan, John. *U.S. and Soviet Policy in the Middle East, 1945-56* (New York: Facts and File, 1972)

Douglas-Home, Charles. *The Arabs and Israel* (London: The Bodley Head, 1968)

Eckhardt, Alice and Eckhardt, Roy. *Encounter with Israel* (New York: Association Press, 1970)

Eddy, William A. *F.D.R. Meets Ibn Saud* (New York: American Friends of the Middle East, 1954)

Ellis, Harry B. *The Dilemma of Israel* (Washington: American Enterprise Institute for Public Policy Research, 1970)

Elmessiri, Abdelwahab M. *The Land of Promise* (New Jersey, New Brunswick – North America, 1977)

Epp, Frank H. *The Palestinians: Portrait of a People in Conflict* (Toronto: McClelland and Stewart, 1976)

Esco Foundation for Palestine. *Palestine, A Study of Jewish, Arab and British Policies* 2 Vols. (New Haven: Yale University Press, 1947)

Fanning, Leonard M. *American Oil Operations Abroad* (New York: McGraw Hill Book Co., 1947)

Feis, Herbert. *Seen From E.A.* (New York: Alfred A. Knopf, Inc., 1947)

Field, James A. *America and the Mediterranean World, 1776-1882* (Princeton, NJ: Princeton University, 1969)

Fiedlander, Saul and Hussein, Mahmoud, *Arabs and Israelis. A Dialogue* (New York: Holmes and Meier, 1975)

Fink, Reuben (ed.), *America and Palestine* (New York: American Zionist Emergency Council, 1944)

Fisher, Carol Ann. *The U.S. and the Middle East Crisis: Ideals and Realities in the Making of Foreign Politics* (Syracuse: Maxwell Graduate School of Citizenship and Public Affairs, Syracuse University, 1957)

Fisher, Eugene M. and Cherif, Bassiouni M. *Storm Over the Arab World* (Chicago: Follett Publishing Co., 1972)

Fisher, Sydney N. *The Role of the Military in the Middle East* (Columbus: Ohio State University, 1963)

Frankenstein, Ernst. *Palestine in the Light of International Law* (London: Narod Press, 1946)

Friedrich, Carl J. *American Policy Toward Palestine* (Washington, DC: Public Affairs Press, 1944)

—— *American Policy Towards Palestine* (Westport, Conn.: Greenwood Press, 1971)

Frye, Richard N. (ed.), *Islam and the West* (Gravenhage: Mouton and Co., 1957)

Gabbay, Rony. *A Political Study of the Arab-Jewish Conflict* (Geneva: Librairie E. Droz, 1959)

Gibb, H.A.R. *Modern Trends in Islam* (Chicago: The University of Chicago Press, 1947)

Glubb, Lt Gen. Sir John. *A Soldier with the Arabs* (London: Hodder and Stoughton, 1957)

Goitein, S.D. *Jews and Arabs* (New York: Schecken Books, Inc., 1955)

Gordon, Kermit (ed.), *Agenda for the Nation* (Washington: The Brookings Institution, 1968)

Gordon, Leland J. *American Relations with Turkey, 1830-1930: An Economic Interpretation* (Philadelphia: University of Pennsylvania Press, 1932)

Graubard, Stephen R. *Kissinger: Protrait of a Mind* (New York: 1973)

Gravill, Joseph L. *Protestant Diplomacy and the Near East's Missionary Influence on Foreign Policy, 1810-1927* (Minneapolis: University of Minnesota Press, 1971)

Hadawi, Sami. *Palestine: Questions and Answers* (New York: Arab Information Centre, 1961)

Halperin, Samuel. *The Political World of American Zionism* (Detroit: Wayne University, 1961)

Hamady, Sania. *Temperament and Character of the Arabs* (New York: Twayne Publishers, 1960)

Hamzeh, Fuad S. *United Nations Conciliation Commission for Palestine, 1949-1967* (Beirut: Institute for Palestine Studies, 1968)

Hart, Parker T. *America and the Middle East*, special edition of this volume. (Philadelphia: American Academy of Political and Social Science)

Hawadi, Joh, Hawadi, Robert, and Hawadi, Sami. *The Palestine Diary* Vols. I and II. (Beirut: Palestine Research Centre)

Hawadi, Sami. *Bitter Harvest: Palestine Between 1941-67* (New York: New World Press, 1967)

—— *Palestine in Focus* (Beirut: Palestine Research Centre, 1968)

Hazen, William F., and Jureidini, Paul A. *The Palestinian Movement in Politics*

(Lexington, Mass.: Lexington Books 1976)

Hazen, William F., *et al. Middle Eastern Subcultures* (Lexington, Mass: D.C. Heath and Company, 1975)

Hindi, Khalil, *et al. The Palestine Resistance and the Jordanian Regime.* In Arabic (Beirut: PLO Research Centre, 1971)

Hirst, David. *The Gun and the Olive Branch: The Roots of Violence in the Middle East* (London: Faber and Faber, 1977)

Hohn, Robert, and Hawadi, Sami. *The Palestine Diary*, Vols. I and II (Beirut: Palestine Research Centre, 1970)

Hopkins, Harry. *Egypt and Crucible* (Boston: Houghton Mifflin Co., 1970)

Hoskins, Halford L. *The Middle East: Problem Area in World Politics* (New York: The Macmillan Co., 1954)

Hourani, Albert. *Arabic Thought in the Liberal Age, 1739-1939* (London: Oxford University Press, 1962)

—— *A Vision of History. Near Eastern and Other Essays* (Beirut: Khayats, 1961)

Howard, Harry N. *The King-Crane Commission: An American Inquiry in the Middle East* (Beirut: Khayatz, 1963)

Howe, Russell Warren and Trott, Sarah Hays. *The Power Peddlers* (Garden City, New York: Doubleday and Co. Inc., 1977)

Howley, Dennis C. *The United Nations and the Palestinians* (New York: Hicksvill, 1975)

Hull, Cordell, *Memoirs of Cordell Hull*, 2 Vols (New York: The Macmillan Company, 1948)

Hurewitz, John Coleman. *Changing Military Perspectives in the Middle East* (September 1970)

—— *Middle East Dilemma: the Background of U.S. Policy* (New York: Published for the Council on Foreign Relations by Harper, 1953)

—— *Middle East Politics: The Military Dimension* (New York: Praeger, 1968)

—— *The Struggle for Palestine* (New York: W.W. Norton Company, 1950)

—— *(ed.), Soviet-American Rivalry in the Middle East* (New York: Academy of Political Science, Columbia University, 1969)

Hussaini, Hatem I., and El Boghdady. *The Palestinians* (Washington DC: Arab Information Office, 1976)

Institute of Arab-American Affairs. *Papers on Palestine* (New York: 1945)

Ionides, Michael. *Divide and Lose* (London: Geoffrey Bles, 1960)

Jansen, Michael. *The United States and the Palestinian People* (Beirut: Institute for Palestine Studies, 1970)

Johnson, Julia M. (ed.), *Palestine: Jewish Homeland?* (New York: H.W. Wilson Co., 1946)

Jones, Shepherd S. *America's Role in the Middle East* (Chicago, Ill.: Laidlaw, 1966)

Jureidini, Paul A. *The Middle East: A Study in Conflict* (Washington DC: American University, Centre for Research in Social Systems, 1969)

Kadi, Lula S. *A Survey of American-Israeli Relations* (Beirut, Lebanon: 1969)

Kanaan, Hussein. *Confessionalism as a Matrix of Lebanese Domestic and Foreign Policy* (Washington, DC: George Washington University, 1969)

Karpat, Kemal H. (ed.), *Political and Social Thought in the Contemporary Middle East* (New York: Frederick A. Praeger, 1968)

Kerr, Malcolm H. (ed.), *The Elusive Peace in the Middle East* (New York: 1975)

Kerr, Malcolm H. *The Middle East Conflict, Headline Series No. 191* (New York: The Foreign Policy Association, 1968)

—— *Regional Arab Politics and the Conflict with Israel* (Santa Monica: The Rand Corporation, 1969)

Kertesz, Stephen D. (ed.), *American Diplomacy in a New Era* (Notre Dame, Ind.: University of Notre Dame Press, 1961)

Khadduri, Majida (ed.), *The Arab-Israeli Impasse* (Washington: Robert B. Luce, Inc., 1968)

Khalid, Muhammad. *From Here We Start* (Washington: American Council of Learned Societies, 1953)

Khalidi, Walid (ed.), *From Haven to Conquest: Readings in Zionism and the Palestine Problem Until 1948* (Beirut: Institute for Palestine Studies, 1971)

Khalil, Muhammad. *The Arab States and the Arab League* Vol. II. *International Affairs* (Beirut: Khayats, 1962)

Khouri, Fred J. *The Arab-Israeli Dilemma* (Syracuse: Syracuse University Press, 1968)

Kimche, Jon. *The Second Arab Awakening* (New York: Holt, Rinehart & Winston, 1970)

Kimche, Jon and Kimche, David. *Both Sides of the Hill* (London: Secker and Warburg, 1960)

Klieman, Aaron S. *Soviet Russia and the Middle East* (Baltimore: The Johns Hopkins University Press, 1970)

Laqueur, Walter. *The Road to Jerusalem* (New York: The Macmillan Co., 1968)

—— (ed.), *The Israeli-Arab Reader* (New York: The Citadel Press, 1968)

Learsi, Rufus. *Fulfillment, the EDIC Story of Zionism* (Cleveland and New York: World Publishing Co., 1951)

—— *The Jews in America: A History* (Cleveland and New York: World Publishing Co., 1954)

Lenczowski, George. *Russia and the West in Iran: 1918-1948* (Ithaca, NY: Cornell University Press, 1949)

—— (ed.), *United States Interests in the Middle East* (Washington: American Enterprise Institute for Public Policy Research, 1968)

Leonard, L. *The United Nations and Palestine* (454 International Conciliation 603, 1949)

—— *The Middle East and the West* (Bloomington, Ind.: Indiana University Press, 1964)

Lilenthal, Alfred M. *The Other Side of the Coin: An American Perspective and the Arab-Israeli Conflict* (New York: Deven-Adair, 1965)

Litvinoff, Barnett. *Ben Gurion of Israel* (London: Weidenfeld and Nicolson, 1954)

Lowdermilk, Walter. *Palestine, Land of Promise* (New York: Harper and Brothers, 1944)

McCarthy, Eugene J. *A Position Paper on Israel* (Midstream 17:51-3, June, July 1971)

MacDonald, Robert W. *The League of Arab States* (Princeton: Princeton University Press, 1965)

Magnus, Ralph H. *Documents on the Middle East: U.S. Interests in the Middle East* (Washington, DC: American Enterprise Institute, 1969)

Manuel, Frank E. *The Realities of American-Palestine Relations* (Washington, DC:

Public Affairs Press, 1949)

Mason, Herbert (ed.), *Reflections on the Middle East Crisis* (The Hague: Mouton and Co., 1970)

Menuhin, Moshe. *The Decadence of Judaism in Our Time* (New York: Exposition Press, 1965)

Mikesell, Raymond F. and Chenery, Hollis B. *Arabian Oil: America's Stake in the Middle East* (Chapel Hill, N.C.: University of North Carolina Press, 1949)

Miller, David W., and Noore, Clark O. (eds.), *The Middle East Yesterday and Today* (New York: Praeger Publishers, 1970)

Moore, John Norton (ed.), *The Arab Israeli Conflict: Readings and Documents* Abridged and revised edition. (Princeton: Princeton University Press, 1977)

Morris, Roger. *Uncertain Greatness* (New York, London, Hagerstown, San Francisco: Harper & Row, Publishers, 1977)

Muhammad, Fadil Zaki. *The American Congress and the Palestinian Question.* In Arabic (Baghdad: 1964)

—— *The Evolution of the American Policy in Palestine, 1945-52* (Baghdad: Times Press, 1953)

Noam, Chomsky. *Peace in the Middle East* (New York: 1969, 1974)

Nuseibeh, Hazem Zaki. *The Ideas of Arab Nationalism* (Ithaca: Cornell University Press, 1956)

Parkes, James W. *A History of Palestine from 135 A.D. to the Modern Times* (New York: Oxford Press, 1949)

Peretz, Don. *Israel and the Palestine Arabs* (Washington: The Middle East Institute, 1953)

—— *The Palestine Arab Refugee Problem* (Santa Monica: The Rand Corporation, 1969)

—— Wilson, Evan M., and Ward, Richard J. *A Palestine Entity?* (Washington, DC: Middle East Institute, 1970)

Perkins, Frances. *The Roosevelt I Knew* (New York: The Viking Press, 1946)

Philipson, David. *The Reform Movement in Judaism* (New York: The Macmillan Co., 1970)

Polk, William R. *The United States and the Arab World* (Cambridge, Mass.: Harvard University Press, 1969)

—— Stamley, David H., and Asfour, Edmund. *Backdrop to Tragedy: The Struggle for Palestine* (Boston: Beacon Press, 1957)

Porath, Y. *The Emergence of the Palestinian-Arab National Movement*

Porter, Kirk H., and Johnson, Donald Bruce. *National Party Platforms 1860-1960* (Urbana: University of Illinois Press, 1961)

Pranger, Robert J. *American Policy for Peace in the Middle East, 1969-71; Problems of Principle, Maneuver and Time.* (Washington: American Enterprise Institute Public Policy Research, 1971)

Quandt, William B. *United States Policy in the Middle East* (Santa Monica: The Rand Corporation, 1970)

—— *A Decade of Decisions: American Policy Toward the Arab Israeli Conflict 1967-1976* (Berkeley: University of California Press, 1977)

Quandt, William, Jabber, Fouad and Lesch, Ann, *The Politics of Palestinian Nationalism* (Berkeley, Los Angeles: University of California Press, 1973)

Rama Zani, R.K. 'The Changing U.S. Policy in the Middle East' (*Virginia Quarterly Review*, 40:369-82, Summer 1964)

El Rayyes, Riad, and Nahas, Dunia. *Guerrillas for Palestine* (New York: St. Martin's Press, 1976)

Reich, Bernard. *Quest for Peace: United States-Israeli Relations and the Arab-Israeli Conflict* (New Brunswick, New Jersey: Transaction Books, 1977)

Reisman, Michael. *The Art of the Possible* (Princeton: Princeton University Press, 1970)

Robinson, Maxime. *Israel and the Arabs* (Baltimore, Md: Penguin Press, 1968)

Roosevelt, Elliott (ed.), *F.D.R.: His Personal Letters, 1928-1945* Vol. II (New York: Duell, Sloan and Pearce, 1950)

Safran, Nadav. *The U.S. and Israel* (Cambridge, Mass., Harvard University Press, 1964)

Sakran, F.C. *Palestine Dilemma: Arab Rights versus Zionist Aspirations* (Washington: Public Affairs Press, 1948)

Sayegh, Faye Z.A. (ed.), *The Dynamics of Neutralism in the Arab World* (San Francisco: Chandler Publishing Co., 1964)

Schachner, Nathan. *The Price of Liberty: A History of the American Jewish Community* (New York: The American Jewish Committee, 1948)

Schechtman, Joseph B. *The Arab Refugee Problem* (New York: Philosophical Library, 1952)

—— *The United States and the Jewish State Movement* (New York: Thomas Yoseloff, 1966)

Schriftgiesser, Karl. *The Gentleman From Massachusetts: Henry Cabot Lodge* (Boston: Little, Brown and Co., 1944)

American Friends Service Committee. *Search for Peace in the Middle East* (Philadelphia: American Friends Service Committee, 1970)

Sharabi, Hisham. *Palestine and Israel: The Lethal Dilemma* (New York: Pegasus, 1969)

—— *Palestine Guerrillas: Their Credibility and Effectiveness* (Washington: Centre for Strategic and International Studies, 1970)

Sheehan, Edward R.F. *The Arabs, Israelis and Kissinger* (New York, Readers' Digest Press, 1976)

Shub, Louis. *The U.S. and Israel in the Mediterranean* (Los Angeles: Centre for the Study of Contemporary Jewish Life, University of Judaism, 1970)

Silverburg, Robert. *If I Forget Thee, O Jerusalem — American Jews in the State of Israel* (New York: Morrow, 1970)

Smith, Wilfred Cantwell. *Islam and Modern History* (New York: The New American Library, 1957)

Speiser, Ephraim Avigdon. *The U.S. and the Middle East.* Rev. Ed. (Westport, Conn.: Greenwood Press, 1971)

Stettinius, Georgiana G. (ed.), *The U.S. and the Middle East* (Englewood Cliffs, NJ: Prentice-Hall, 1964)

Stevens, Richard P. *America Zionism and U.S. Foreign Policy* (New York: Pageant Press, 1962)

Stookey, Robert W. *American and the Arab States: An Uneasy Encounter* (New York, London, Sydney, Toronto: 1975)

Sykes, Christopher. *Crossroads to Israel: Palestine from Balfour to Bevin* (London: A New English Library, 1967)

Taylor, Alan R., and Tethe, Richard N. (eds.), *Palestine: A Search for Truth: Approaches in the Arab-Israeli Conflict* (Washington, DC: Public Affairs Press, 1970)

Truman, Harry S. *Memoirs: Years of Trial and Hope, 1946-1952* (New York: New American Library, 1962)

Vance, Vick and Laver, Pierre. *Hussein of Jordan: My War with Israel* (New York: William Morrow and Co., 1969)

Ward, Richard Y., Peretz, Don and Wilson, Evan M. (eds.), *The Palestine State: A Rational Approach* (London: National University Publications, 1977)

Welles, Sumner. *We Need Not Fail* (Boston: Houghton Mifflin Co., 1948)

Whitman, Marjorie M. *Digest of International Law, Vol. V*, (Washington, DC: Government Printing Office, 1965)

Wilber, Donald. *The United Arab Republic, Egypt* (New Haven: Human Relations Area Files, 1969)

Wilson, Evan M. *Jerusalem, Key to Peace* (Washington, DC: The Middle East Institute, 1970)

Yaari, Ehud. *Strike Terror: The Story of Fatah* (New York: Sabra Books, 1970)

Young, T. Cuyler (ed.), *Near Eastern Culture and Society* (Princeton: Princeton University Press, 1966)

Zeine, Zeine N. *The Struggle for Arab Independence* (Beirut: Khayats, 1960)

Zurayk, Constantine. *The Meaning of the Disaster* (Beirut: Khayats, 1956)

Periodicals

Abdallah, H. 'Weapons of the Fifth War', *Shu'un Filastiniya* nos. 50-51 (October-November 1975): 174-85. (In Arabic)

Abu-Lughod, I. 'Arab Information and Breaching the American-Zionist and Information Blockade in America: The Role of Palestinian and Arab Organizations since the June 1967 War', *Shu'un Filastiniya* nos. 41-42 (January-February 1975): 154-65. (In Arabic)

—— 'Palestinian Options', *Middle East International* 41 (November 1974): 11-15

Abu-Lutf. 'PLO Speech before UN Security Council', *Palestine* 9 (February 1976): 30-4

Abu-Nidal, N. 'Attitude of the Palestinian Revolution to the Issues in the Dispute within the International Communist Movement', *Dirasat 'Arabiya* 1 (November 1975): 47-54. (In Arabic)

Abu Rudeneh, O. 'The Shift of American Jews to Support for Nixon', *Shu'un Filastiniya* 28 (December 1973): 98-106. (In Arabic)

Adams, Michael. 'Summing up of the Future of Palestine', *Middle East International* 47 (May 1975): 29-32

—— 'The Search for Settlement in the Middle East', *Political Quarterly* 29 (October-November 1968): 427-38

Ahmad, I. 'A Return to a World that Washington Wants', *Shu'un Filastiniya* 43 (March 1975): 33-58. (In Arabic)

'Alarm Signals for U.S. and Russia', *Il US News* 69 (20 July 1970)

Allush, N. 'The Palestinian People and Legitimate National Rights', *Shu'un Filastiniya* 33 (May 1974). (In Arabic)

'The American Peace Plan', *New Outlook* 3, no. 1 (January 1970): 3-6

Al-Amin, M. 'Palestinian Arabism in History', *Shu'un Filastiniya* 26 (October 1973): 141-52. (In Arabic)

Amira, M. 'Municipal Elections and Self-Rule', *New Outlook* 18, no. 4 (December 1975): 20

Aptheker, H. 'Toward Peace in the Middle East', *Jewish Affairs* 5, no. 3 (June 1975): 9-17

'The Arab Dimension of the Palestinian Liberation Movement', *Palestine Lives* 4

(May 1975): 24-27

'The Arab-Israeli Conflict', *Trans-Action* Special Issue (July-August 1970)

'Arafat's Moscow Trip', *Israel and Palestine* 39/40 (June 1975): 1-2

Arafat, Y. 'Abu Ammar at the UN', *Palestine* 1, no. 1 (January-February 1975): 12-21

—— 'The Way to Restoring the Violated Rights of the Palestinian People', *World Marxist Review* 18, no. 2 (February 1975): 123-32

Arey, J.F. 'The Sky Pirates', *American Behavioural Scientist* 15, no. 5 (May-June 1972): 766

Aruri, N. 'Kissinger's Legacy to Carter: Containment in the Middle East', *Mid East* 29 (March 1977): 50-2

Ashhab, N. 'The Balance of World Forces and the Middle East Crisis', *World Marxist Review* 10, no. 3 (March 1976): 116-23

—— 'For an overall Settlement in the Middle East', *World Marxist Review* 19, no. 12 (December 1976): 25-32

Al-Asir. 'Israel's Role in the Events of Lebanon', *Shu'un Filastiniya* 66 (October-November 1976): 155-66. (In Arabic)

Avineri, S. 'Israel and the Palestinians', *Middle East Information Series* 17 (February 1972): 30-6

Avineri, S. *et al.* 'An Exchange on the Middle East', *Foreign Policy* 21 (Winter 1975-76): 212-23

Avnery, U. 'Reflections on Mr. Hammami', *New Outlook* 19, no. 1 (January 1976): 50-52

Awad, M. 'The Palestinian Character and Jewish Settlement', *Shu'un Filastiniya* 36 (August 1974): 73-87. (In Arabic)

Al-Ayyubi, H. 'The Responsibility for Kissinger's Failure', *Qadays Arabiya* 1 (April 1975): 37-47 (In Arabic)

—— 'Ten Years in the Life of Palestinian Armed Struggle', *Shu'un Filastiniya* 41/42 (January-February 1975): 237-55. (In Arabic)

Badeau, J. 'Let's Broaden our Options', *Middle East* 10, no. 5 (October 1970): 34-7

Begin, M. 'Facing the Truth', *American Zionist* 64, no. 3 (December 1973): 13-35

Bein, N. 'Confederation: The Way to Peace', *New Outlook* 18, no. 4 (May-June 1975): 38-41

Ben-Horin, M. 'Toward a Renewal of Political Zionism', *American Zionist* 64 no. 6 (April 1974): 7-8

Berger, Elmer. 'The Old Politics Grow Older. Arab Israeli-Zionist Problems; U.S. Role in the Near East', *Arab World* 14, nos. 4-7 (July-August, 1968)

Bergue, Jacques. 'Palestine 1971: The Future Outlook', *Interplay* 4 (January 1971): 22-5

Binder, D. 'Israel and the Bomb', *Middle East International* 59 (May 1976): 6-8

Brecher, M. 'Israel and the Rogers Peace Initiatives', *Orbis* 18, no. 2 (Summer 1974): 402-26

—— 'The Four Questions: A Dialogue in Cairo', *New Outlook* no. 2 (February-March 1976): 30-8

Brownfield, A. 'American Jews Growing Restive', *Middle East International* 61 (July 1976): 13-15

Bruzonsky, M. and Kipper, J. 'Washington and the PLO', *Middle East International* 69 (February 1977): 14-15

Bryson, T. 'US Middle East Policy and the National Interest', *Middle East International* (October 1974): 7-9

Budeiri, M. 'West Bank's Firm Answer', *Middle East International* 56 (February 1976): 10-12

Calvert, P. 'The Diminishing Returns of Political Violence', *New Middle East* 56 (May 1973): 25-7

Caradon, Lord 'What can the U.N. Do?' *Middle East International* 65 (November 1976): 8-10

—— 'Middle East Impressions', *New Outlook* 19, no. 1 (January 1976): 31-4

Cockburn, P. 'West Bank Anxieties', *Middle East International* 64 (October 1976): 7-8

'Contact in Bologna', *Israel and Palestine* 21 (June-July 1973): 5

Darraj, F. 'Dr. Kissinger and the Policy of Homogeneous Zones: On the Political Implications of the Egyptian-Israeli Agreement', *Shu'un Filastiniya* 50/51 (October-November 1975): 105-11. (In Arabic)

Dmitriyev, I. and Alexeyev, V. 'U.S. Policy in the Middle East', *International Affairs* (Moscow). (November 1971): 39-43

Dorsey, W. 'Washington Ready, Willing and Available to Play a Role', *New Middle East* 46 (July 1972): 4-6

'FBI-CIA Activities against Arab-Americans', *Palestine* 2, no. 8 (January 1976): 14-17

Flub, F. 'When Terrorism is Legal', *Palestine* 2, no. 10 (March 1976): 26-7

Fulbright, J. 'Getting tough with Israel', *Washington Monthly* 6, no. 12 (February 1975): 23-7

Fulbright, J.W. 'The Clear and Present Danger', *Middle East International* 43 (January 1975): 17-19

Gaspard, J. 'Who's Who Among the Guerrillas', *New Middle East* 18 (March 1970): 12-17

Gershman, C. 'The Jews and the Elections', *The American Zionist* 63, no. 1 (September 1972): 19-21

Gershman, C. 'Senator Jackson and the Jews', *The American Zionist* 62, no. 6 (February 1972): 16-19

Ghilan, M. 'Is There a Black September?' *Israel and Palestine* 16/17 (December 1972, January 1973): 1-2

Gillon, D. 'America and Israel: Who can Break the Spell? *Middle East International* 58 (April 1976): 4-6

—— 'Growing Concern among American Jews', *Middle East International* 67 (January 1977): 6-8

Glubb, F. 'Hussein and the Rabat Verdict', *Middle East International* 42 (December 1974): 18-19

Goldman, N. 'The Psychology of Middle East Peace', *Foreign Affairs* 54, no. 1 (October 1975): 113-26

Gottlieb, G. 'Palestine: An Algerian Solution', *Foreign Policy* 21 (1975/76): 198-211

Graham, J. 'Israel's Voice in the US', *Middle East International* 43 (January 1975): 15-17

Griffin, J.J. Martin and Walter, O. 'Religious Roots and Rural American Support for Israel during the October War', *Journal of Palestine Studies* 6, no. 1 (1976): 104-14

Griffith, W. 'The Fourth Middle East War, the Energy Crisis and U.S. Policy', *Orbis* 17, no. 4 (Winter 1974): 1161-88

Gross, L. 'Voting in the Security Council and the PLO', *American Journal of International Law* 70, no. 3 (July 1976): 4-5

Halpern, Ben. 'The Making of U.S. Middle East Policy', *American Academic Association for Peace in the Middle East* (1969): 54-68

Harris, F. 'The American People and the Arab-Israeli Conflict', *Middle East Forum* 43, nos. 2-3 (1967): 57-64

Hart, P. 'An American Policy toward the Middle East', *Annals of the American Academy of Political Science*, no. 390 (1970): 98-113

Hart, Parker T. 'America and the Middle East', *Annals of the American Academy of Political Science*, no. 401 (May 1972): 142

Herman, E. 'From Arab Majority to Jewish State', *Israel and Palestine* 44/45 (December 1975): 5, 11-12

Hottinger, A. 'U.S. Interests in the Middle East', *Bulletin of the American Professors for Peace in the Middle East* 2, no. 2 (January 1972): 4-5

Howard, H.N. 'The U.S. in the Middle East Crisis', *Current History* 53 (December 1967): 337-40 and 366-7

—— 'The U.S. in the Middle East Today', *Current History* 57 (July 1969): 36-41

Hudson, Michael. 'The Palestinian Arab Resistance Movement: Its Significance in the Middle East Crisis', *Middle East Journal* 23 (1969): 291-307

Hudson, Richard. 'What Future for the Palestine Arabs?' *War/Peace Report* 10 (June/July 1970): 3-11

Huston, J.A. 'The Eisenhower Doctrine', *Current History* 57 (July 1969): 24-40, 53

Ismael, Tareq Y. 'The Palestine Emergency and U.S. Foreign Policy', *Middle East Forum* XLVI, nos. 2-3 (February-March 1970); 61-5

'Israeli-Palestinian Contacts', *Israel and Palestine* 53/54 (November-December 1976): 1-10

'Israel's Counter-Terror', *Israel and Palestine* 19 (March 1973): 1-9

Jiryis, S. 'A PLO Moderate Speaks out', *New Outlook* 18, no. 6 (September 1975): 11-17

—— 'The Legal Status of the Arab Population of the Occupied Areas', *Shu'un Filastiniya* 34 (June 1974): 30-45 (In Arabic)

Johnson, Joseph E. 'Arab versus Israeli: A Persistent Challenge to Americans', *Middle East Journal* 18 (Winter 1964): 1-13

Kaplowitz, N. 'Psychopolitical Dimensions of the Middle East Conflict: Policy Implications', *Journal of Conflict Resolution* 20, no. 2 (June 1976): 279-318

Katz, N. 'Hebrew Anti-Zionists and the Palestinian Resistance', *Israel and Palestine* 43 (October 1975): 8-9

Keatley, Robert. 'Why the United States needs a Suez Peace', *Wall Street Journal*, February 4, 1971

Khalidi, Walid. 'Plan Dalet', *Middle East Forum* 37 (November 1961): 22-8

Khouri, F. 'Don't put the cart before the horse', *Middle East International* 70 (April 1977): 16-18

Kimche, J. 'Kissinger Diplomacy and the Art of Limited War', *Midstream* 20 (November 1974): 3-12

Krenz, Frank E. 'The Refugee as a Subject of International Law', *International and Comparative Law Quarterly*, 15 (1966)

Lewis, B. 'The Palestinians and the PLO', *Commentary* 59, no. 1 (January 1975): 32-48

'Links Between Official Terror and Private Outfits Revealed', *Israel and Palestine* 22 (August 1973): 1-3

Majtales, M. 'The Arab Scene-Palestinian Outlook', *Israel and Palestine* 9 (April 1972): 5

Malawer, Stuart S. and Joseph, Jeffrey. 'Peace keeping Forces, imposed Treaties and regional Conflict. U.S. Policy in fostering an interim', *International Problems* 11: 34-42

Mandel, D. 'Fighting for Left Jewish Strength in the US', *Israel and Palestine* 20 (May 1973): 8

Mark, M. 'United States Foreign Policy in the Middle East', *New Outlook* 15 (March-April 1972): 48-54

Marshall, C.B. 'Reflections on the Middle East', *Orbis* 11, no. 2 (1967): 343-59

Masannat, G. 'Arab Neutrality and American Policy in the Middle East', *Political Quarterly* 1, no. 3 (1967): 19-26

Meyer, J. 'Modes of Arab Political Discourse', *Middle East Review* 5/6 (Autumn 1975): 95-103

Mezvinsky, Norman. 'America and Israel: Special Relationship under Strain', *Middle East International* 32 (February 1974): 10-12

'Middle East Crisis and Washington Manouvers', *International Affairs* (Moscow) 4 (1970): 30-5

Mosher, L. 'Carter: A Waiting Game?', *Middle East International* (January 1977): 4-5

—— 'Kissinger's Blind Alley', *Middle East International* 43 (January 1975): 4-6

—— 'Scepticism on the Hill', *Middle East International* 53 (November 1975): 4-6

—— 'Special Relationship Wearing Thin', *Middle East International* 57 (March 1976): 4-6

Muslih, M. 'Moderates and Rejectionists within the Palestine Liberation Organization', *The Middle East Journal* 30, no. 2 (Spring 1976): 127-40

Nahumi, Mordechai. 'The Kennedy Line and the Middle East', *New Outlook* 4 (October-November 1961): 18-24

News, D. 'American Policy in the Middle East before and after the June War', *Middle East Newsletter* 2, no. 8 (October 1968): 183-99

Neuberger, B. 'The Arab-Israeli Conflict and the Principle of National Self-Determination', *International Socialist Review* 33, no. 7 (July-August 1972): 32-5

'The Palestinian Arab Resistance Movement: Its Significance in the Middle East Crisis', *Middle East Journal* 23, no. 3 (Summer 1969): 291-320

Parzen, H. 'The Roosevelt Palestine Policy 1943-1945', *American Jewish Archives* 26 (April 1974): 31-65

Peled, M. 'American Jewry: More Israeli than Israelis', *New Outlook* 4 (May-June 1975): 18-22, 26

Peretz, D. 'Dilemmas of Palestinian State', *New Politics* 11 (Spring 1974): 52-60

—— 'Arab Palestine: Phoenix or Phantom?', *Foreign Affairs* XLVIII (January 1970): 322-33

Perlmutter, Amos. 'Israel's Fourth War, October 1973: Political and Military Misperceptions', *Orbis* 19 (1975): 434-60

—— 'Sources of Instability in the Middle East: Two Decades of Nationalism and Revolution', *Orbis* 12 (Autumn 1968): 718-53

Piety, H. 'Who Speaks for Judaism?' *Middle East Perspective* 8, no. 10 (February 1976): 3

'The PLO at the UN and in the Future', *Merip Reports* 33 (December 1974): 28-30

'The PLO's International Victories', *Palestine* 2, no. 10 (March 1976): 28-32

Price, D. 'Jordan and Palestinians: The PLO's Prospects', *Conflict Studies* 66 (December 1975): 1-16

Prlja, A. 'The Jordanian Crisis and Intra-Arab Relations', *Review of International Affairs* 21 (July 1970): 31-2

'Prospects for Peace in the Middle East', *Bulletin of the American Professors in the Middle East* 2, no. 3 (March 1972): 3-4

Qazzaz, A. 'The American View of the Arab, as depicted in American Elementary and High School Social Science Textbooks', *Dirasat Arabiya* 8 (June 1975): 3-22 (In Arabic)

Quandt, William J. 'The Middle East Conflict in U.S. Strategy, 1970-1971', *Journal of Palestine Studies* 1 (Autumn 1971): 30-52

Rafael, Gideon. 'The Role of the Two Super-Powers in the Middle East', *Israel Yearbook* (1971): 59-62

Reich, B. 'Change and Continuity in Israel', *Current History* 63 (February 1975): 58-60, 84-5

—— 'Israel's Time of Tranquility', *Current History* 72 (January 1977): 22-4

—— 'America in the Middle East: Changing Aspects of U.S. Policy', *The New Middle East* 1 (October 1968): 9-13

—— 'The Jarring Mission and the Search for Peace in the Middle East', *The Wiener Library Bulletin* 26, nos. 1-2

—— 'United States Policy in the Middle East', *Current History* 60 (January 1971): 1-6

Richmond, J. 'West Bank: The Pot Boils Over', *Middle East International* 59 (May 1976): 13-14

—— 'What Should the Palestinians do next?', *Middle East International* 66 (December 1976): 15-16

—— 'After the Hussein Plan: What Hope for Palestinian Arabs?', *The New Middle East* 46 (July 1972): 34-7

—— 'The Future of Palestine after the Rogers Plan', *The New Middle East* 29 (February 1971): 38-40

Rivlin, H. 'American Jews and the State of Israel: A Bicentennial Perspective', *Middle East Journal* 30 (Summer 1976): 369-89

Rosen, S. and Indyk, M. 'The Temptation to pre-empt in a fifth Arab-Israeli War', *Orbis* 20, no. 2 (1976): 265-86

Rosenblum, S. 'New Chapter in the Palestine-Israel Conflict', *New Politics* 11, no. 12 (Spring 1974): 67-72

Rosenne, S. 'On the Definition of Aggression', *International Problems* 15 (Spring 1976): 24-34

Rostow, E. 'America, Europe and the Middle East', *Commentary* 57 (February 1974): 40-55

Rouleau, Eric. 'The Palestinian Quest', *Foreign Affairs* 53 (January 1975): 264-83

Rustow, Dankwart A. 'Balancing Power in the Middle East: A Policy Proposal',

New Leader 52 (February 3, 1969)

Ryan, S. and Stork, J. 'U.S. and Jordan, Thrice Rescued Throne', *Merip Reports* 7 (February 1977): 3-11

Safran, N. 'Arab Politics, Peace and War', *Orbis* 2 (Summer 1977): 337-401

—— 'The War and the Future of the Arab-Israeli Conflict', *Foreign Affairs* 52 (January 1974): 215-36

Said, A. 'The U.S. and the Middle East and North Africa', *Naval War College Review* 22 (June 1970): 41-7

Said, E. 'The American Perceptions of Palestinians and Arabs', *New Outlook* 19 (January 1976): 27-30

Saleim, Q. 'Resistance and National Self-Determination in Palestine', *Merip Reports* 28 (May 1974): 3-10

Samed, A. 'The Proletarization of Palestinian Women in Israel', *Merip Reports* 50 (August 1976): 10-15

Sams, J. 'U.S. Policy and the Middle East Crisis', *Middle East Forum* 43 (1967): 45-55

Sams, James F. 'United States Policy in the Middle East', *Middle East Forum* XLIII, nos. 2-3 (February-March 1967): 45-55

Schiff, Z. 'War on Terrorism', *The American Zionist* 63, no. 3 (November 1973): 14-16

Schulz, A. 'United States Policy in the Middle East', *Current History* 68 (February 1975): 54-7, 81-2

Sharabi, H. 'Next Phase for Palestinian Guerrillas: People's War', *Mid East* 10 no. 3 (July 1970): 15-17

—— 'The Transformation of Ideology in the Arab World', *Middle East Journal* 19 (Autumn 1965): 471-86

Sheehan, E. 'Step by Step in the Middle East', *Foreign Policy* 22 (Spring 1976): 3-70

Sid-Ahmed, M. 'When the Guns Have Stopped', *New Outlook* 18, no. 5 (July-August 1975): 20-3

Stone, Elihu. 'The Zionist Outlook in Washington', *New Palestine* 34 (March 17, 1944): 305

Stevens, Georgiana. 'Arab Refugees, 1948-1952', *Middle East Journal* 6 no. 3 (Summer 1952): 281-98

Tomeh, G. 'Zionist Violence', *Arab Palestinian Resistance* 5 (August 1973): 65-90

Touma, E. 'Limits of Partnership in U.S. Israeli Relations', *World Marxist Review* 18 (June 1975): 91-7

Turki, F. 'Don't Ask too much of me', *Middle East International* 68 (February 1977): 16-18

'Twenty-seven years of Terrorism', *Palestine* 1 (May-June 1975): 22-4

Weisman, H. 'New Directions for American Zionism', *The American Zionist* 63 (September 1972): 10-14

'What Future for the Palestine Arabs?' *War/Peace Report* 10, no. 6 (June-July 1970): 3-11

Wolf, John B. 'The Palestinian Resistance Movement', *Current History* 60 (January 1971): 26-31

Yizhar, M. 'The Origins of the American Involvement in the Middle East', *International Problems* 13 (January 1974): 335-46

Younger, S. 'Jordan's Quiet Comeback', *Middle East International* 70 (April 1977): 4-6
Zahlan, A. 'The Economic Viability of a West Bank State', *Middle East International* 66 (December 1976): 20-2

Serial Publications and Newspapers

Al-Ahram (Cairo)
Al-Hadaf (Beirut)
Al-Nahar (Beirut)
Arab Report and Record
Atlantic
The Boston Globe
The Boston Herald American
Contemporary Jewish Record
Filistin Al-Thawra (Beirut)
Informational Bulletin of the American Council for Judaism
Israel/Palestine
Jewish Frontier
Jewish Outlook
Los Angeles Times
The Manchester Guardian Weekly
Middle East
Middle East International
New Palestine
Newsweek
New York Times
Palestine
Times (London)
Washington Post
Washington Star

INDEX

Abd al-Hadi, Salim 16
Abdullah, King 31, 45, 145
Abourezk, Senator James 128, 169
Afghanistan 12, 192, 195
AFL-CIO 171, 176
Africa 156; Organization of –
    Unity 182
Afro-Asian Conference 182
aid, economic 12, 50, 56-7, 61, 64,
    73, 96, 137, 163, 171, 173, 174,
    176, 178, 190, 195; see also
    development
AIPAC 162-73
Algeria 124, 126
Alsop, Joseph 162
America, Latin 70, 124
American Council for Judaism 163;
    – Friends Service Committee
    141; – Jewish Committee 167,
    172; – Zionist Conference 163;
    – Zionist Council 163, 164
Americans for Democratic Action
    171, 173
Amitay, Morris J. 165-7, 170-3
Amnesty International 192
Anfuso, Representative 65
Aqaba, Gulf of 84
Arab Congress 14-15; – League 48,
    60, 155; League of – States 182;
    – Nationalist Youth Organization
    for Liberation of Palestine 112;
    – Organization for Liberation of
    Palestine 112
Arab-Americans 144, 161-2; AAUG
    162; NAAA 162, 166
Arafat, Yasser 102, 103, 104, 120,
    121, 123, 140, 142-5, 172, 184,
    185, 189
arms, to Arabs 171, 173, 174, 185,
    190, 191; to Israel 72, 104,
    165-6, 177, 191; embargo 36-7,
    50, 163, 171, 173, 191
Assad, President 102, 123, 133,
    182
Atherton, Alfred Jr 139-40, 144
Austin, Ambassador 37-8
Australia 25, 70
de Azcarate, Pablo 54, 55

Badeau, John 88

Bahrain 124
Balfour Declaration 11, 15, 25-7, 33,
    40, 147, 200
Ball, George 179
al-Banna, Sami 125
Bayh, Senator Birch 166
Bedell Smith, Walter 43
Begin, Menahem 138, 139, 144,
    148-56, 191, 194, 215
Ben Gurion, David 52, 53, 179
Bentsen, Senator Lloyd 172
Berman, Jay 166
Bernadotte, Count Folke 48-9, 51
Bernstein, Rabbi Philip S. 164
Bingham, Representative Jonathan
    165, 173
'Black September' 97, see also
    Jordan, civil war; – Organization
    (BSO) 112
Blackstone, W.E. 24
Blandford, John B. Jr 62-3
Blum, Jack 166
Blum, Yehuda 154
Bolivia 183
Bolling, Landrum 87, 142
Bonn summit meeting (1978) 127
Bookbinder, Hyman 167, 168, 172
Brandeis, Louis 25
Breira 167
Brezhnev, President 100, 183
Britain 11, 15, 16, 24, 25, 27-30, 34,
    37, 38, 39, 50, 51, 56, 57, 61, 82,
    84, 127, 171, 188
Brody, David 166
Bryen, Stephen 166
Brzezinski, Zbigniew 133
Bumber, Dale 169

Cambodia 176
Camp David accords 12, 139, 141,
    145-56, 183, 188, 194, 210-15
Canada 70, 127
Caradon, Lord 143
Carter, President 13, 133-4, 136-42,
    144, 148, 155, 156, 168, 171,
    174, 176, 177, 183, 194, 215;
    Doctrine 13
Case, Senator Clifford 173
Ceausescu, President 183
Cecil, Lord Robert 25

Celler, Representative 50
China 25, 34, 37, People's Republic
　72, 140
Church, Senator 166
Churchill, Winston 15
Clapp, Gordon 57, 59
Clark, Ramsey 172
Clifford, Clark 39
compensation, to Palestinians 49,
　51-3, 57, 62, 65-8, 71, 84, 86, 88,
　91, 137, 189
Cooley, Representative 61-2
Cuba 127, 140
Cyprus 191

Davis, John 88
Dayan, Moshe 101, 136, 137, 152,
　153
development, economic 56-9, 63, 74,
　65, 67, 68
Dewey, Governor 36
diaspora, Jewish 17; Palestinian 16,
　17, 22, 87, 183, 184, 194; *see
　also* refugees
Dinitz, Simcha 101, 177
Dominican Republic 124, 195
Drew, Joseph 33
Dulles, John Foster 13, 63, 65, 145,
　168

East Bank 17, 44
Eban, Abba 163
Ecuador 124
Eddy, William A. 35
Egypt 31, 35, 57, 73, 82, 85, 88,
　92-3, 95, 106, 124, 133, 142,
　156, 173, 174, 179, 180-2, 185;
　and Israel 17, 83, 92-4, 99, 100,
　101, 104, 106, 138, 145, 147-8,
　151-2, 210-15; and Palestinians
　16, 46, 56, 138, 144, 146-8,
　212-14
Eisenhower, President 63, 179,
　185; Doctrine 67
Esmail, Sami 128
Ethiopia 35
Ethridge, Mark 54
Europe 183, 191, 195
Eytan, Walter 53

Fahd, Crown Prince 180
Faisal, Amir 15, 145
Faisal, King 99, 100, 180
Fanon, Frantz 111, 112

Fateh 112, 145
fedayeen 90-3, 96, 99, 120, 123,
　129; *see also* guerrillas, violence
Feldman, Myer 168
Feldman, Trude 134
Filastin 15
Fish, Representative Hamilton Jr
　26
Fisher, Max 168
Ford, President 105, 141, 168,
　171-4, 176, 183
Forrestal, James V. 36
France 11, 37, 52, 56, 57, 61, 82,
　84, 124, 127
Frankfurter, Felix 25
Friedrich, Carl J. 177
Fulbright, Senator William 88-9,
　164, 169
Fuller, Melville 24

Gaza 17, 44-7, 54, 58, 73, 74, 84,
　87, 89, 93, 103, 134, 136, 138,
　140, 141, 144-52, 154, 179, 184,
　185, 192, 212-14; *see also* self-
　rule
Geneva peace conference 100-2,
　120, 135-8, 142, 143, 184
Germany 124, 127; East 140
Gibbons, Cardinal 24
Golan Heights 100, 106, 153, 192
Goldberg, Arthur 74, 75
Goldman, Nahum 168
Greece 35, 176
Griffin, Stanton 51
guerrilla activities, Palestinian 85, 86,
　89, 91, 93, Ch. 5 *passim*, 188, 193

Haig, Alexander 191
Haiti 35, 124, 183
Halpern, Representative 72
Hamilton, Representative Lee 90-2
Harding, President 27
Hare, Raymond 54, 61
Harrison, President 24
Harrop, Deputy Assistant Secretary
　144
Hatfield, Senator Mark 87, 90, 169
homeland, Jewish 24, 25-8, 33, 39,
　90; Palestinian 12, 13, 87, 112,
　129, 133-5, 140, 188, 189, 194,
　195, 196, 199, 201; *see also*
　Palestinian state, repatriation
Hooks, Benjamin 176
Hopkins, Harry 29, 30

House, Colonel 25
Howard, Harry 88
Hull, Cordell 29, 30
human rights, violation of 146,
    192; Swiss League of 192
Humphrey, Senator Hubert 67, 85,
    166, 172
Hunter, Representative 66
Hurwitz, Harry 154
Hussein, King 45, 85, 89, 91, 93, 95,
    101, 102, 103, 120, 122, 123,
    133, 173, 182

Ibn Sa'ud 31, 33
immigration, Jewish 11, 27-8, 30,
    32, 49, 152
International Labor Organization
    182
Iran 12, 190
Iraq 14, 31, 57, 59, 66, 67, 68, 70,
    123, 124, 128, 141
Isaacs, Stephen 174
Islam 195, Conference (Algiers
    1973) 182
Israel 11, 12, 16, 17, 24, 39; and
    Egypt 83, 92, 94, 99, 100, 101,
    104, 106, 138, 145, 147-8, 151-2,
    210-15; and Palestinians 13, 17,
    43, 49, 52-5, 62, 71, 74, 84, 86,
    88, 91, 101, 103, 104, 136, 137,
    138, 143-56, 167, 192, 212-15,
    see also compensation, repatria-
    tion, self-determination; and
    security 53, 62, 69, 85, 91, 98,
    134, 140, 150, 153-4, 176, 179,
    185, 195; and US 12, 53, 65,
    85, 94, 95, 104, 123, 127-8, 133,
    137, 143, 145, 147-56, 166-8,
    178-80, 191, 195; Palestinian
    attacks on 85, 92, Ch. 5 *passim*,
    193; recognition of 39, 50, 88,
    97, 104, 133, 135, 140-3, 179,
    184, 191, 193; *see also* Zionism

Jabari, Sheikh 144
Jackson, Senator Henry M. 165,
    166, 171, 172
Jacobson, Eddie 37, 168
Japan 112, 127, 191
Jarring, Gunnar 82, 94
Javits, Senator 56, 69, 165, 166, 172
Jerusalem 15, 26, 34, 43, 50, 84,
    94, 152-3, 181, 206-7; East 89,
    102, 153
Jessup, Philip C. 63

Jewish Agency 37, 39, 163, 164;
    World – Congress 168; *see also*
    USA, – lobby in
Jiryis, Sabri 141
Johnson, Joseph 70-2
Johnson, President 74-5, 82, 86
Johnston, Eric 63-4; Plan 63-7
Jordan, 17, 57, 68, 82-5, 92, 93,
    100, 101, 106, 123, 124, 133,
    138, 142, 155, 173, 180, 182,
    185, 190, 193, 195; and Palestin-
    ians 12, 16, 44-6, 57, 59, 66,
    85, 86, 89-93, 99, 123, 129, 134,
    135, 139, 141, 144, 148, 150,
    151, 182, 184, 193, 212-14; civil
    war in 45, 89, 90, 93, 95, 120,
    122, 123, 182
Jordan, Vernon 176
Joseph, Senator 73

Kane, Irving 164
Karameh, Battle of 86
Kee, Representative 59
Kenen, I.L. 88, 163-4, 166, 170,
    171, 172
Kennedy, Howard 62
Kennedy, President 68-9, 71
Khaled, King 180
King, John 96
Kirkland, Lane 176
Kissinger, Henry 85, 98-106, 120,
    136, 141, 162, 177, 179, 180,
    182
Kuwait 124

Lakeland, Albert 166
land, loss of 44, 66, 87, 150, 192,
    194; *see also* compensation
Lausanne Protocol 53
League of Nations Mandate 147, 171,
    194, 200; *see also* Britain
Lebanon 14, 31, 35, 47, 57, 68, 88,
    99, 124, 133, 190, 195; and
    Palestinians 12, 44, 47-8, 56, 86,
    91, 129, 182, 184, 193; civil war
    in 105, 182; Israeli attacks on 13,
    14, 99, 121, 191
Lehman, Herbert 35
Levison, Jerome 166
Liberia 35
Libya 124, 141
Lindsay, Representative 69
Lipskey, Louis 164
Litvinoff, Barnett 37
Lodge, Henry Cabot 26

Loeb, Bob 167
Long, Senator Russell 123
Lovett, Robert 34, 36, 39

McDonald, James G. 53, 66
McGhee, George 56-7, 59, 61
McGovern, Senator George 86, 88, 95, 142, 176
Mack, Julian 25
Marshall, George C. 39, 50; – Plan 163
Mauritania 124
Meany, George 176
Meir, Golda 101
Mexico 124
Milehlm, Mayor Muhammed 13
Miller, Rabbi Israel 85, 168
Mondale, Vice-President Walter 134, 136, 140, 172
Moore, Curtis 122
Morgan, C. Pierpoint 24
Morocco 124
Morse, Wayne 169
Mosad 125, 127

NAACP 176
Nashashibi, Ali 16
Nasser, President 87, 93
nationalism, Arab 16, 29, 36, 195; Palestinian 15-18, 21, 87, 90
navigation, freedom of 82, 84, 94
Near East Report 88, 164-5, 169, 170
Nelson, Senator Gaylord 172
Niles, David 39
Nixon administration 83, 85, 92, 95, 98, 124, 176; President 92, 95, 100, 123, 124, 168
Noel, Cleo 122
Nolte, Richard 89
non-aligned Conference 146, 182

occupation/occupied territories 82, 86, 96, 136, 138, 148-55, 181, 191-4, *see also under individual headings*; Organization of Sons of – – 112; Organization of Victims of Zionist – 112
oil 36, 99, 100, 128, 161, 190-1, 193; companies 36, 160-1; embargo 180, 181
Oman 124
OPEC 161, 181
Ottoman Empire 14-16, 40

Palestine Congress of North America 162; Society of Friends of a Jewish – 27
Palestine Liberation Army 72, 73, 122, 123
Palestine Liberation Organization (PLO) 12, 17-18, 22, 23, 98, 103, 120, 122, 172, 182-5, 191, 193, 197-201, 208-10; and Israel 101, 103, 136, 137, 140-3, 177, 179, 191; and US 12, 97-8, 102, 103, 104, 106, 121, 128, 130, 137, 141-5, 162, 172, 179, 182, 183, 188, 191
Palestinian, liberation movement 13, 72, 86, 95, 96, 184, 190, 198-9, *see also* nationalism, PLO; – National Charter 17, 140, 197-201; – state 87, 89, 102, 133, 134, 137, 138, 139, 141, 146, 154-5, 182, 184-5, 192, 195, *see also* self-rule, West Bank
Palmer, Ely 55
Pan-Arabism 16
participation, Palestinian, in negotiations 86, 90, 96-7, 98, 100-2, 134-7, 139, 140, 143-5, 155, 179, 188, 189, 194, 212
partition 34-8, 50, 53, 134, 145, 147, 189, 199, 203-4
PDFLP 112, 120
Percy, Senator Charles 172, 177
Peretz, Don 87-8
Perle, Richard 166
petrodollars 161, 181, 190, 191, 193
PFLP 112, 120, 121, 122
Philippines 35
Porter, Paul 54
Prouty, Representative 64
PSF 112

Qatar 124
Quandt, William 177

Rabat summit conference (1974) 102-3
Rabin, Yitzhak 95, 133
Rayburn, Sam 31
recognition, of Israel *see* Israel; of Palestinian people/PLO 12, 14, 75, 88, 97, 98, 103-6, 129, 130, 137, 143, 145, 182, 183, 184,

188, 191, 208-9, *see also* self-determination
Red Army 112
Reed, Thomas 24
refugees, Jewish 32, 61-2; Palestinian 11, 16, 17, Ch. 3 *passim*, 83-6, 88, 90, 91, 97, 105, 128, 129, 143, 146, 167, 169, 179, 188, 189, 192, 207, 216, 223-4, *see also* compensation, repatriation, resettlement
rejectionists conference (Tripoli) 144, 184
repatriation 43, 45, 49-52, 54, 56-60, 62, 64-7, 69, 70, 71, 73, 74, 84, 86, 88, 91, 103, 146, 150-2, 179, 180, 189, 195, 207, 208
resettlement 12, 49, 52, 55-9, 63-71, 75, 84, 88, 128, 146, 188, 189, 192, 207
Ribicoff, Senator Abraham 165, 167, 168, 172
Rockefeller, John D. 24
Rockefeller, William 24
Rogers, Secretary of State 83, 85, 93-7, 99, 120, 121, 124, 125, 126; Plan 83-5, 91, 146
Roosevelt, F.D. Jr 35, 36
Roosevelt, President 11, 25, 29-33, 171, 185
Roosevelt, Representative James 69, 72
Rothstein, Raphael 127
Rusk, Dean 121

Saba, Michael 166
Sadat, President 94, 95, 99, 101, 102, 106, 120, 121, 133, 138, 139, 144, 149, 155, 156, 179, 182, 184, 190, 215
Sage, Russell 24
al-Sa'id, Hafiz 16
Saudi Arabia 31, 35, 57, 68, 99, 100, 124, 133, 142, 153, 174, 180-1, 185
Saunders, Harold 105, 180, 182
Saxbe, Senator William 172
Schindler, Rabbi Alex M. 168
Scott, Senator Hugh 69, 165
Scranton, Governor William 142
self-determination, Palestinian 33, 40, 87-92, 97, 103, 120, 133, 134, 138, 139, 140, 146, 180, 181, 182, 188, 191, 192, 194, 196, 208

self-rule/autonomy proposals 138, 139, 147-52, 155, 156, 188, 193, 194, 212-14
settlements, Jewish 11, 138, 149-50, 152-3, 155, 167, 191, 192, 194
al-Shawa, Sa'id 144
Shukairy, Ahmad 72
Silver, Rabbi Abba Hillel 28
Sinai 61, 67, 70, 92, 100, 106, 145, 150, 153, 154, 179, 185; Agreements 104, 106, 168
Sisco, Joseph 96, 99
Smith, Representative Lawrence 64
Socony Vacuum 36
South Africa 148, 195
Soviet Union 51, 52, 82, 84, 100, 106, 138, 193, 195; and Arabs 36, 94, 141, 173, 190; and Israel 85, 191; and US 83, 90, 92, 99, 128, 138, 183, 192, 193, joint statement 136, 137, 143, 174; Jewish emigration from 171-3
Spiegel, Dan 166, 172
Spiegel, Mark 168
Stalin, Marshal 31, 32
Stettinius, Edward 30, 33
Stimson, Henry 29
Stone, Senator Richard 165, 172
Sudan 120, 124
Suez Canal 92, 94; agreement 94, 120
Sunday Times (London) 192
Symington, Senator Stuart 165
Syria 14, 15, 16, 17, 31, 35, 57, 59, 73, 99, 106, 124, 128, 133, 134, 138, 142, 180, 181, 182, 193, 214; and Palestinians 12, 44, 46, 57, 66, 70, 123

Taft, Senator 28
al-Tal, Wasfi 120
Talisman, Mark 166
Talmadge, Senator Herman 165, 172
Tenzer, Representative Herbert 73
terrorism 11, 12, 82, 111, 112, 121-6, 188, 189; anti- 124-7, 188, 189
Tiran, Straits of 84
Tito, President 183
trade 181, 191, 193; – Reform Act 165, 171-2
Transjordan 31
Tripartite Declaration (1950) 163
Trucial States 124
Truman, President 11, 25, 32-9, 49, 53, 57, 61, 163, 168, 179

Tunisia 124

UNESCO 174, 182
United Arab Emirates 124
United Nations 29, 32, 34-5, 37-8, 43,
   48, 51-6, 58, 60, 62-3, 71, 73,
   75, 82, 84, 103, 126-7, 146,
   150-1, 172, 174, 182, 183, 189,
   192; Conciliation Commission
   52-5, 57, 60, 62, 68, 70, 205-8;
   partition plan 34-5, 37-8, 53,
   134, 145, 147, 189, 203-4; peace
   keeping force 100; Resolution
   194 (III) (1948) 51-2, 54, 55, 57,
   60-3, 69; Resolution 242 (1967)
   75, 82, 83, 91, 93, 94, 97, 104,
   130, 139-43, 145, 147, 184, 202,
   210, 211, 213; Resolution 338
   (1973) 104, 203, 211; Resolution
   3236 (1974) 137, 208-9; Resolution 3237 (1974) 183, 209-10
United States, and Arabs 36, 69,
   180-2; and Israel 12, 53-7, 61, 65,
   73, 74, 83, 93, 95, 101, 104,
   112, 123, 127, 130, 137, 143,
   145-52, 154, 156, 162-80, 190-1,
   194, 195; and PLO 12, 97-8, 102,
   103, 104, 106, 121, 128, 130,
   137, 141-5, 162, 172, 179, 182,
   183, 188, 191; and Soviet Union
   83, 90, 92, 99, 128, 138, 183, 192,
   193, joint statement 136, 137,
   143, 174; and terrorism 120-30;
   and UNRWA 60, 68, 72, 73, 121-2,
   128, 188; Arab-Americans 144,
   161-2, 166; Jewish lobby in 12,
   35, 85, 137, 162-76, 190, CPMAJO
   162, 167-8, 171, *see also* Zionism
UNRWA 43-4, 48, 51, 60-2, 64-6, 68-70,
   72, 73, 91, 121-2, 128, 146, 188,
   217-22

Vance, Cyrus 133, 136, 137, 142,
   153
Vanik, Representative Charles A.
   165, 166, 171
Vietnam 13, 72, 191
violence, revolutionary/commando
   12, 14, Ch. 5 *passim*, 145, 184
Vorys, Representative 65

Wadsworth, George 35
Wagner, Senator 28
war (1948) 38, 43, 44, 66, 84;

(1956) 67, 179; (1967) 14, 16,
   17, 44, 73, 82, 84, 86, 121, 129,
   162, 183; (1973) 14, 99, 100,
   177, 179, 180; civil, Jordan 45,
   89, 90, 93, 95, 120, 122, 123,
   182, Lebanon 105, 182; World
   I 162, World II 11, 29, 90, 188
water projects/resources 12, 58,
   63-5, 69, 150
Weiss, Congressman Samuel 30
Weizmann, Chaim 37, 39, 145
Welles, Sumner 32, 34, 35
West Bank 13, 17, 44, 45, 58, 73,
   74, 84, 87, 89, 91, 93, 102, 103,
   134, 136, 137, 138, 140, 141,
   144-9, 152-5, 179, 182, 184-5,
   192, 212-14, *see also* Palestinian
   state, self-rule
Wheeler, Winslow 166
White Paper (1939) 27-8, 30
Wilson, President 11, 25, 33, 40
Wise, Rabbi Stephen 25, 31-4
Wright, Representative James A. 28

Yemen 31, 124
Yost, Charles W. 96-7
Young, Andrew 176

Zablocki, Representative 66
Zimbabwe 191
Zionism/Zionists 12, 15, 16, 18,
   24-30, 32-5, 37, 39, 111, 152,
   154, 163, 164, 185, 188, 193,
   197, 199, 200; American –
   Conference 163, Council 163,
   164, – Emergency Council 28;
   Federation of American – 25;
   Provisional Executive Committee
   for General – Affairs 25; World
   – Congress 24
Zutty, Sam 125